To Dennis —

To a columnor columnor.

Best personal wishes,

Ray Chen
11/7/97

In the past only the largest companies had the resources to develop a truly professional salesperson. Roy Chitwood has finally and comprehensively documented professional sales training that any company or any aspiring professional salesperson can thrive on. If you are for customer satisfaction as a basis for increased sales success, you can't afford to let *World Class Selling* pass.

> *Howard P. Stevens, The H.R. Chally Group*

I am glad to see the Track Selling System™ in book form. It has helped me — and will help many others — become a professional salesman.

> *Kenley Lawton, Senior Vice President*
> *The Principal Financial Group*

World Class Selling is outstanding! Our company has rigorously utilized Track Selling™ as our primary sales tool for the last two years. Our growth rate has tripled that of the rest of the industry! Track Selling™ is a tremendous competitive advantage. I encourage all selling professionals, except our competition, to utilize it. Our results speak for themselves.

> *William Holl, Vice President & General Manager*
> *Coca-Cola Bottling Company of Michigan*

This down-to-earth new book contains real life experiences and a proven method of effective selling. A must have for all sales professionals.

> *Stewart Coombe, President, EnerCom Geothermal*

Finally someone addresses what today's business environment requires from the sales reps who sell them. *World Class Selling* combines the strategic partnership with customers and the training of salespeople in the best handbook for how-to selling ever.

> *George Kemptner, President, Copyprint*

Chitwood's experience, professionalism and success comes clear in the reading. So many of our people start shortcutting and lose the sale in the process. With this track and the proven methods this is a must book for all salespeople.

> *David Miller, Senior Vice President, Franchise Sales*
> *Coldwell Banker Residential Affiliates*

World Class Selling is a masterful book written by a masterful salesperson. This step-by-step guide will help novice and seasoned professionals improve their level of sales and increase their sales income.

> *Bill Bethel, Co-Founder/CEO, Bethel Institute*

The techniques behind Track Selling™ work! I heartily recommend that anybody interested in selling anything to anybody run to the book store and buy two copies — a personal copy and a copy to give to their boss.

> *Rick VonderBrink, Managing General Agent*
> *Med-Care Advantage*

After attending a Track Selling™ program, I didn't think Track Selling™ could ever be improved or enhanced. *World Class Selling* completes the process started with Track Selling™ in the best written, best formulated and operationally beneficial book relating to sales I have read.

> *James L. Watson, Senior Vice President and Salesman*
> *National American Insurance Company*

We have introduced the Track Selling™ concepts and techniques to nearly 1,000 of our channel partners and have trained our internal sales staff on it as well. I predict that *World Class Selling* will rise to the top of the growing list of books devoted to effective selling in the business climate of the 1990s.

> *Dave W. Hanna, President and CEO, State of the Art*

World Class Selling makes professional sales an exciting process of continuous improvement. This systematic sales track steps up sales naturally. It is so practical and easy to follow, all of my associates use it to build quality relationships while meeting customer needs. *World Class Selling* will enhance anyone's sales productivity.

> *Martin Garff, Regional Sales Manager*
> *Dynatech Laboratories*

Every person desirous of a successful sales career should commit themselves to the relevant principles outlined in *World Class Selling*.

> *Thomas N. Fuelling, President, Lawry's Foods, Inc.*

Successful selling involves the art of persuasion. Therefore it can be taught and learned. *World Class Selling* provides an excellent roadmap for helping to accomplish that objective.

F. G. (Buck) Rodgers, Former Vice President
of Marketing, IBM

In this fast paced world of computer to computer contact there is an even greater need for excellent personal contact selling. If you follow this book from cover to cover, you can become the best there is to be. It is full of basic information that salespeople can use immediately.

Donald C. North, CSE, President
Sales & Marketing Executives International

Roy Chitwood unscrambles the simple process of getting people to put their money down and buy something, which has become so complicated.

Nick Carter

World Class Selling combines the best of research and practice into a must read handbook for salespeople of all types. Roy Chitwood has integrated many years of proven sales techniques into a practical handbook that makes the sales process easy to learn and profitable to use. Managers should own this tool and buy it for all of their sales and customer contact personnel.

William H. Crookston, Ph.D., The Entrepreneur
Program, University of Southern California School of
Business Administration

I am continually amazed at how weak so many salespeople are at closing a sale. If they would only embrace a step-by-step procedure, a simple method, their incomes would sky rocket. *World Class Selling* provides that method.

Dick Boudreau, Western Region Manager
American Linen Supply Co.

As the business world gets more competitive, there is no room for an amateur in selling. Roy Chitwood can teach everybody the skills, techniques, scripts and strategies they need to compete. If you are only going to read one book on selling it has to be *World Class Selling*. This is the only sales book you will ever need.

Patricia Fripp, CSP, CPAE, Past President
National Speakers Association

World Class Selling is full of truisms directed toward true professionalism and the elevation of the selling process. No matter what the product, it all begins with people to people communication.

> *Larry Tucker, Vice President Sales and Marketing*
> *Thermalloy, Inc.*

Finally, a book that vividly explains what the world of selling is all about. No more buzz words and overused clichés. This is practical, in the trenches, real life selling.

> *Les Hewitt, President and Founder*
> *Achievers Canada Seminars, Inc.*

Chitwood takes a no-nonsense approach to the art and craft of selling as it must be practiced in the highly competitive world of today and tomorrow. If you want your customers to see you as an integral partner in the success of their business, the process described in *World Class Selling* will help you make a quantum leap in that direction.

> *George Morrisey, Author, Morrisey on Planning*

Over the years, I have interviewed many people who wanted to go into sales, but had not had formal training. *World Class Selling* will help those who want to go into the sales profession to understand what sales is all about and prepare them for a successful career in sales. It will also be useful to train new sales employees with little experience.

> *Abdullah Mat Zaid, President, MAS Catering*
> *Malaysia Airlines*

World Class Selling is a great combination of technique and the practical experience of a superb salesman and teacher, Roy Chitwood. It is not a book to read and put away. *World Class Selling* is a must for the beginner and a vibrant review for the professional of the success patterns of world class salesman and companies.

> *Jack Root, Business Consultant To Management*

Important training for salespeople and sales managers. Outstanding examples make all the important points easy to grasp. Sales today must depend on sincerity, believability and credibility. This book attests to that.

> *Claudia J. Bowers, CSE, Chairman of the Board*
> *Sales and Marketing Executives International*

I've used these concepts in every conceivable situation, including business selling, family situations, executive management, human resource situations, and dozens of other areas. Track Selling™ is more than selling — it is a communications protocol. *World Class Selling* is bound to become a key addition to the bookshelves and briefcases of leading salespeople, managers and executives throughout the business world.

> *Lee Zinsli, Healthcare executive, Vice President*
> *Brim, Inc.*

Selling investors, strategic partners, regulators, payers and employees all must happen before any product is sold to a customer. Behind every successful medical innovation is a great salesperson. *World Class Selling* teaches selling as a process with skills that are learned. Chitwood's methods are the keys to succeeding, whatever your field.

> *Max Lemberger, Producer*
> *Minnesota Medical Frontiers*

World Class Selling presupposes today's salesperson must be positioned as a professional, with all the educational and experiential credentials necessary to succeed. This book will equip the serious-minded sales practitioner wanting to prepare now to succeed in the 21st century. The contents of this book will provide you with a competitive advantage.

> *John A. Counter, CME, Managing Director, Marketing*
> *AAA Auto Club South*

In my more than 30 years of building, managing, fixing and consulting to sales organizations in all industries, I have missed the availability of one all encompassing textbook and manual, one selling source book. Now we have one with *World Class Selling*. I would recommend this complete and scientifically practical guide to anyone at any level in business. It is a world class book on a very important subject.

> *Kenton Cooley, Managing Partner, Topline Group*

World Class Selling is a very practical book that actually teaches the selling process step by step. It gives salespeople the techniques and procedures they need to make immediate sales.

> *Bill Renfro, President, Renfro Foods, Inc.*

Success in selling an insurance program encourages continued effort. If you know the program will have positive results, the easy part is selling the program if you follow the seven steps of Track Selling.™ Although I use the basic concepts of Track Selling™ toward all areas of my life, *World Class Selling* is a reminder of many areas which need brushing up on.

> *Jack R. Powell, Senior Vice President, Chief Operating*
> *Officer, CalComp Insurance Company*

Pros know sales success is never easy. *World Class Selling* will simplify the path to higher performance and earnings. Roy Chitwood lights the path to success with his classic wisdom, systems and today's techniques.

> *Patty DeDominic, Founder and CEO*
> *PDQ Personnel Services, Inc.*

Since meeting Roy Chitwood over ten years ago, my success in all business matters has increased tremendously. Our company structures everything that has to do with customer relations according to Chitwood's methodology, and it works beautifully. I am extremely pleased to see that Roy has decided to share his knowledge in *World Class Selling*. If it sold for $1,000 it would be an incredible value!

> *Gale Banks, President, Gale Banks Engineering*

World Class Selling is an excellent compilation of the Track Selling System™ concepts. Beyond that it represents a forward look into the future of selling products to purchasers that buy for their reasons. This book can become the frame work for any successful sales organization.

> *H. K. Broxey, Longview Fibre Company*

When I was introduced to Track Selling,™ I was a good salesman. Roy Chitwood aided me in becoming an excellent salesman and manager. *World Class Selling* is a way of communicating that you must know to be truly successful!

> *Jerry D. Beck, CEO, TEC International*
> *Former COB-CEO Mighty Distributing System*

Roy Chitwood has accomplished the Herculean task of pulling together all the sequential steps and fundamentals of making a sale and of making a sale stick. Pros can use *World Class Selling* as a check-up. Beginners, as a shortcut, crash course.

> *Dan S. Kennedy, Author, No B.S. Sales Success*

World Class Selling is one of the most comprehensive guides to professional selling that I've ever read. Chitwood addresses individual attitude and purpose, deals with technique and then goes on to deal with process in depth.

> *Bryan Bennett, Executive Chairman/CEO*
> *Movers International*

World Class Selling is the definitive text on the profession of selling. Chitwood provides a true win-win situation for all involved! This book is a very readable discourse on the track method — a can't-put-it-down thriller!

> *Chris Billat, President, Benchmark Strategies*

Yesterday and today's success does not guarantee tomorrow's. *World Class Selling* provides critical material on Track Selling.™ When fully grasped, it will make your success in the future much more obtainable. Having taken my first sales course from Roy Chitwood in 1978, I have found this to be one of the most valuable learning tools anyone could ask for.

> *Gerald A. Johnston, President and CEO*
> *Johnston & Culberson, Inc.*

Reading and following the guidelines vividly described in *World Class Selling* will help anyone gain insight and lead to the road of success. The short chapters with hard hitting points will keep your attention and the exercises and Things to Remember reinforce the major points. This book is a practical compendium of sales understanding, sales techniques and procedures synthesized in pragmatic rather than theoretical prose.

> *Jack Bunis, Chairman of the Board, CEO and*
> *President, Cair Systems*

World Class Selling takes an approach that works and converts it to a simple, understandable process that increases the salesperson's chance of success and subsequent client satisfaction due to the reliable qualification process. This shouldn't be a book you read and put on the shelf — like the quality process, it should be used, refined and adapted on a daily basis.

> *Roger Stedronsky, President, Motivation Media Inc.*

Most selling books are pure motivational hype. It's nice to see a book that finally teaches the selling process. The techniques used in *World Class Selling* are invaluable.

> *Louis Csabay, Assistant Vice President, Cosmair Inc.*

World Class Selling is an excellent text for salespeople, regardless of experience or years at the job. It is an excellent tool to organize not only thoughts, but actions, that will lead a salesperson toward a successful close.

Jackson C. Oswald, National Account Manager
Graybar

Whether you have been in sales two weeks, two months, two years or twenty years, you cannot help but get ideas to help you be a better salesperson if you read *World Class Selling*.

Mike Frank, CSP, CPAE, Past President
National Speakers Association

Roy Chitwood's seven-step process of selling has changed my life. My income has increased more than ten times in ten years. *World Class Selling* is one of the greatest gifts I have given myself.

Stephan Helbock, Tao Communication

The new salesperson and the seasoned professional will both find a lot of value in *World Class Selling*. The key word is: complete. This book covers the whole sales process.

James W. Newman, CPAE, President
The Pace Organization; Author, Release Your Brakes

We at Senco have been using the Track Selling System™ for over fifteen years. *World Class Selling* will be a requirement for all of our salespeople, both new hired and experienced, for a follow-up to their on going training..

Jerry Carter, Senco Products Inc.

World Class Selling cuts straight to the heart of the sales process. This book reflects the author's deep understanding of sales as a value-building process, and every page offers sound advice for the sales professional.

Tom Ingram, Professor and Chair
Colorado State University College of Business

World Class Selling does an excellent job of explaining the effective sales process. This new book is an excellent tool for enhancing anyone's skills in both selling and communications!

James L. McCarty, Senior Vice President
Ecolab Center

Having trained over 25,000 salespeople I eagerly read this new book to see what new light could be shed on the problem of ideas that would apply to selling any product, service or idea. Roy Chitwood is a genius to be able to invent a book full of workable, practical ideas for any of us that sell. You will be underprivileged if you do not have this book.

D. John Hammond, CEO
American Motivational Association;
Past President, National Speakers Association

Every once in a while a book comes along which spells out the basics with simplicity and great insight. This is one of those books. Practice Roy Chitwood's methods. The results will speak for themselves.

Linda Ehlenberger, Vice President of Sales
Holland America Line - Westours Inc.

World Class Selling is without doubt the best and the most powerful sales tool a professional salesperson can, and should possess. If you purchase the book for no other reason, purchase it to learn the best closing question anyone has ever come up with. I use it in both my professional and personal life with equal success.

Alan G. Julier, Sales Manager
Krautkramer Branson-Hocking Inc.

Chitwood has an incredible knack for taking something as complicated as the selling process and making it simple. *World Class Selling* is an educational program that anyone can use and from which they can easily learn. Chitwood not only provides leadership to the sales profession, he has elevated it.

David Yoho, The Professional Educators Group

Finally a book that is more than motivational hype. *World Class Selling* teaches the selling process and techniques that are invaluable.

Rolf Benirschke, President, Eastman & Benirschke

World Class Selling is truly world class and will be regarded as such — as the seminal work on the subject — long into the future. I've given it to my daughter, Mary, with my enthusiastic endorsement as she started a new job.

Harry G. Bubb, Chairman Emeritus
Pacific Mutual Life Insurance Company

I have employed the Track Selling System™ successfully in telemarketing, third party retail selling networks and other marketing programs. The unique mix of a straight forward process and sophisticated marketing concepts make it a useful tool, for the beginner and seasoned professional. If you are seeking to improve effectiveness by being of greater service to your customer, I highly recommend that you read and study *World Class Selling*.

> *Steve Tonissen, Senior Vice President, Comshare, Inc.*

UCLA's retired coach, John Wooden was Basketball's Master of detail. Roy Chitwood is selling's master of detail. He has turned the art of selling into a science. *World Class Selling* is your blueprint for superstar sales performance.

> *Neil Cannon, Chairman of the Board*
> *Schmidt Cannon, Inc.*

A book on selling which is incredibly useful for everyone even if "sales" isn't in your title.

> *Todd Hartwell, Director of Marketing, Diesel Jeans & Workmen*

World Class Selling provides logical and understandable material that will help any sales person become more effective. If you really want to understand what a true sales professional is and how to become one, then you need to read this book. Roy Chitwood has provided a great service for the sales profession.

> *Donald Gessel, President, Washington Energy Services*

During a 40 year career in sales, sales management and executive management, I've studied and implemented many sales processes. Roy Chitwood has developed the best I've seen. All of our sales consultants have been trained in this discipline and our results have increased significantly. I have become an ambassador for this process.

> *Richard M. Nelson, President & CEO*
> *The Grant Nelson Group*

Roy Chitwood is in a class by himself with *World Class Selling*. Buy it, read it, and reap the rewards.

> *John Imlay, Chairman, Dun & Bradstreet Software;*
> *Author, Jungle Rules*

World Class Selling is a bible for the sales professional. As I hire additional sales directors, it will become part of their orientation and ongoing professional development. This book will assist us in developing and retaining our key business partners — our customers.

> *Jay Youell, Vice President of Sales*
> *Human Affairs International, Inc.*

I recommend this book to all firms committed to serving their customers' needs through relationship building. The process recommended in *World Class Selling* recognizes the customer's needs and commits the sales professional to connect directly with and fulfill the needs of the customer not the product. This approach lays the foundation for longer term customer relationships and sales.

> *Wendy Weir, Manager, DSM, BC Gas Utility Ltd.*

Chitwood has done what other writers have tried and failed to do — represent the selling cycle from beginning to end. No matter how long you have been in sales, a day or a life time, you will find areas in *World Class Selling* that will help you to be even more successful. I highly recommend this book to anyone who wants to be a professional salesperson and even more so to the individual who is in the world of sales.

> *Ken McCrocklin, President, Ke-Re, Inc.*

The active learning that is promoted by the skill-building exercises in *World Class Selling* virtually guarantees that readers will not only remember, but will also be able to skillfully use all of the techniques and strategies that they have learned. The steps in the sales process and the strategies of selling are illustrated with fascinating examples and case studies that breathe life and drama into every page of this outstanding book.

> *Donald J. Moine, Ph.D., Sales Psychologist;*
> *President, Association for Human Achievement, Inc.*

Successful selling requires a process based on integrity, a sincere concern for the needs of the customer and a set of skills that assures a high probability of a mutually beneficial relationship with a customer. *World Class Selling* fulfills that need admirably. Mastering his seven-step selling process is a must for every salesperson regardless of the product or service being sold.

> *Jack Asgar, President, Practical Management, Inc.*

Roy Chitwood is one of the very important sales tools that has contributed to the success of our company. Through the focus on Track Selling,™ our Account Executives have been able to close business that would have otherwise gone to other people selling a similar service. The investment we have made in training has paid outstanding dividends. The methods in *World Class Selling* give an excellent return on investment.

Bob Waldorf, President, Idea Man, Inc.

Bravo! It was long overdue and I thoroughly enjoyed reading *World Class Selling*. It is the ultimate guide on how to properly sell anything to anyone. It definitely works as we have established company sales records every year over the past four years!

Victor W. Sterne, Vice President, Medicus Systems

World Class Selling is the first of its kind which focuses in on the specific issues and problems of the expert professional salesperson and delivers usable, practical and unique ideas and solutions. It teaches the techniques and processes that can be used every day and it provides the materials, forms and guidelines necessary to make the process happen. Chitwood brings the selling process to an all new state-of-the-art.

Raymond J. Hall, Executive Vice President and CEO
Electronics Representatives Association

As Roy Chitwood states: "When selling becomes a procedure, it ceases to become a problem." *World Class Selling* shows that sales is a method of communicating and provides a procedure of communicating which will always ensure that the customer is satisfied. This procedure is not only valuable in a person's professional life, but also in their everyday life. Professional salespeople are the result of following the seven steps correctly.

K. M. Dowlson, Western Regional Manager. CFM Inc.

World Class Selling is first-class reading! As a salesperson for over twenty years, I can honestly say the selling principles so well covered in Roy Chitwood's new book work in the real world. *World Class Selling* should be required reading for every salesperson. It will be for all Mighty Distributing salespeople!

Gary Vann, Senior Vice President of Sales and
Marketing, Mighty Distributing System of America, Inc.

The quality of material, insight, depth of logic, and new ideas, give Roy Chitwood's efforts a five star rating. *World Class Selling* is must reading for the serious sales professional trying to either move to the next level or greatly enhance his or her income.

> *Bill Shearer, President*
> *East-West Broadcasting Company, Inc.*

At last, a book that takes the reader through a simple seven-step, world class selling process. Recommended reading for everyone in the sales profession.

> *Jack I. Criswell, CSE, Executive Director*
> *Sales and Marketing Executives International*

No sales office should be without this book! While newly hired salespeople will find a solid blueprint for sales success, the experienced salesperson will appreciate the finer points that will help them reach the highest level of sales success.

> *Gerhard Gschwandtner, Publisher*
> *Personal Selling Power*

World Class Selling is an easy-to-read book with great ideas to help every salesperson increase their sales, their self-esteem and their customers' satisfaction.

> *Dr. Tony Alessandra, Author*
> *Non-Manipulative Selling; People Smarts*

An outstanding book by a most respected professional. Clear. Complete. Highly recommended.

> *Nido Qubein, Chairman, Creative Services, Inc.*

Chitwood's three decades of sales experience come out clearly in this logical and systematic new book. No matter what the product or service, *World Class Selling* is the backbone to success in sales.

> *Jeffrey M. Abrahams, President, Qualyvendas, Brazil*

Top rate material! I have used the seven steps of Track Selling™ to close most of my biggest deals. To say that was worth millions would be an understatement.

> *David H. Schwartz, President, Super Marketing*

Roy Chitwood's seven step process served as the foundation for my final presentation to the search committee to obtain my current position. *World Class Selling* packages Chitwood's philosophy and process as an ongoing, working document for all of us in sales.

George J. Twiss, Vice President, Sales and Marketing
Fox Communications Corp.

Finally a definitive step-by-step sales process is explained in a fast moving, well-written book by a true master of sales!

Robert A Chesney, Executive Producer
Window on Wall Street

World Class Selling will be considered a classic for today's market and for years to come. Roy Chitwood and his Track Selling System™ is a combination that has no competition.

Don Estrin, CME, Founder and Former Chairman,
Move Management by Ryder; Former President,
Sales and Marketing Executives International

Roy Chitwood's profound analysis of the psychology of both seller and buyer in *World Class Selling* has a global value. It is the principles of marketing wherever you are — in New York, Tokyo or even Beijing. I am learning a lot from this great book.

Tom Ikehata, Former President, CEO and
General Manager Far East, Spalding Japan Co., Ltd.

What a whale of a product! Lots and lots of good stuff for everyone in sales. I've been selling since age 12, yet I'm digging into Roy Chitwood's *World Class Selling* almost daily for new and helpful ideas.

"Rocket" Ray Jutkins, Professional Speaker and
Marketing Consultant

World Class Selling professionally sells to salespeople exactly what they need most. Chitwood not only stresses professionalism, but defines clearly how all salespeople can be professional. *World Class Selling* provides a track that will lead salespeople to success, not only in achieving that original order, but in establishing repeat customers and clients.

Jack Berman, Berman Publications

Roy Chitwood has done it again! One of the real sales masters has taken sales to a whole new level. This book is a must resource and a must read. Marvelously done and masterfully written!

Bill Brooks, Author, Niche Selling; You're Working Too Hard To Make The Sale

If you want your sales in the world class category you've got to find world class material and a world class teacher. You've got them both right here. Go directly to the cash register.

Danny Cox, Speaker; Author, Leadership When the Heat's On; Seize The Day

Instead of creating reverence for past answers, *World Class Selling* flings the door open to a new paradigm for sales. Roy Chitwood goes beyond traditional hype to provide the sales professionals with a workable roadmap to a value-based, client-centered selling process. This principle-based book is money in the bank. It's something sales professionals need to read, right now.

Terry L. Paulson, Ph.D., CSP, CPA, Author, Paulson on Change; They Shoot Managers Don't They?

Roy Chitwood correctly spots the problem: the buyer has become sophisticated. In *World Class Selling* he covers why and how to establish the long-term relationship that creates profit through stability. His seven steps to Track Selling™ are a blueprint for success.

Jim Tunney, Ed.D., CSP, CPAE, Professional Speaker and Former NFL Referee

The techniques in *World Class Selling* were instrumental in helping me launch a successful career at Hewlett Packard in the 1960s and later has helped Scott Blum and myself build Pinnacle Micro into a world class company in the 1990s.

Bill Blum, President and CEO, Pinnacle Micro, Inc.

Anyone interested in becoming a sales representative should buy *World Class Selling*. It contains instructions and examples that, if followed, will help you to become successful.

G. W. Hogue, Assistant Vice President of Sales Lance, Inc.

World Class Selling is a practical and proven approach that explains the "how to" of the sales process. The application of the insights and process outlined in this remarkable book will give your professional sales team a competitive advantage.

> *Thomas J. Bligh, Principal, Deltapoint*

Most books emphasize what should be done and leave out the how to do it. *World Class Selling* provides Roy Chitwood's proven step-by-step Track Selling System,™ which provides the tool for a person to become a productive salesperson.

> *Robert M. Randolph, Chairman and CEO*
> *Professional Management Institute*

An irresistible read; educational, inspiring, enlightening, full of proven basic skills, techniques and philosophies in a simple how-to-use format. The reader is likely to feel a renewed pride and respect for the important and ever shifting role of a professional salesperson.

> *Don K. Covington, Jr., CSE, Senior Vice President*
> *Sales and Marketing Executives International*

Roy Chitwood really understands the selling process. His seven steps of selling are practical, powerful and results oriented. *World Class Selling* is a must read for every new sales professional as well as the veterans working in today's challenging and exciting markets.

> *Ted Kemper, President*
> *The Canadian Training and Development Group Inc.*

World Class Selling is the cornerstone to my personal and professional success. Chitwood's book on his selling process is the most comprehensive, understandable treatment of the subject I have yet read. Selling is a skill everyone should have, and Chitwood's publication is absolutely a "must" addition to the library and knowledge base of any serious professional.

> *Kirby Fox, Founder and CEO*
> *EXCELL Executive Leadership Exchange*

World Class Selling is a great text and one every sales professional should buy and read, as it will help sharpen their skills in the selling process, utilizing invaluable techniques.

> *Robert R. Sharp, President and CEO*
> *AAA Auto Club South*

World Class Selling is one of the best training-type books I have seen. It provides step-by-step procedures for becoming a consultative sales professional, but it is practical enough that the user still keeps his own personality. Each step in the process is explained clearly and thoroughly with dialog that adds clarity and life to each step of the system.

> *Don Butler, President & CEO, Employers Group*

I have attended Roy Chitwood's seminars several times both in the United States and Japan. At the conclusion of the training, all of the participants understand what selling is and how to sell. *World Class Selling* contains the techniques Roy Chitwood has spent half of his life developing.

> *Tomio Joichi, President, Business Brain Co., Ltd.*
> *Japan*

Roy Chitwood embraces the ethical selling strategies that have made today's top professionals successful. Readers that will invest in themselves and take the time to implement the techniques and strategies described in *World Class Selling* will quickly develop the skills that will set them apart from the competition.

> *Joe Scharbrough, Consultant*
> *McGladrey & Pullen, LLP*

I have consistently prescribed Roy Chitwood's training programs. Now, with the publication of *World Class Selling*, I can send my clients and students to the bookstore to have their prescriptions for effective, professional selling filled.

> *"Dr. Revenue" John Haskell, Sales and Marketing*
> *Consultant; Instructor, USC Business Expansion*
> *Network, Fast Trac Entrepreneurial Training*

World Class Selling covers every aspect of the selling opportunity in a format that is easy to read, understand, and implement. Anyone can enjoy success in the sales profession if they take the time to read this book and apply it to their business. Chitwood covers the smallest details such as attire, and not accepting drinks, which can be lethal to success.

> *Bob Aldridge, Senior Vice President - Marketing*
> *Forest Lawn Memorial Parks and Mortuaries*

In *World Class Selling*, Chitwood looks at the entire selling process from top to bottom and gives the reader a new perspective on what it takes to be a world class seller. Salespeople who work through this program will become better communicators and enrich their professional career — and their personal life as well. If you want to reach your goals, this is a path well worth taking.

> *Christen Heide, Executive Editor, Sales and Marketing Publications, The Dartnell Corporation;*
> *Editor, Marketing Times, The Official Publication of Sales and Marketing Executives International*

World Class Selling is not only an excellent "how to" quantitative guide to high sales achievement but an in-depth qualitative "how to" guide as well. Chitwood combines all of the softer skill sets with proven sales techniques and successfully marries all the elements in an easy to use format. *World Class Selling* will bring participants to the top 2 or 3% of achievers in the sales profession.

> *L. Bryant Barry, CSE, Director of Sales,*
> *Animal Health Division, Sandoz Agro, Inc.*

In *World Class Selling*, Roy Chitwood speaks from a world of experience. That experience, so generously shared with me over time, is what I attribute to the fact that today, I too have become a world class salesman. *World Class Selling* is a good start for anyone who desires to be among the best.

> *James C. Naleid, President*
> *Lokken, Chesnut & Cape Inc. Investment Counsel*

Roy Chitwood's system offers a crisp, clear and organized method of selling that is easily understood by our sales professionals and management. It has proven tremendously effective in converting interested shoppers into satisfied customers. In all my years in retail I have never seen a sales method that compares! It really works!

> *Rick Haux, President, The Bedroom Super Store*

After nearly 30 years in the marketing business, I have yet to see a book that builds the reader's self esteem and confidence the way *World Class Selling* does. There is no doubt that if a sales organization embraces the philosophy and follows the system, they will be successful beyond their expectations.

> *John D. Eastham, Managing Partner, EMB Partners*

World Class Selling is unique, different and certainly applicable to selling any product or service. It is a must for all sales personnel. It should be studied and constantly referred to as different types of sales customers, objections and competitive situations materialize. In time, it should be the most "dog-eared" book in the sales library. Track Selling™ is the best sales habit any true professional salesperson can develop.

> *Douglas Hill, President*
> *California Moving and Storage Association*

The fundamental principles of Roy Chitwood's method of Track Selling™ have brought many rewards to me and my family. His system of planning and development lends itself to more than selling. It makes your whole life easier to manage.

> *Kenn Baroni, Salesman*

World Class Selling is practical and gives people the actions, techniques and procedures they need to make sales now.

> *Robert D. Johannsen, CSE, President*
> *Entre Computer Center*

World Class Selling is a wonderful text on selling to adapt for today's competitive industrial society. It precisely analyzes the complete selling process leading to successful results with not only a scientific, but also humanistic, approach. I recommend this valuable work to all sales professionals throughout the world.

> *Hiroh Kuno, Executive Director*
> *International Marketing Council of Japan*

World Class Selling is indeed a well-thought-out, comprehensive approach to sales. Chitwood moves the field, in a very practical way, in a direction so likely to yield both higher ethics and higher performance.

> *Jeff Cox, Cox Creative Works*

Roy Chitwood provides a selling philosophy that creates a caring and dependable approach of partnership in serving the prospects or clients needs. *World Class Selling* should provide many sales managers and salespersons with a unique track to follow in dealing with all situations that arise in communicating ideas to others. The system has great merit.

> *Jack O'Loughlin, CME, Past President and Chairman*
> *Sales and Marketing Executives International*

It's great to see such a no-nonsense, practical guide to selling. Follow the seven outlined steps and you will be on the way to *World Class Selling*.

Janice M. Szur, CSE, CME
Automation Resource Corporation

World Class Selling is a common sense guide that enables a salesperson to make more sales, build long term customer relationships, and out perform the competition every day. Roy Chitwood has given us a proven formula for success and prosperity.

Charles Gordon, President, Renewal Concepts

Learning and using Roy Chitwood's highly-effective selling method has changed my career and life. I always shunned selling — feeling uncomfortable and ill-prepared to sell. I especially encourage those who feel they cannot sell to use this scientific approach to selling. It provides the selling differential that is so vital to success in our hyper-competitive markets.

Ron Holm, R. W. Holm & Associates

WORLD CLASS SELLING

The Science of Selling

The Complete Selling Process

Roy E. Chitwood, CSP, CSE

BEST SELLERS PUBLISHING

Minneapolis, Minnesota USA

Publisher's Cataloging in Publication

Chitwood, Roy E.
    World class selling: the science of selling, the complete
selling process / by Roy E. Chitwood.
        p.   cm.
    Includes bibliographical references, index.
    ISBN 0-9636268-3-3

    1. Selling.   I. Title.

HF5438.25.Q32   1996   95-080723
658.8'5
                                                    CIP

TABLE OF CONTENTS

To Anneli,

my love, my friend, my soulmate

In Memorium

To my brother, Jim,

one of the best salespeople I have ever met

To the Sales Professionals

of the world . . .

They make our world better.

ACKNOWLEDGMENTS

I want to personally thank the many people that have helped me and made a contribution to *World Class Selling*.

A special thank you to all the clients of Max Sacks International that I have had the opportunity of working with for the past twenty years. And to the thousands of participants who have responded to me in writing, phone and fax thanking me for the impact the Track Selling System™ has made on their lives.

To all the people at Best Sellers Publishing for all their help in making *World Class Selling* a reality. A special thank you to my editor, Shannon Kranz, for her immeasurable contribution.

To the staff of Max Sacks International including Rick Cobb, Al Kauder, Ray Felix, Ron Holm and our facilitators who deliver our World Class Track Selling System™ workshops worldwide.

A super special thanks to my executive assistant, Christine Klinner, for her contribution in keeping me on "track."

Also, to the many people on our staff of consultants who have contributed to *World Class Selling*, including Betty Platts, Bert Barer, Ph.D., Rose-Lise Obetz, Ph.D. and Tim Branning. These people have contributed their brilliance, creativity and hard work to making *World Class Selling* a reality and to the many clients we have served.

And last but not least, to all my friends and relatives who have supported me during the past several years as I have grown to be a better salesperson, teacher, business person and above all a more loving and caring human being.

PREFACE
THE NEW AND CRITICAL ROLE OF SALESPEOPLE

Recently the H. R. Chally Group completed the first World Class Sales Benchmarking study. This 18-month project was sponsored by: AGT, Alcoa Building Products, Hobart Corporation, Johnson & Johnson, The Mead Corporation, Northern Telecom Limited, Reynolds & Reynolds, Steelcase, Unisource and the International Benchmarking Clearinghouse, arm of The American Quality and Productivity Center.

The results of this research project focus on what customers want from sellers, critical salesperson skills, and the eight most important sales Benchmark Areas that contribute to bottomline profitability.

WHAT CUSTOMERS WANT FROM SELLERS

Interviews with over 1,000 corporate customers established three major needs customers expected vendors and sellers to address, even though they were not confident they could get them.

1. Customers want to narrow their own focus to the few things they do best, and outsource the rest without the added overhead costs of supervising their suppliers.

2. Customers want sellers to know their business well enough to create products and services they wouldn't have been able to design or create themselves.

3. Customers want proof — hard evidence — that their supplier has added value in excess of price.

THE CRITICAL SALESPERSON ROLE

To evaluate a vendor or seller's potential to fulfill these three needs, these corporate customers specifically judged salespeople on combinations of only seven factors. These seven, listed in descending order of the frequency they were cited, are:

1. Managing our satisfaction personally

2. Understanding our business

3. Recommending products and applications expertly

4. Providing technical and training support

5. Acting as a customer advocate

6. Solving logistical and political problems

7. Finding innovative solutions to our needs

Customers believe that salespeople who excel at these seven factors can best fill their three basic business needs.

Our interviews with these corporate customers also resulted in their "voting" a group of sellers as "best" or "world class." While none of these sales forces were viewed as perfect, they have committed themselves to the goal of meeting all three major customer needs.

By benchmarking these top ten sales forces, we identified the critical success factors for sales and the standards of sales excellence. Benchmarking pinpoints how world class sales forces manage customer satisfaction, understand their customers' business and deliver the other critical benefits.

THE BASICS OF WORLD CLASS SELLING

The overriding philosophy of the best sales forces, simply stated is: "Be the outsource of choice."

The basic priority, therefore, is to provide salespeople who add value to the customers' business.

Adding value requires at least three critical elements:

1. Identify the business needs of customers.
2. Develop the added services to wrap around products which will guarantee the customers' business improvement.
3. Measure for continuous improvement refinements as well as proof for customers that their business was improved.

NEW REQUIREMENTS, NEW CULTURE

To be the "outsource of choice" forces a seller to refocus the corporate culture. Creative engineers or other technical experts who invent new products are not enough to sustain a competitive advantage. Too many new products do not match customers' priorities, are too difficult to understand or use, or are simply not needed.

The focus must change from product to benefit or business result. Grandiose products and services with more capacity, features or options are often just seen as overpriced. Additionally, products and services must be simple to use and manage, either in their own right or because the seller manages the complexity as part of the sale.

The focus must also change from price and delivery to utility and ease of use, not only of the product but in doing business with the seller. The salesperson of choice will take responsibility for managing the relationship — the "partnership" — between seller and customer. This will require the role of the salesperson, and consequently, the role of the sales manager who trains and develops the salespeople, to change.

Our top sellers are changing from peddlers to relationship managers, from order-takers to consultants. In some cases, order taking, service, technical support and product expertise need not be directly provided by the salesperson.

While the requirements are changing and many of the solutions are new, the approach the top sellers use is remarkably consistent, either intentionally by benchmarking others, through partnerships, or coincidentally by addressing their own needs. Through a "total quality" styled approach they are investigating and analyzing their customer needs and problems. They are reorganizing their processes, developing new skills, creating new measures and new standards and, most of all, committing to the need for continuous improvement.

The most basic tenets of total quality management require the biggest investments to be in people and measurement. In fact, the hallmark of how the world class selling companies can be recognized is in their approach to people and their approach to information and its management.

This leads the greatest single effort toward selecting, developing and supporting a new kind of salesperson — a fully professionalized, competent businessperson who delivers real added value.

In short, we're taking about salespeople who understand *World Class Selling*.

Howard P. Stevens

CEO, The H. R. Chally Group

Co-Author, The Quadrant Solution

INTRODUCTION

The sales profession is undergoing a historic change. Each salesperson must decide where he or she stands in relation to this change. On the path from the past, pseudo salespeople maneuver, ambush, trick, and cajole customers into buying a product or service. On the path to the future, up-front, empathetic, professional salespeople serve their customers as advisors, counselors, and even partners.

Thirty-five years of sales experience and contacts with thousands of salespeople have convinced me beyond the shadow of a doubt that to succeed, today's salesperson must make the customer's needs primary. If the customer doesn't benefit from a sale, the sale shouldn't take place.

Today's competitive marketplace is forcing companies to scale back costly sales operations, leaving room only for top performing salespeople. The seller's market which existed for many years has become a buyer's market. Companies don't need salespeople to take orders; they need salespeople who can sell. Incompetent salespeople are becoming unemployed salespeople.

Only the cream-of-the-crop salespeople will remain. Out of necessity they will practice partnership selling. They will be actively engaged in their clients' business affairs as consultants and counselors. Companies are reducing the number of vendors they deal with, and want partnerships with those they retain. Customers will turn from salespeople who cannot or will not forge such partnerships to salespeople who are willing and able to help them succeed. A salesperson's success will depend on the success of his or her customers.

Today's more sophisticated customers no longer tolerate the fast-talking, back-slapping salesperson whose only concern is his or her pocketbook. Nor are clients satisfied with a salesperson who simploy promotes a product or service as the best on the market. Clients want salespeople who help them solve problems and who enlighten them on new ways to improve their business.

World Class Selling is an about-face from obsolete hard-sell tactics. As a World Class Salesperson, you help eliminate the popular stereotype of a salesperson as an insincere, pushy individual who would happily sell the proverbial "refrigerator to an Eskimo." *World Class Selling* involves doing things for the client rather than to the client. This helping relationship, similar to the doctor-patient or lawyer-client relationship, is the key to successful selling.

World Class Selling is a scientific process that covers all bases and leaves nothing to chance. It includes the Track Selling System™ that takes you through each step in the sales process, from the approach to the close and follow-up. Behind these procedures is an ethical philosophy — a win/win philosophy of serving the customer that you can rely on when you need to make a decision. It works when you are selling for your company, yourself, within an organization as a CEO or manager, and even in your personal life.

Whether you're a seasoned professional or a newcomer to sales, you'll find your confidence skyrocketing when you learn and practice *World Class Selling*. As Dick Boudreau of American Linen Supply puts it, "I went into it thinking, 'Okay, what are they going to show *me*?' I think many guys my age have this attitude: 'I've been kicking in this business for 26 years. What are you going to teach me about selling?' But the Track Selling System™ takes people from where they are to the next level. I embraced it immediately."

THE FUTURE DEPENDS ON SALES

In today's competitive marketplace, a company's future depends more on its sales and marketing ability than on any other facet of its business. Without sales, nothing happens. Even knowledge of what a products and services to provide flows from the partnership between a company's sales force and its clients. W. Edwards Deming says that a company must "focus on the consumer, not the product, as the most important part of the production line."

Deming founded the Total Quality Management (TQM) movement. TQM shifted the focus in manufacturing from profits to quality, and from the individual to the team. TQM is working well. Costs are down; profits are up; consumers are more satisfied; team work is replacing old win/lose ways; and new methods and processes ensure that the consumer receives quality service as well as a quality product.

TQM works because it insists that a logical, step-by-step process is central to improving production. And the TQM process can be applied to any product, from potato chips to computer chips. Now, just about every organization has a production process, as well as an accounting process, a distribu-

tion process, and an administration process. But what about
sales? Which organization has a sales process? Sales tend to be
left to chance. Typically, salespeople are given some product
knowledge and some motivational hype, then sent out to sink or
swim. Is it any wonder that salespeople feel pressured, panic,
and don't close sales? Without training, a process, and assistance, how can salespeople enhance the quality of their relationship with the customer? How can they become true sales
professionals?

For the past thirty-five years, I have developed, practiced and
taught the principles, skills and techniques covered in *World
Class Selling*. Like TQM, *World Class Selling* can be applied
to any product or service that benefits a consumer. It can even
help you sell an idea. Our organization has worked with
150,000 salespeople from over 3,000 companies. We know
World Class Selling works, because it has helped these salespeople increase their productivity. This increase in productivity
and profits flows from the basic premise of *World Class Selling*:
Serve the customer. It's that simple.

Becoming A Sales Professional

World Class Selling is founded on ethics, caring and service.
Therefore a World Class Salesperson must be well schooled in
building relationships. Most sales literature and training focuses
on closing the sale. Sales trainers talk about identifying customers' needs and building long-term relationships, but they tend to
make these goals secondary to the sale itself. That distorts the
process. To serve the customer, and therefore to maximize your
own success, the sale must be considered another stepThe sales
role of today can be such that the sale is considered yet another
step — an important one, to be sure — toward establishing a
long-term helping relationship.

Today's corporate environment imposes this new paradigm of
integrity. The sleazy salesperson in the baggy blue suit is a relic
of the past. Today's top salespeople bring their honesty to work
with them. They know that prospects don't false promises; they
want salespeople to "tell it like it is." Buyers demand more
than a good price. They want honest value for their investment.

It's human to be a little nervous about operating in a changing
environment. The Track Selling System™ prepares you to

calmly handle most of the situations you will encounter. Because it's based on a win/win philosophy of serving the customer, you never need to con or pressure a prospect, or do anything against your standards or contrary to your personality.

There is nothing wrong with selling. There is only something wrong with trying to manipulate people into buying.

THE PROFITS OF ETHICS

Here is what a few of the many *World Class Selling* professionals have to say:

"I thought you might be interested," reports Nancy Christenson of the Employers Group, "in knowing that I closed a $300 sale over the phone the first time I used the Track Selling System.™"

"The Track Selling System,™" says Greg Weir, Project Manager of BC Gas, "is just a far more effective and efficient use of everybody's time. For example, I sat down with a committee the other day to get their approval on $80,000 worth of funds. I sat down with a sales plan in front of me, and in twenty minutes, I had their approval of $80,000."

"Within three months of learning The Track Selling System,™" relates Brian Soliday, sales manager of Genasys, "I became complacent in administering the Track method. Hence I accepted a Sales Manager position with a leading computer mapping software developer. After a single week with my new firm, I decided to review my notes from the The Track Selling System™ training, and reorganized my sales efforts. In an almost unheard-of amount of time — seven weeks — I closed a sale with a major systems integrator for the U.S. military. Although the initial sale was not a tremendous amount, the success of the development of the prototype will generate sales that may exceed three to four million over the next two or three years."

RESEARCH POINTS TOWARD THE FUTURE

The H. R. Chally Group recently completed a study of 56 Fortune-500 corporations. Based on their findings, complied

over an 18 month period, the Group made these recommendations:

 • Position customers as drivers of strategy.
 • Form a partnership with the customer.
 • Develop high quality salespeople.
 • Implement team selling.
 • Professionalize the sales profession.
 • Standardize training procedures and certification.
 • Commit to lifelong learning.

The recommendations of the Chally Group confirm the principles of *World Class Selling*.

WHAT YOU CAN LOOK FORWARD TO

In *World Class Selling*, you will learn a process that covers all
aspects of sales. This process will enable you to successfully sell
any valid product, service or idea. It is flexible and adaptable to
your personality, and the personalities and styles of your customers.

You will learn about the buyer's hidden agenda: the Five Buying Decisions that every prospect must make before buying. If
you don't know what these decisions are, or the precise order in
which they are made, you can't reach your potential in sales. In
World Class Selling, you will learn the Seven Steps of the
Track Selling System™ that carry you smoothly through each of
the prospect's buying decisions in that correct order.

You will also learn the Six Buying Motives — the hot buttons
in selling. By adapting your presentations to your prospects'
motives you will increase your sales and your customers'
satisfaction.

Most sales literature focuses on closing. But asking for the
order and closing the sale are logical conclusions to a well given
presentation. That's why *World Class Selling* covers each point
in the sales process, from the approach to the close — and
beyond.

You'll learn new ways — ways that help the customer — of
dealing with objections such as ''I want to think it over,''
''Your price is too high,''and ''I want to shop around.''

The skills, techniques and philosophies of *World Class Selling* will give you a sustainable advantage over your competition. *World Class Selling* will show you how to sell more, earn more, and have more fun in the process.

PART 1

WHAT EVERY PROFESSIONAL SALESPERSON NEEDS TO KNOW

I n the next nine chapters, you will learn everything you need to know to become part of the twenty percent of peak performers in sales. You will learn:

- ◆ What really makes a buyer buy.
- ◆ What buyers must say yes to before they say yes to the sale.
- ◆ How to serve your prospects by filling their needs and solving their problems.
- ◆ How to listen more than talk, to establish rapport.
- ◆ How to ask questions that yield a gold mine of information — information you can use to fill your prospects' needs.

In short, you will learn to become a sales professional — a giver rather than a taker — and make a ton of money doing it.

GETTING CLEAR ON YOUR OBJECTIVES

Before you start learning about the Track Selling System,™ take a look at what your own objectives are at this point. Goals — personal and professional — help you get where you want to go.

For example, why are you reading this book? Perhaps your main objective is to make more sales...and more commissions. Or, it may be to gain more confidence as you develop a better understanding of the sales procedure and how to conduct your day-to-day sales calls. You may want to learn to close your sales more easily. Or, you may just want to brush up on existing skills, and to find out what you're doing right and where you can improve.

Whatever your reasons, you are devoting a lot of time and effort to reading and implementing this material. You expect that time and effort to pay off for you, and so do I.

Take a few moments to think carefully about your main reasons for reading this book. In the space below, write the main benefits that you hope this book will help you achieve.

Be assured that you will be given all the tools you need to accomplish the objectives of your choice.

And now, welcome to the world of the sales professional.

1

THERE'S NOTHING WRONG WITH SELLING

Say the word "salesperson" and what picture comes into your mind? A guy in a baggy, blue suit that looks like it cost $49.95 and hasn't seen the dry cleaners since its first day off the rack. Or, a fast-talking, back-slapping, suede-shoed, high-pressure con artist. Salespeople are pictured as people who are totally absorbed in touting the virtues of the product or service they sell, with no concern about what their customers really want or need.

This image doesn't *have* to be true, but unfortunately, it is often well deserved.

I first began in sales as a young man, answering the classified ads: "Get rich quick. Work four hours a day, earn a thousand dollars a week, drive a new Cadillac!" If you've never had this experience, you're better off, but when I got to meet the person behind the ad, it was the man in the baggy, blue suit. "Things are a little rough right now," he'd say, "But as soon as you come on board, everything will be wonderful."

THE SALESPERSON'S NEGATIVE IMAGE

In most people's minds, the image of a salesperson is negative. If you doubt that, try a little experiment next time you're at a a party. Announce in a loud, clear voice that you're a life-insurance salesperson, and watch how fast you're left alone.

CREDIT AND BLAME

Why is this image so negative? In addition to being justified, there's another reason: It's a basic human trait to take credit for our wise purchases and blame the seller if something goes wrong.

Let's suppose you counsel with a prospect for months. You make dozens of calls on that prospect. You find out exactly what that person wants or needs. You put together a custom-made program, designed to solve the person's problems and needs precisely.

You've worked hard. You've practically performed a miracle. When it's time to ask for the order, you say, "Jane, if we can schedule delivery by the first of the month, can you think of any reason why we shouldn't go ahead?" Jane says, "No," and you've made your sale.

What happens next? Jane's company prospers like it's never done before. As a direct result of making that purchase, the company is able to function more quickly and easily. Profits zoom.

When that happens, does Jane's company call you in? Throw a banquet in your honor? The company might throw a banquet for Jane. After all, in their eyes it was *she* who made that astute purchasing decision.

But if something goes *wrong, then* they call you in. It's a basic trait of human nature to take the credit for our own wise purchases and blame the seller if anything goes wrong. There's not a single thing any one of us can do to change that fact.

Think about how you react after making a purchase. Suppose you buy an absolutely perfect car at a downright bargain price. Who was responsible for that purchase? Who made that astute purchasing decision? Who recognized the good deal when he or she saw it? You or the salesperson?

If, however, the car turns out to be a lemon, whose fault is it? It's the salesperson's fault, isn't it? The salesperson talked you into it. You didn't *buy* the car at all; the salesperson *sold* it to you.

Everyone loves to buy, but no one likes to be sold. Normally, the image of a salesperson is someone who sold you something you didn't want, didn't need, couldn't afford...and it didn't wear well.

WHEN MEDIOCRITY SETS THE STANDARD

A major electronics firm went to a university campus to interview graduating seniors for the position of sales engineer. They put up fliers all over the campus announcing the date, place and time that interviews would be held.

Jobs were scarce at the time and seniors were voicing genuine concerns about finding any jobs at all. Do you know how many students showed up for interviews? Do you know how many of those university seniors were eager to have a job carrying the title, "salesperson?"

Zero. Absolutely none.

Over twelve million people in the United States give themselves the title of "sales professional," yet eighty percent of all sales are made by just twenty percent of those salespeople.

Four out of every five salespeople a customer meets are mediocre, incompetent or downright ineffective. Even some of those in the upper twenty percent are borderline mediocre. At best, when we're talking about *professional* salespeople, we're talking only about that upper ten percent.

The average prospect tends to meet people who *call* themselves "salespeople" but haven't the foggiest notion what selling is about. They aren't really salespeople at all, but simply pretending to be.

The negative image of a salesperson is well deserved, but this, we *can* change.

Remember those fantastic, get-rich-quick ads I mentioned earlier? After combing through those ads for several weeks (and weathering the effects of the con artists behind them), I finally landed a sales job I could believe in. Because I believed in it, I stayed there for sixteen years before moving on and purchasing my own sales company, Max Sacks International.

I know from experience that you can't just "sell anything to anyone, anytime." You have to believe in what you sell, the company you sell it for, the one doing the selling (you), and the one you're selling to (your prospect). Once you do, the whole game changes for the better, for everyone.

There's nothing wrong with selling. There's just something wrong with the way most people sell.

GOOD MONEY IS GREAT BUT IT'S NOT ENOUGH

An insurance salesperson once declared, "I can make it big selling anywhere...just find me a hot product, I'll sell it. Don't care what it is."

If all I wanted was lots of money, this philosophy would have worked well for me. However, my main mission in life is not to have as much money as possible, but to teach others how to better themselves. I always appreciate what money can bring, but beyond that, I want to help people grow and develop.

I don't see selling as a matter of separating the prospect from his wallet. Selling is a matter of serving the prospect so well that the product or service wears well over time and a trusting relationship develops. These well-served customers will return to do more business, refer other prospects to you, and contribute to your success and prosperity in ways beyond your current dreams.

"True professionals go by a code of conduct that directs them to abide by ethical standards," says Ray Bagley, my friend and former president of Westland Life Insurance Co. "One standard says that professionals should serve the needs of clients with integrity. A doctor does this with a patient, a lawyer with a client, a banker with investors. When a salesperson is bent on making money rather than serving a customer's needs, that seller is not performing as a professional."

The more you sell as a professional, the more you elevate the caliber of selling, and the prospect respects you more for your high standards. "When the seller maintains professional standards,'' Ray continued, ''the prospect becomes more trusting and open to your proposal.''

There's nothing wrong with selling, except the image that shoddy, untrained salespeople have left in the mind of the general public — *your* prospects.

You can change all that by becoming one of the twenty percent of salespeople who actually make the sales and serve the prospects with complete integrity, pride and professionalism.

INTEGRITY PAYS

Contrary to the image of salesperson-as-con-artist, integrity will get you through difficult situations more effectively and profitably than manipulation. Here is one real-life example.

Russ Shamun, the senior vice president of Right-O-Way, a transportation company, had to present a rate increase to a long-term customer, despite his general manager's conviction that this company would never accept a rate increase. ''My approach was simple,'' he recalled. ''I remembered what I always admired most in a salesperson: an individual who told me the truth, and sold honesty and integrity.''

Russ decided to *be* that person. ''My approach was to explain the current situation to the vice president — our costs were steadily increasing, yet we had not taken an increase from his company in two years. 'We don't want to lose your business,' I assured him. But I also reminded him that 'it's extremely important for our two companies to stop negotiating as adversaries and work together to reduce each other's costs. Part of that process is to mutually understand each other's business and the variables involved.' I presented him with our airline contracts and several articles about our industry's condition and the need for us to increase our rates.''

What happened as a result of this straight talking? Did Russ lose the sale?

''Before I had an opportunity to close,'' he chuckled delightedly, ''the customer responded: 'What can I do to help you with your present condition?' What most amazed my general manager was that we did not even have to *ask* for a rate increase. All we had to do was explain our situation. Not only did we receive a ten percent rate increase — and retain the business — but we expanded our business to include additional areas.''

Russ Shamun is a strong believer in integrity in the sales situation. ''People want to see companies survive and prosper,'' he said from experience, ''so they can develop long-term business partnerships as opposed to short-term deals. What we sell is transportation, but let us not forget that we sell solutions — and, more importantly, honesty and integrity.''

BEING A SALES PROFESSIONAL IS MORE FUN

Most people in selling today don't actually *like* to sell. Why? Because they don't do a very good job of it.

Think about the things you do for fun. Maybe you jog, or play tennis or handball. Maybe you swim, play golf, or go fishing or dancing. Maybe you do gourmet cooking or watercolor paintings. Whatever it is, I bet you do it reasonably well. If you *didn't*, you wouldn't do it for fun.

The same is true in selling. Skilled, professional salespeople have *fun* selling. They're interested and genuinely enthusiastic for each day's work. What makes selling fun for the skilled professional and a sweaty-palm experience for the untrained salesperson? *Confidence*...the confidence that comes from knowing what to do and how to do it. A *positive attitude*...the kind of thinking that expects and creates success. And *energy* to carry him or her through.

The skilled professional has methods — precise, step-by-step procedures that cover all points in the selling process and leave nothing to chance. The skilled professional also has *success* — the self-satisfaction of accomplishing important things.

The skilled, professional salesperson has all the training, skill and inner resources required to do the job well. Because the job is done well, each day's work is challenging, rewarding and *fun*.

If you make an effort to get a little better and a little more professional every day, imagine the impact it could have on your career. If you get just a little better each day, imagine the impact it will have on the image of salespeople as a group.

When you make your next call on a new prospect, do you think that person is expecting to talk with a truly professional salesperson?

Not on the basis of their own past experiences with salespeople.

How many times in the past do you suppose your prospects have experienced a salesperson who came into a meeting with a written plan — a plan that could carry them from their initial greeting straight through to closing the sale, and even one step beyond that successful sale, to ensure that the sale will wear well?

How many times in the past do you suppose your prospects have worked with salespeople who asked on-target questions to uncover exactly what they wanted or needed, really *listened to* what they had to say, and offered ways to solve their problems or fill their needs precisely?

How many times in the past do you suppose your prospects have worked with salespeople who had their prospects' own best interests in mind every step of the way — who were more concerned with providing genuine, beneficial service than the commissions they were earning?

You can be one of the new breed of salespeople. You can achieve more success in your career by helping your prospects meet their real needs.

In this book, you will learn a precise method to use on every sales call you make — a method that incorporates integrity every step of the way. You will learn how to view situations through your prospects' eyes and make a sales call for one reason only: to provide genuine, beneficial service. After reading this book, you will conduct yourself and your sales calls differently, and you will be more successful.

Several years ago, Nelson Rockefeller posed for the cover of *Fortune* magazine above the caption, "Salesman." Now, if someone with the success and stature of Nelson Rockefeller can call himself a salesman, maybe you and I should be proud to be in this profession, too.

There's nothing wrong with selling. What's wrong is the eighty percent of sales amateurs that pretend to be salespeople. *World Class Selling* can keep you out of the low-producing eighty

percent, and keep you firmly entrenched in the top twenty
percent who truly deserve the title, "salesperson."

IMAGINE A POSITIVE IMAGE

Imagine what it could be like to shed that negative image — to
learn the philosophy and principles that will help you make the
right decision every time — to take pride in your expertise,
your professional appearance, your listening skills and your
ability to establish warm, sincere rapport with your prospects.

Wouldn't that make you feel better about calling yourself a
"salesperson?"

You have no idea how many well-intentioned salespeople shy
away from the word that describes their profession. "I'm a
sales[burble]," one salesperson may mumble deliberately,
hoping to move on to the next subject. "I'm an account executive," another may say with a quick, defensive smile. Anything
to avoid being associated with the guy in the baggy, blue suit.

If you were truly professional — if you could take legitimate
pride in your work, your human relations skills, and your ability
to really be of service to your prospects and long-term customers — don't you think you'd be able to utter that word without
flinching?

What would it be like to make a cold call and know you were
really going to help someone? Most salespeople walk into a
prospect's office with their hands sweating, their heads almost
bowed, and grateful to be given an audience with the prospect.
They walk in apologetic and on the defensive from the start.

Why? They think they have to sell their prospects something —
talk them into it. A professional salesperson knows that he or
she is there to serve. whether the prospect buys or not. So how
can he or she lose? Either way, he or she wins. If the prospect
buys. the salesperson has been of service, and if the prospect
truly does not need what the salesperson is selling. then leaving
gracefully is in the prospect's best interest. The salesperson
can't lose, because either way, he or she will be of service to the
prospect.

If that salesperson were you, and you knew you were prospecting to serve the potential customer, wouldn't you walk into the prospect's office with your head held high?

MAKING THE PARADIGM SHIFT

In selling you on *World Class Selling*, I'm really suggesting that you make what's known as a *paradigm shift* — a shift to a whole new way of seeing the world of selling.

Taking a new view of reality has often been met with resistance. When Columbus suggested that the world was round rather than flat, his new idea was initially met with suspicion. When Copernicus suggested that the earth revolved around the sun rather than the other way around, his new idea so upset the scientists of his time that they rejected it outright.

World Class Selling, on the other hand, meets with no real resistance among salespeople, and none at all among prospects, because they feel understood by professionals who use the Track Selling System.™

Why don't salespeople balk at seeing the world of sales as a place to do service? In the real world, salespeople understand that the old ways of selling don't work any more. The young salespeople tend to be more consumer-oriented to begin with, and the more seasoned salespeople are relieved to find answers to what has stopped going right for them.

In a recent training seminar, I talked about outmoded closes, like the Assumptive Close. At the break, a participant came up to me. "Listen, Chitwood," he said irritably. "Don't tell me the Assumptive Close doesn't work. I've been using it for years!"

"I didn't say it doesn't work," I replied. "I said it doesn't work *as well as* the Guaranteed Close." (You will learn the Guaranteed Close in Chapter Fifteen, "Step Six: Act of Commitment.")

Unconvinced, he stalked back to his seat. After he had heard more, he came back with a friendlier look on his face. "You know," he said, "You're right. In fact, the reason I'm here is because I've had trouble with my closing. Now I know why."

Here's another actual scenario. Chuck, the vice president of sales, was concerned about Harry, a veteran salesperson who used to be one of his best producers. These days, Harry was working harder than ever, but his sales were down. He just wasn't cutting it.

One day, Chuck took the bull by the horns and called Harry into his office.

> *Vice President:Harry, you know we value you as an important part of our sales team, but something's been off for a while. What's going on?*
>
> *Salesperson: Oh, it's that new, young, punk buyer at Acme Manufacturing.He doesn't know what he's doing, so we lost the account.*
>
> *Vice President:How about Phoenix Industries?*
>
> *Salesperson: Well, it's that new woman they just added. She's not qualified to be a buyer.*

What's really going on? Harry's not relating to today's young, educated buyers and he "blames" success on nonprofessional factors like "luck" and "charm." He knows his old ways aren't working, but he doesn't know why.

Is Harry a dinosaur? Will he soon become extinct? His years in the field can only be a plus, but if he doesn't recognize the world has changed — that buyers don't want to be conned, they want real service, and giving service is the most profitable, self-esteeming thing a salesperson can do — then he *may* go the way of the dinosaur.

It sounds severe: "Change or die." *World Class Selling* offers a philosophy that serves not only the customer, but the salesperson. What's to lose in changing to win/win? If serving the customer will ensure that your sales wear well, that you will have more pride in yourself and more fun, and that your profits will increase as a matter of course, can you think of any reason why you shouldn't read the rest of this book and make the paradigm shift to becoming a sales *professional*?

THINGS TO REMEMBER

- Most people have a negative image of salespeople that is often well deserved.
- It's human nature to take the credit for wise purchasing decisions, and blame the salesperson when things go wrong.
- A professional salesperson uses integrity, not empty promises, to serve the customer and make the sale.
- Eighty percent of all sales are made by only twenty percent of the salespeople, and only ten percent of those are professionals.
- When selling becomes professional, selling becomes fun.

EXERCISES

1. What have been your own negative associations with salespeople?

2. What would you need in order to become a professional salesperson?

3. What would make selling more fun for you?

2

THE FIVE BUYING DECISIONS:
WHAT YOUR PROSPECTS DON'T TELL YOU

We buy countless things that are not *sold* to us. We buy on our own initiative to satisfy our needs and desires. When we do, we buy almost without thinking.

However, when something is being *sold* to us, we *do* think.

To be a successful salesperson, you need to know *how* people think when they're being sold. Your prospects won't tell you, but if you pay attention, it's easy to tell. Putting yourself in your prospects' place is a great way to understand how they think. In fact, you probably *have* been in their place.

Suppose you're driving a long distance on an important journey. Suddenly, you notice your gas gauge registers empty. The road stretches before you, suddenly longer and lonelier than before. You need gas in a hurry and you don't care what brand it is, where you buy it, or who services you. You don't even care about paying a few more pennies per gallon.

"Gas Next Exit." With a sign of relief, you roll into the gas station on your last drop of gas and stop in front of the fuel pump. You hardly notice the attendant as he fills your tank and cleans your windshield. Nothing matters except that you're out of trouble — or so you think.

Then the attendant gives you a funny look. "I wouldn't drive another mile on that tire," he says unexpectedly. "We can replace it for you right away."

"Eh?" you respond. "What tire?" Suddenly, the whole picture changes. Who *is* this guy, anyway? Is he honest? Does he really know tires? Does he truly care about you and the safety of your journey, or is he trying to make a quick buck because he guesses that you're over-anxious to arrive somewhere? "If I need a tire, I need a tire," you think, "but not at just any price." On the other hand, you don't want to waste money on an off-brand cheapie. What kind of place is this, anyway?

You become acutely aware of your surroundings. Details that didn't matter at all now matter very much. Is this a proper service station? Is it well-rated? Are the attendants trained and knowledgeable? Can they really replace your tire "right away," or will it take hours? And does the tire really need replacing *now*? It has already gotten you this far safely, but dare you postpone it until you get home? These and many other conflicting thoughts flash rapidly through your mind while you listen to the attendant's words, but you don't tell him what you're thinking. Why would you? You don't even know if you trust him.

Without intending to, you have become a prospect, and the unknown gas attendant has become a salesperson. You are having these thoughts because you're not buying on your own initiative and timing. Someone is trying to sell you something that you may or may not need. Without prior preparation, you have to make a decision. Will it be yes or no?

YOU'RE AN UNKNOWN QUANTITY TO YOUR PROSPECT

When *you* make a sales presentation, this is essentially the situation your prospect is in. The kinds of questions and doubts that flashed through your mind at the service station are exactly what flash through your prospects' minds as you discuss your product or service. Understanding this will help you. It will increase your chances of selling successfully and keeping control of the sales presentation.

There are five buying decisions *everyone* makes when you are trying to sell them something. It is different when the person has made the decision to buy something. At that time, he or she is only interested in two things, the product or service and the price. However when you are selling something the decisions always come into play even though the other person may not be aware of making the decisions.

Once you know about these Five Buying Decisions, you can address them so that each of your prospect's decisions is a yes. This leads your presentation to a successful close — and another happy customer.

THE ORDER OF THE FIVE BUYING DECISIONS

The Five Buying Decisions *always* occur when you are selling and they occur in this *precise, psychological order*.

1. About you, the salesperson
2. About your company
3. About your product or service
4. About your price
5. About the time to buy

THE FIRST BUYING DECISION: ABOUT YOU, THE SALESPERSON

The prospect's first impression is not the product or service you sell, but *you*. *You* have come to sell him or her something. He or she may be ever so friendly, but he or she is sizing you up just the same.

Wouldn't you?

The prospect's unspoken concerns about you revolve around two particular issues.

1. Your integrity
2. Your judgment

YOUR INTEGRITY: In your prospect's mind, this translates to whether you are there to take or to give. "How interested is this salesperson in serving my needs?" your prospect wonders. "Or is this person just interested in making a fast buck? Is he or she capable of understanding my needs? Do I trust this person? Do I like this person?'' The prospect wants to see you — both now and in the future — as a helpful, valuable consultant, advisor, and counselor — to trust you as he or she would a close friend.

YOUR JUDGMENT: This translates to whether your understanding of how your product or service is matched by an understanding of how it fits the prospect's needs. "Does this person really have a handle on what he or she is selling?'' your prospect wonders. "Does he or she know my business, and how this product or service could really help me?''

So in your first contact with your prospect, *you* will be assessed. This means you need to make a good connection with the prospect — establish good rapport. Chapter Seven: "The Art of Asking Questions'' and Chapter Ten: "Step One: Approach'' will show you how.

THE SECOND BUYING DECISION: ABOUT YOUR COMPANY

In addition to liking you, trusting you, and feeling that you know what you are doing, the prospect also wants to be convinced that your *company* is dependable — that it supports service after the sale and will be there to back you up.

Just as you would wonder, "Who manufactured this tire?'' when you suddenly had to buy a tire, your prospect wants to know: "Who backs you up? Can your company deliver what you promise? How long has it been in business? How much do I really know about your company?''

Your prospect also wants to know, "What does your company stand for? Do you have faith in your own employers? Do you have faith that your other customers will recommend you favorably? If your company is new, why has it entered the business? What does it offer that is better than its competitors?''

You may make a distinction between yourself and your company, but your *prospect* doesn't. When *you* serve your prospect's needs well, that person views your *company* in the same light. Potential buyers resist saying yes to a close until they have been persuaded that both *you* and the *company* have a good reputation and deliver on your promises. If you convince them that both you and your company have integrity, they will be open to accepting the rest of your presentation.

THE THIRD BUYING DECISION:
ABOUT YOUR PRODUCT OR SERVICE

Now that your prospect is satisfied with *who* is representing the product or service, he or she is ready to focus on *what* you're selling — the product or service itself.

Of course your prospect wants to know the factual details: "Our widget is compact, portable and weighs only 10 pounds." But the real *emotional* concern (and people buy for emotional, not logical reasons) is: "Does this product or service really meet my needs — emotional as well as practical? Does it solve my problem? If not, can I count on you to back out gracefully instead of trying to persuade me to buy something that I may regret?"

At this stage, the prospect is also mulling over the quality of the wares, the installation, the delivery schedule, and many other factors.

THE FOURTH BUYING DECISION: ABOUT YOUR PRICE

Now the prospect is ready to consider price: "Is the product or service affordable?"

Prospects don't really buy because of price; they buy because of *value*. Buyers want more than a good price; they want value for their investment. Until prospects are convinced that your product or service has value to them — until they see the *benefits* — no price is right. Too low a price arouses instant suspicion, and they view all other prices as too high.

Don't push price: sell value. As long as prospects are convinced they are buying real value. they will be less resistant to price and can *afford* to buy what they want.

THE FIFTH BUYING DECISION: ABOUT THE TIME TO BUY

If the prospect's answer to all the previous decisions is yes, you have almost closed the sale. The prospect has decided to buy — but when?

This is a valid question, like "*When* should I have that tire replaced?" No one wants to spend money before it's necessary. However, if you can give the prospect sound advice on why to buy now, he or she wants to hear it.

Now is the time to ask for the order — and give a delivery date. Your prospect will decide whether your timetable for delivery and installation fits with his or her requirements, and make a decision accordingly. (Don't worry if that decision turns out to be no. You will learn how to close not only once, but five times — easily and without embarrassment — in the Guaranteed Close, detailed in Chapter 15: "Step Six: Act of Commitment.")

WE MAKE THE FIVE BUYING DECISIONS ALL THE TIME

We may not consciously be aware of making the Five Buying Decisions, but they occur for all of us, in this order, whether we're buying tires, swimming pool maintenance, a new car, a new job...or even a new relationship. The more you know about these decisions, the better you can serve your customers — and yourself.

Years back I wanted to enter the sales field, and I interviewed for a sales job at Midland National Life. In this case, I was not only a seller (for myself as a prospective employee) but also a buyer (of this company as an employer). I asked questions that would help me make the Five Buying Decisions and be able to answer the question, "Is this job for me?"

1. ABOUT THE SALESPERSON

My first buying decision was made about the salesperson — in this case, the manager who interviewed me. After some opening chitchat to establish rapport, he asked me, "Why did you leave your previous job?"

I responded, "I was looking for a management opportunity, a chance to use the skills and talents I have."

"What do you know about the insurance industry?" he went on.

"Very little, other than that insurance agents seem to make a lot of money."

"How important is a weekly paycheck to you?"

"If a weekly paycheck were a must," I told him, "I'd still be punching a time clock at my old job."

He shifted in his chair and looked straight at me. "Roy, we're looking for people who are sincerely looking for a management opportunity in a dynamic organization," he said. "We want you to feel that you're not only working for Midland, but for yourself as well."

I decided to check out the sincerity of his earlier assurance that I could go as far as my talents and drive would allow. "How long has your boss been with the company?" I asked him. "What is his background?"

He responded, "My boss is the district manager, in charge of several offices. He's just been with Midland Life a short time. He's new to the insurance business. He was in the retail furniture business before."

This seemed to support his earlier assertion about management opportunity. I asked him, "What traits should a person have to be successful in this business?"

"The person needs to be honest, energetic, hardworking, and able to follow instructions."

I knew I had these traits. This gave me confidence that I could succeed with this company.

"Selling insurance is not easy. You have to know the business. It's hard work and long hours."

"Long hours don't turn me off." I told him. "I'm looking for the right opportunity."

Later I was interviewed by the District Manager. He told the same story, so I thought it must be true. I had long ago learned that you can tell when someone is not being truthful by asking the same question in different ways. If the answers don't match, you know you're getting a lot of smoke and mirrors. Fortunately, they did.

2. ABOUT THE COMPANY

My next decision was about the company. The manager went on to explain the philosophy of the founder. "Mr. Sammons was a self-made millionaire," he said. "He built an empire by taking ordinary people and giving them an opportunity that was limited only by their ability and how hard they were willing to work. They could advance as quickly as their talent would allow. Mr. Sammons amassed a fortune by giving the average person unlimited opportunity to build a career."

As the prospect, I was really happy to hear that. I thought, "How could anyone ask for anything more? If what he says is true, then this is what I've been looking for." I was seeking an opportunity, not just a job. What sold me was that Sammons Enterprises was the embodiment of Charles Sammons. He urged his people to go for the top, to be the best they could.

3. ABOUT THE PRODUCT OR SERVICE

My third decision was about the product or service. The product Midland offered me was opportunity — not only the opportunity of selling insurance, but also the opportunity of advancing into management.

4. ABOUT THE PRICE

What would I be paid? "You'll have to support yourself for about thirty days," the manager told me. "From that point on you'll be working on a commission basis, so you can earn as much money as you're capable of producing. Your paycheck is limited only by your talents and how hard you're willing to work."

Was I willing to "pay the price?" Was I willing to risk going to work on a straight commission, with no guaranteed salary?

5. ABOUT THE TIME TO BUY

My response was yes. My drive to succeed and better myself would go nowhere without the right opportunity. The time was right. The career opportunity and outlook at Midland Life were what I wanted and I decided to accept their offer.

So what were my buying decisions based on?

1. The manager (the salesperson) — his integrity and judgment
2. Sammons Enterprises (the company)
3. The opportunity to sell insurance and advance to management (the product or service)
4. The willingness to risk working on a straight commission with no guarantees (the price)
5. To go for it (time to buy)

CONVICTION IS CONVINCING

People buy because it's clear to them that the seller truly believes in what his or her company offers. This conviction is more important to buyers than all the facts in the presentation. Your ability to meet the prospect's Five Buying Decisions will give them that conviction.

When you understand the inner workings of the Five Buying Decisions, you're in a better position to design a presentation that serves the prospect's real needs — and gets results.

THINGS TO REMEMBER

- People buy for *their* reasons, not yours.
- There are five psychological buying decisions. When someone is selling these always occur, and always in this precise order:

    1. About you, the salesperson
    2. About your company
    3. About your product or service
    4. About your price
    5. About time to buy

- People buy because you truly believe in what you are selling.

EXERCISES

1. How do you react when salespeople try to sell you something for *their* reasons?

2. Recall how you, as a consumer, experienced an incident that illustrates how the buying decisions work. Describe when and why you made each of the Five Buying Decisions.

    a. About the salesperson:

    b. About the company:

    c. About the product:

    d. About the price:

    e. About time to buy:

3

SALES IS SERVICE: THE SALES PROFESSIONAL FILLS A GENUINE NEED OR SOLVES A GENUINE PROBLEM

What *is* a salesperson, really? Everyone seems to have a different idea of what a salesperson really is. Some say, "a problem-solver." Others say, "a communicator," or "an educator," or "someone who motivates a prospect to buy."

I say: *The professional salesperson is one who has the ability to help the prospect buy now and wear well, or get an act of commitment and wear well.*

This definition is a central principle of the Track Selling System,™ so please fix it in your mind and write it below.

WEARING WELL

"Wearing well" means that the sale is right for both the seller and buyer. It means that your sale has helped create a happy, satisfied customer and helped build an ongoing relationship in which your prospect becomes a long-term client.

A sale wears well when everything you promised your prospect on the front end to get the sale is delivered on the back end. This means that your customers receive the benefits they expect: your product or service works as you described it; any extra service or training that you promised is delivered; and they feel respected, considered, and well taken care of. You promise a lot and always deliver more.

It may be a new idea to think of wearing well as part of a salesperson's responsibilities, but a professional salesperson has integrity every step of the way. This means you sell your prospects what they need. The job does not end as soon as the prospect signs on the dotted line. You learn as much as possible about the prospect's problems, fill the prospect's needs or solve those problems, and then make sure that the prospect gets everything he or she expects. For example, "wearing well" means that:

- The product or service fits the customer's needs precisely.
- Delivery is made on the date promised.
- The service turns out to be even better than the customer expected.
- The salesperson checks back with the customer to make sure all details have been handled to the customerÆs complete satisfaction.

A sale can only wear well if the salesperson stands behind the product or service that is of value to the customer, and if the company standing behind the salesperson is honest. In my view, anyone working under less than these conditions isn't a salesperson at all.

There is a big distinction between a person who happens to work in sales and a *professional* salesperson.

QUALITY AND INTEGRITY — LIKE MONEY IN THE BANK

A professional salesperson does more than sell quality products and services. His or her whole way of *operating* says "quality." When you sell the *World Class Selling* way, you assure your prospect you can be counted on, and you can take pride in having integrity and the long-term success that comes with integrity.

Integrity and quality. In manufacturing, these traits are a must. In sales, can we get by without them? Can a salesperson really be successful when selling a product or service that has little or no value to the prospect? Can he or she really be successful when working for a company that is less than honest?

The answer is no. How can a sale like that wear well? Even if we *could* get by without integrity and quality, why *should* we? It's much more fun, challenging, satisfying, and profitable to serve your prospect, not your wallet.

Do you know what happens when you truly give service? You get back more than you can even imagine.

THE RIGHT TO HELP YOUR PROSPECT BUY

As a professional salesperson, you have the right — and the responsibility — to help your prospect buy and buy now.

MAKING THE PURCHASE HELPS YOUR PROSPECT

Why? First, your prospect will be *better off* by making the purchase. It will help your prospect fill a need or solve a problem. If it doesn't, you shouldn't be selling it to that person.

Let's say that you're a publisher's rep selling medical and scientific reference works and textbooks. Your first prospect is the acquisitions librarian for a large medical school who is under pressure to provide reference materials that include recent findings on the new drug-resistant strain of tuberculosis. You sell her two new titles on this disease from a German medical publisher, and she is happy because you solved her problem and filled her need.

Your second prospect, however, is your local physician. You would not use powerful persuasive skills to try to push these same books onto him, even though he has many new TB patients. Why not? You know — being a professional salesperson who researches your prospect's needs — that his applications are clinical, not academic. Therefore, to solve his problem you would do better to offer abstracts of the latest medical journal articles on TB, which he could access through on-line medical databases at the local hospital.

Now let's say that your third prospect is your neighborhood bookseller. You certainly wouldn't use your persuasive skills to sell him these academic tomes; he could never sell them to *his* customers. In this case, once you discovered his needs, you would thank him and leave gracefully. After all, a professional salesperson only sells to prospects whose needs and problems fit your specific products or services. (To determine whether there is a match, you will use Step Two: Qualification, which is discussed in Chapter Eleven).

If you really believe that your prospect will prosper by buying your product or service, then you have the responsibility to act. If you didn't, the prospect's needs would go unmet. You are doing the prospect a service — helping him or her solve problems or fill genuine needs.

GETTING AN ACT OF COMMITMENT

When it is not immediately appropriate to make the sale, your right and responsibility is to get an *act of commitment* from your prospect — an agreement on the next step that will eventually lead to a successful sale. The next step could be a future appointment, or the prospect's agreeing to mail you detailed specifications the following week, or agreeing to inspect your facilities at a later date. (For more on Step Six: Act of Commitment, see Chapter Fifteen.)

WHEN NOT TO SELL

This does not mean talking the prospect into buying, then talking yourself into believing the prospect "needed" what you sold. A real professional knows when the prospect does *not* need the product or service. You must clearly see how it will benefit your prospect; otherwise, don't go on with the presentation. Instead, end gracefully, apologize for not being able to help the person, perhaps suggest another supplier who can meet his or her needs, and be on your way.

More than once, I served prospects' needs by not talking them into buying. A while back, a senior vice-president of a Minnesota bank asked Max Sacks International's Minneapolis office to present a training program that we don't do. I didn't want to take the time to develop a new program, nor did I want my Minneapolis manager to spend time on it. So instead of trying to sell the bank our existing training program (which wouldn't have fit their needs) or just leaving them high and dry (which didn't fit my need for integrity), I asked my manager to call several other training companies and find out: (1) did they offer the kind of training program this bank needed, and if so, (2) could they meet the bank's needs? If the answers were yes, then my manager was to figure out which of those companies seemed to offer the most value for the money and relay this information to the senior vice-president of the bank.

Which he did. "We're sorry that Max Sacks International can't meet your needs at this time," my manager told him, "but we would like to recommend three companies that we checked out on your behalf."

The senior vice-president was amazed. "Every other sales training company I called assured me they could do *any* type of training, *any* time," he exclaimed. "I want you to know that I appreciate your honesty — and I'll take your recommendations."

We did not make that sale. However, we did make a friend.

One year later, that same bank *did* purchase a training program from us — a much larger training program.

THE VALUE TO THE CUSTOMER EXCEEDS THE PROFIT YOU WOULD MAKE

The second reason why your job is to help your prospect buy now has to do with money: You truly believe that your product or service is *more valuable to the prospect* than the money you would earn from the sale is to you.

Think about it: In the years ahead, you'll be making a good deal of money in commissions and/or salary. Do you suppose it will take you a relatively long time or a relatively short time to get those checks cashed and spent? A relatively short time, don't you think? However, in the years to come, your prospects will be buying a great deal of the product or service you sell, and quite likely still be receiving the benefits of those purchases years after your own commissions are gone. Remember: The sales process has a long time span. *World Class Selling* is not about a win/lose situation; it's win/win. When the salesperson is a professional, it's the customer who wins the most.

This is not an idealistic objective. It's highly *realistic*. Increasingly, the marketplace demands this kind of honesty. Research evidence shows that the glib, fast-talking smoothies are no longer the high performers. Individual consumers and corporate buyers are more educated and more enlightened. They are "on to" the smoothies. Companies and buyers require salespeople who are knowledgeable, client-oriented counselors and consultants. Larry Wilson wrote a book called *Changing the Game: The New Way to Sell,* in which he observed: "salespeople of the nineties must provide adequate solutions and serve as trusted consultants to the customers they sell. They must be creative, strategic thinkers — team players and leaders — and develop long-term relationships with their clients."

By definition, you have every right and full responsibility to convince your prospect to buy a product or service that will fill an actual need or solve an actual problem.

As a professional salesperson, when neither a sale nor an act of commitment is possible, your underlying goal remains to provide a genuine, beneficial service.

HOW TO SPOT A PROFESSIONAL SALESPERSON

Putting this all together, how do professional salespeople differ from those who simply work in sales?

  ◆ Professional salespeople are *effective*.

They close most of their sales and make high earnings. When they don't close a sale, they get an act of commitment from the prospect which will further the sales process.

  ◆ Professional salespeople have *confidence*.

They enjoy the selling process and enjoy their working relationship with their prospects and customers. Their prospects and customers like and trust them. Prospects become loyal customers.

  ◆ Professional salespeople become thoroughly familiar
    with their prospects' businesses.

Because they are givers, not takers, professional salespeople serve as counselors and consultants. By patiently discovering their prospects' needs, they can determine how their products or services will fill those needs. Professional salespeople are honest and forthright. They do not lie or manipulate. They don't need to.

Are most people who sell professionals? Unfortunately, only twenty percent of the salespeople make eighty percent of the sales. Four-fifths of all salespeople are ineffective — *un*professional. These people don't close many sales. They don't earn the money they could be earning. They don't have the confidence and enjoyment they could have. They don't become experts in their customers' businesses, and they certainly don't create long-term loyalty in their customers.

In another study, 69 percent of corporate buyers in a recent survey rated salespeople calling on them as "fair" or "poor." Considering the lack of training (and the well-deserved bad rep of most salespeople), this is not surprising.

PROFESSIONAL SELLING PAYS
OFF IN CUSTOMER LOYALTY

Shortly after Leanne Sipple, an account executive for the Right-O-Way Transportation Company, learned the Track Selling System,™ she was chosen Right-O-Way Salesperson of the Year. Her selection was based on her total revenue and revenue over quota.

I asked her, "What kind of service and follow-up do you use to win new accounts and keep customers coming back?"

"First I try to develop a professional, yet personal, relationship with my prospects," she told me. "I act as a consultant to help them solve their unique problems. I try to become an advisor for them, as one of their team." Leanne uses *World Class Selling*, and this helps forge prospect loyalty and friendship, and assures her clients that she will help them meet their commitments to their own companies.

"After I've closed the sale," she continued, "each account gets my personal attention to make sure that my own company can provide what I've promised."

What kind of personal attention? "This can be by communicating details of customers' needs via memos and reports," she explained, "or, if necessary, helping our own staff get the job done." Sometimes she also brings her company's operations and customer service people to the customer's site so they too can understand the customer's needs clearly.

Has Leanne's income suffered with this personal attention and customer teamwork — this professional follow-through.

"Hardly," she laughed. "After adding these techniques to my sales approach, my sales increased *300 percent* over the previous year."

Leanne Sipple is not an exception to the rule. *World Class Selling* enhances the process, the product, and the profits for everyone involved. I get letters every day from salespeople who tell me how this approach has changed their lives.

Patricia Duhn, Director of Sales and Marketing for the Decathlon Athletic Club, responded, "Your material, particularly the 'guaranteed close.' offers a truly scientific 'track selling' approach that is humane and encourages developing relationships that last, as opposed to manipulating people for the sake of the sale."

Bruce L. Paul of Scott & Lauritzen Associates informed us, "I cannot thank you enough for the increased level of professionalism and practicality that the Track Selling System™ has employed in my business and personal life. I can read it in my clients' eyes. They have told me of their increased level of satisfaction of my services. The client becomes convinced that I thoroughly understand their concerns, goals, and objectives. The result is that the client wants to work exclusively with me. and that helps me concentrate on the task at hand more clearly and effectively. It is actually a satisfying experience to see the client and my business relationship grow. By working together with them as a team, I am clearly effective at helping them make wise and intelligent real estate investment decisions. Our company is growing in leaps and bounds."

If learning how to solve the prospect's problems or fill their genuine needs could have that kind of effect on *your* sales. can you think of any reason why you shouldn't make the commitment to becoming a professional salesperson?

THINGS TO REMEMBER

- There is a big difference between someone who works in sales and a professional salesperson.

- The professional salesperson has the ability to help the prospect buy now and wear well, or get an act of commitment and wear well.

- You have the right — and the responsibility — to help your prospect buy, and buy now.

- As a professional salesperson, you learn your prospect's needs so well you know whether your product or service truly fills your prospect's need or solves a problem.

- As a professional salesperson, you believe that your product or service is of more value to your prospect than the money you would earn from the sale is to you.

- The underlying goal is to provide genuine, beneficial service.

- Today's changing business environment demands this kind of honesty and integrity from salespeople.

- The professional approach to sales yields high income and rich personal rewards.

EXERCISES

1. Suppose you discover that a prospect has no need for your product or service. You would:

   a. Persuade the prospect to buy now.

   b. Make an appointment with someone else in that company who might be easier to persuade to buy.

   c. Thank the prospect for talking with you and conclude the meeting on a positive note.

2. Your prospect expresses a genuine need for your product or service, but does not have the authority to make the buying decision. You would:

   a. Persuade the prospect to buy now.

   b. Find out who the decision maker is, and make an appointment to meet with that person.

   c. Thank the prospect for talking with you and conclude the meeting on a positive note.

3. Your prospect expresses a genuine need for your product or service, has the authority and budget to buy, but says he or she wants a week or so to think it over. You would:

   a. Persuade the prospect to buy now.

   b. Make an appointment to come back in a week or so.

   c. Thank the prospect for talking with you and conclude the meeting on a positive note.

4

SELLING IS SELLING IS SELLING

World Class Selling works if you sell cars. It works if you sell real estate. It works if you sell heavy equipment, life insurance, interior decorating, counseling, or oyster farming. No matter *what* product or service you sell, the basic sales process is exactly the same. The only thing that's different is the *sales cycle* — the time between your first meeting with your prospect and the conclusion of your successful sale.

A THERMOS IS A THERMOS IS A THERMOS

Let me suggest an analogy. Suppose you take a thermos bottle to work every day. One day you decide to drink hot coffee, so you fill that thermos with hot coffee. Later in the day when you open the thermos, what do you pour out? Hot coffee. The next day, you decide to drink ice cold lemonade instead. So you fill the same thermos with ice cold lemonade. And when you open it later on, what do you find? Ice cold lemonade. One day hot coffee, another day cold lemonade. But the thermos — *the vehicle you use to accomplish those two, very different goals* — remains exactly the same.

I'm not saying that you don't have your own individual sales problems. Every salesperson is different from every other, and you may face sales problems that other salespeople never run into. What I *am* saying, however, is that the *same process can be followed in every selling situation.*

The same process can help you accomplish your goals on each sales call, no matter how varied those goals may be.

The method you will learn from this book is a structured process, not a canned one. It's not my goal to turn readers into think-alike, talk-alike sales robots who are programmed to invade the countryside, armed with products and a glib manner. Quite the opposite: The words you will use on your sales calls will be, for the most part, your *own* words. What you will be learning, however, is a series of seven steps, to be followed in precise order, that will carry you straight through every sales call you make.

You will not find this difficult. After all, you are following all kinds of procedures in your life right now. You eat your dessert after you've finished your main course. That's a procedure, in precise order, that you follow without a second thought. If you plan to take a plane flight, you first make your reservation, then pick up your ticket, drive to the airport, check your bags, and get on the plane. That's another procedure, in precise order. Again, you do it without a second thought. You know very well that you won't be very successful if you try to change the order of that procedure. You're not going to be successful boarding that plane, for example, if you haven't first made your reservation and purchased your ticket. When you *do* follow the procedure, in precise order, you know it *will* work for you no matter where you're flying, what airline you're using, or what airport you're departing from. It's a procedure that is completely adaptable to whatever unusual situations you face.

That's what I mean when I say selling is selling is selling.

For 35 years I have been telling this to my own sales force and to the more than 150,000 salespeople my company has trained. Over the years I've gotten some pretty strong reactions to that statement.

"What do you mean, 'selling is selling is selling'?" one salesperson might say. "My territory has just been cut to three square blocks of downtown Manhattan, and I sell fertilizer! Don't tell *me* selling is selling is selling."

Or someone will say, "Go call on 'King' Sam Wilson once. *Then* tell me that selling is selling is selling."

My response is that if the selling procedure is effective with one problem or set of circumstances, it will be equally effective with a different set of problems or circumstances. It is the *procedure itself* that is effective.

THE ACTIVITIES OF SELLING

What kinds of activities do you commonly do as part of your normal day in selling your product or service? For example, do you make phone calls? Do you drive to meetings? Your own experience will tell you: Your daily activities remain pretty much the same, no matter what product or service you sell. Do you think the same sales procedure can be used on every sales call, regardless of differences in each specific situation?

Think about everything you do (or think you should do) on a normal sales call. This might include the following:

- Introducing yourself to your prospect and establishing warm, sincere rapport (Step One: Approach in the seven-step procedure)
- Qualifying your prospect as a genuine, prospective buyer who has the authority, and the budget to buy (Step Two: Qualification)
- Understanding what your prospect wants or needs to buy (Step Three: Agreement on Need)
- Establishing in your prospect's mind the reliability and integrity of the company you represent, and giving your prospect specific information about your company (Step Four: Sell the Company)
- Helping your prospect understand the benefits that your product or service provides, and, specifically, how it solves your prospect's problems or fills his or her needs (Step Five: Fill the Need)
- Asking for the order (Step Six: Act of Commitment)
- Thanking the new customer for doing business with you (Step Seven: Cement the Sale)

I think you will agree (especially after reading Part II of this book) that each of these steps is necessary on any sales call.

This is true whether you are selling a fleet of aircraft or a gross of rivets, selling futures options or 30-second radio spots. You can demonstrate this to yourself by imagining three different prospects you now call on or three different customers you service currently. Think about their different personalities, work environments, available budgets, and unique needs and problems. Couldn't you use all of the seven steps with each of them?

You could — and should. Because selling is selling is selling.

KNOWING EXACTLY WHAT TO DO, NO MATTER WHAT THE SPECIFICS

Did you know you are already doing a lot of things right, right now? Do you know *why* they are right?

As you keep reading, you will find out why. You will find the names for some of the procedures you're now using and discover why they're working for you. You will learn techniques and procedures that will give you *consistent* success, because you will be operating in the same way and in the same order on every sales call you make. You will learn techniques and procedures that are practical — ideas you can really use that will adapt to your own personality and any selling situation. You will know *exactly* what to do on *every* sales presentation, and this will make you a lot more successful in selling your product or service, no matter what it may be.

Factors will vary, of course. Every sales situation is unique and you might have special sales problems. For example:

- The territory could be too large or too small.
- The territory could be unsuitable. You could be assigned to sell heavy equipment in suburbia.
- The sales quota could be too high for the territory.
- Your own, unique personality could work well with certain kinds of people, but not with others.
- Some prospects could be difficult, though others are cordial.
- The competition could have the market ''sewn up.''
- Something about your company could put off certain prospects.

Regardless of these variable factors, *the same basic selling process will work in every case* whether your territory is Rhode Island or the six western states. The same sales process will work whether you and your customers are introverts, extroverts, or any shade in between. The same sales process will work whether your company is large or small, progressive or conservative...whether you're selling real estate or stereo parts, plumbing supplies or banking services.

Why? Because *everyone* makes the same Five Buying Decisions in the same precise order. As long as you have a step-by-step selling process — one that addresses all Five Buying Decisions in the correct order — you have the tools you need for *any* selling situation.

Here is an example: A few years ago, I was asked to teach the Track Selling System™ to members of an electrical association, which is made up of most of the electric utility companies on the West Coast. Because of the energy crunch, the utility companies had to suddenly conserve energy, so they needed to sell their customers on the idea of using *less* electricity. Not too many years earlier, these were the same companies who were trying to convince customers to use *more* electricity — promoting all-electric kitchens, for example, or the prestige of Medallion Award homes.

"How can we sell the opposite of what we used to sell?" they asked me.

"Your task today is no different than it was twenty years ago," I advised them. "Your 'product' is different, but your task — and procedure — is the same."

I taught the Association's customer service representatives the Track Selling System,™ and they went out and sold their customers on the idea of energy conservation. And their customers *did* use less energy!

Who do you think was the most successful in meeting this challenge? It was the same salespeople who had previously convinced customers to use more electricity, who now convinced the same customers to use less electricity. They were able to apply the Track Selling System™ to very different — and in this case, opposing — sales situations.

So again I say: Selling is selling is selling.

There is no problem that directly relates to selling that cannot be handled *by knowing precisely what to do in each step of the selling process.* You will learn to do this expertly in Part II: The Seven Steps to Successful Sales.

THE SALES CYCLE

There is, however, one major difference in the sales process that depends on the specific product or service you sell. The difference is the *sales cycle.* The sales cycle is the length of time between your first contact with a prospect and the time until the sales transaction is completed — until the person becomes the satisfied owner of whatever product or service you sell.

An average sales cycle for a retail store transaction is very short. From the time the salesperson greets the customer, answers a few questions, rings up the sale, and hands the product to the customer, perhaps only five or ten minutes have elapsed.

Other sales cycles may last weeks, months, or even years. For example, suppose that you sell a computerized system for controlling an office building's heating, cooling, and lighting operations. Your sales procedure might begin long before the ground under the proposed building is even broken. You might be working first with the architect, getting the equipment into the design specifications. Then, as the building is under construction, you would be coordinating plans with construction engineers and crews. Even after the structure was finished, you might continue working with building inspectors and building engineers, making sure that everything functioned exactly as promised. In this kind of situation, it would not be unusual for the sales cycle to take two, three or four years, or longer.

Two factors most influence the sales cycle:

1. The price
2. The complexity of your product or service

What kinds of products or services have *short* sales cycles? Selling air filters to a service station manager, filing cabinets to a local florist, or a janitorial service to a veterinary clinic, for instance. What kinds of products or services have *long* sales cycles? Selling an ad campaign to a national car rental corporation, or a computerized reservation system (complete with software and hardware) to a commercial airline.

Regardless of the length of the sales cycle, *the same basic selling process will apply*. The basic sales process is simply carried out over a longer period of time.

Here's how James Ornest of Digital Equipment Corporation was able to use his knowledge of the sales cycle profitably: "The Track Selling System™ gave me the base to begin my sales career eight years ago," he related. "I have just completed my eighth consecutive year of exceeding my sales quota — over $20 million dollars of computer equipment. It's nice knowing the sales cycle so you are one step ahead of the customers."

SELLING IS SELLING IS SELLING

You can demonstrate to yourself that selling is selling is selling by thinking about the following questions.

STEP ONE: APPROACH: Can you think of any situation — with any of your current or past prospects, or current or past products or services — where you would *not* introduce yourself to your prospects and establish warm, sincere rapport?

If you *can* think of a time where you would not do this, I'd advise you to keep on reading. It seems like "shooting yourself in the foot" not to extend this simple courtesy to a prospect.

STEP TWO: QUALIFICATION: Can you think of any situation where you would *not* qualify the prospect as genuine, prospective buyer?

If you can, why would you want to waste your valuable time, and the time of someone else — someone who couldn't use your product or service?

STEP THREE: AGREEMENT ON NEED: Can you think of any situation where you would *not* find out what the prospect wants or needs to buy?

If you can, perhaps it is because you think you already *know* what the prospect wants or needs. This could be a big mistake for you, as well as your prospect. Or perhaps you believe that regardless of what your prospects want or need, your job is to sell them your product or service. In my experience, this can backfire on you in a number of ways. I hope to convince you of this fact as you read on.

STEP FOUR: SELL THE COMPANY: Can you think of any situation where you would *not* establish the reliability and integrity of your company in your prospect's mind?

If you answered yes, perhaps you are thinking that the quality of your product or service will carry the prospect regardless of your company's reputation. If so, please think again. The reliability and integrity of your company can only enhance the image of your product. Establishing this in your prospect's mind may also lead to more sales later on.

STEP FIVE: FILL THE NEED: Can you think of any situation where you would *not* help your prospect understand the benefits that your product or service provides...and how it solves your prospect's problems or fills his or her needs?

If you answered yes, you may be new to selling. As you grow in experience and confidence, you will realize that this step can be one of the most critical and important in successful selling.

STEP SIX: ACT OF COMMITMENT: Can you think of any situation where you would *not* ask for the order or get an act of commitment?

There's only one situation I can think of where you wouldn't do this: If the prospect asks to buy before you get to this step. Many salespeople neglect to ask for the order or get an act of commitment. You, however, will learn to ask for the order up to *five* times.

STEP SEVEN: CEMENT THE SALE: Can you think of any situation where you would *not* thank the prospect for doing business with you?

Selling is a "people" skill and part of this skill is having good manners. It is always important to thank customers for doing business with you, even though they will probably thank *you* for helping them.

If you are in the sales profession, you are probably doing a lot of these steps right, right now. In the next few chapters you will find out *why* they are working for you. You will learn techniques and procedures that will give you consistent success,

niques and procedures that will give you consistent success, because you will be conducting your sales process the same way, and in the same order, on every sales call you make.

If you are not yet a salesperson, you will have the benefit of not having to unlearn ineffective or inconsiderate sales procedures. You will learn it right the first time.

Whether you're a beginner or a seasoned pro, you can use exactly the same procedure, in the same order, to lead, convince, or inspire people in your personal life. *World Class Selling*, the science of helpfully persuading people, will work at work, at home, among friends, and with your family. The Track Selling System™ will work in *any* situation.

THINGS TO REMEMBER

* No matter what product or service you sell, the basic, step-by-step sales process remains the same.
* The only difference is the sales cycle, the time between your first contact with your prospect and the conclusion of your successful sale.
* In a complex sale with a long sales cycle the same procedures are carried out over a longer period of time.

EXERCISES

1. List your most common sales-related activities.

    a.

    b.

    c.

    Think of all the products or services you have sold in your career.

    Think of the product or service you sell now.

    Are your daily activities somewhat the same, no matter what you sell?

2. What is the average sales cycle for your product or service?

5

THE OBJECTIVES OF YOUR SALES CALLS

once overheard the following conversation while waiting for an appointment.

Salesperson:	*How's it going?*
Prospect:	*Fine.*
Salesperson:	*Anything I can help you with?*
Prospect:	*Nope.*
Salesperson:	*Well. Okay. I'll catch you the next time I'm back around. Bye.*
Prospect:	*Yeah. Bye.*

What was the *purpose* of this sales call?

This salesperson must have read somewhere that according to the law of averages, he could make one sale for every ten sales calls he made. Thus, if he just made enough calls. he'd get lucky and make a sale. You can almost imagine him thinking, "Well, great. Just two minutes on that call. One down and nine to go."

Unfortunately. it doesn't work that way.

THE COST OF A SALES CALL

In today's economy, you cannot afford to spend any time on a sales call just for the sake of "doing the numbers." A single sales call is estimated to cost the company between $99 and $452. All other things being equal, would a purposeless sales call cost your company less, more, or the same, as a purposeful sales call? It would cost the same. Can your company afford — and *should* it afford — to send you on sales calls with no apparent purpose?

Unless you are working for a charitable organization, your company's ultimate goal, beyond serving the customer, is to bring in revenue and make a profit.

What are the profit-making components of a company? Think about all the activities carried out by *your* company. Which of the following, *in itself*, brings in revenue?

- Research and Development
- Personnel training
- Management activities
- Production
- Purchasing
- Quality control
- Pensions and employee benefits
- Bookkeeping
- Customer relations
- Sales

If you checked off "sales," you're right. Sales are the only activities that, *in themselves*, bring cash directly into the company. The other activities are also vitally important — without them there would *be* no product or service to sell — but other activities all *cost* money. Only when the product or service is actually *sold* does cash come into the company.

Since each individual sales call costs from $99 to $452, and successful selling is crucial to your company's income and profits, *never make a sales call without having clear-cut objectives about what you want to accomplish on the call.*

GETTING AN ACT OF COMMITMENT

A professional salesperson, by definition, has the ability to help the prospect buy now and wear well, or get an act of commitment and wear well.

This not only defines what a salesperson *is*, but also what a salesperson *does*. Your primary goal is to make a sale — now, today. If the product or service you sell is simple and inexpensive, and thus has a short sales cycle, you may be able to accomplish your objective on a single sales call.

However, because of the complexity and cost of most products and services, it is impractical to expect to make a sale after just one call. Because most sales have longer sales cycles, *each sales call becomes a "sale within a sale."* Your objective on each of the multiple calls is to get an act of commitment, moving the prospect one step closer to buying your product or service.

What would be appropriate objectives for making a sales call when the goal is not necessarily to make a sale right now?

- Establishing rapport with your prospect
- Making an appointment for a longer meeting, where you *can* make your presentation
- Discovering what the decision-making process is in your prospect's company
- Determining who will be involved in the selection process
- Finding out whether funds are available for the purchase
- Persuading the prospect to *do* something for you, such as review your product's specifications, set up an appointment for your demonstration, or give you needed specifications or facts
- Finding out your prospect's specific problems or needs
- Supplying your prospect with new information about your product or service
- Checking to see if your prospect's needs or problems have changed
- Meeting new people within your prospect's organization — people who may be involved in the buying decision

- Working with your prospect to devise a method of payment that will fit within that person's budget limitations
- Providing your prospect with references from your previous or current satisfied customers
- Determining who the competition is

Any of these could be worthwhile, productive objectives for a sales call, and there are many others. Each could play an important part in helping you reach your ultimate goal of closing the sale.

IDENTIFY YOUR OBJECTIVES
AND PUT THEM IN WRITING

Before you make a sales call, identify specific objectives you want to accomplish on the specific call. This lets you focus on achieving exactly what you set out to do.

When you put these objectives in writing, they remain firmly in your mind. There is some kind of internal ''magic'' that occurs when you write down a goal or objective. It creates a strong, internal ''act of commitment'' that you make with yourself and, in your subsequent behavior, you tend to fulfill.

Writing your objectives down also helps you remember them, since, as the old saying goes, ''The faintest ink is stronger than the strongest memory.'' You can refer to your objectives during your sales call to keep your meeting on target.

Think about the last sales call you made. Did you carefully think through exactly what you wanted to accomplish on the call? Did you put your objectives in writing?

When the meeting was over, were you satisfied with what you accomplished? If you did *not* plan your objectives in advance, do you think the meeting might have gone more smoothly and stayed focused on what you wanted to achieve if you had?

In my experience, setting precise objectives for every sales call and putting your objectives in writing can help you achieve other important benefits as well.

- You'll gain increased self-confidence, because you'll know exactly what you plan to do.

- You'll gain new respect from your prospects. Their time is valuable, and they appreciate doing business with someone who understands this and conducts sales calls in a productive, businesslike way.

- Your own time is valuable too, and worth money to you. Keeping attention focused on achieving specific goals can help you make more sales faster. As you know by now, selling is a win/win situation. When the sales-person is a true professional, the customer wins the most. (The added income in your pocket won't be hard to take either.)

I have met salespeople who sincerely feel they can't set objectives before making actual sales calls. They say that every prospect and every selling situation is totally different from every other — unusual or unexpected circumstances arise that don't fit within the planned framework. Some salespeople feel they demonstrate extra skill and are especially expert if they can think fast on their feet — wing it — live on the edge.

Nothing could be further from the truth. If you want *consistent* success in selling, *you need to set specific objectives for every sales call you make*, and focus your attention on achieving your objectives.

HANDLING THE UNEXPECTED

Although you set objectives for every sales call, unexpected circumstances are bound to arise. Sometimes you're given an opportunity to *surpass* your objectives. For example, suppose your objective for a particular sales call is simply to discover the decision-maker, but the first person you talk to not only has that authority, but also expresses interest in and a need for your specific product or service.

What do you do? You sell the person, of course. By definition, a professional salesperson has the ability to help the person buy now. There is no rule that says you cannot achieve *more* than your targeted objective.

In other cases, you will achieve *less* than your targeted objective. If you stay focused, you can go for an act of commitment, and return to your original objective in the next round of your sales cycle.

BEING REALISTIC

It would be unrealistic to go on a sales call with no objectives in mind, and simply hope things work out. It would be equally unrealistic, as in the example, to adhere to your prepared agenda so rigidly that you pass up an opportunity to serve by helping your customer buy now and wear well.

In Part Two you will learn precise, step-by-step procedures that cover every point in the sales process and leave nothing to chance. All procedures you learn will be adaptable to any situation, your own personality, your prospects' varied person-alities, and whatever specific product or service you sell.

You can apply the same principles in your personal life to convince and persuade friends, co-workers, and family mem-bers. Before the conversation:

  ♦ Identify your objectives.
  ♦ Put them in writing.

When you don't know where you're going, any road will take you there. Set objectives for your sales calls. Know exactly where you're going. Be adaptable to the new information you receive on each sales call you make.

THINGS TO REMEMBER

  ♦ Never make a sales call without clear-cut objectives.
  ♦ A purposeless sales call costs just as much as a pur-poseful one.
  ♦ Sales activities are the only activities that, *in them-selves*, bring your company immediate revenue.
  ♦ Your primary goal on sales calls is to make a sale. However, in a longer sales cycle you can have many other objectives.
  ♦ Put the objectives for your sales calls in writing.

EXERCISES

1. What have you experienced by making sales calls without a written objective?

2. What are the general objectives of your sales calls?

3. Think back to a specific prospect. If you could do the call over again, knowing what you know now, what would be your objective?

4. Think ahead to an upcoming sales call. What is your specific objective?

6

LET YOUR PROSPECTS DO THE TALKING

Why do people buy from you? Because they like your product or service? Ultimately. But that's later down the line. The real reason is:

People buy from you because they like you.

Old-time salespeople say that a prospect doesn't have to like you to buy, just respect you. That isn't true, or if it is, it's true only as long as you're the only game in town. The moment an agreeable competitor shows up, you become the *ex*-supplier.

In my sales experience, observing thousands of salespeople, I have seen that *only* if the prospect likes you do you have a prime opportunity to make the sale. If your demeanor puts off your prospect in any way, the prospect may buy from you once, but *only* once. It's doubtful whether you'll ever sell to that customer again.

I'm certainly not suggesting that *you* may be offensive yourself. I'm just strongly suggesting that being a congenial, likable salesperson is the *first* requirement for any sales transaction. You've probably experienced this yourself.

Have you ever had this experience: You wanted to buy a product or service, but the salesperson had an attitude, tone of voice or behavior that was so offensive you couldn't bring yourself to do business with that person? Have you disliked the clerks at one store so much that you stopped buying there and switched to another? Have you ever switched lines while waiting at the bank, the post office, or the supermarket, primarily because you didn't like the person serving a line?

I'm not saying a prospect buys from you only because you're likable. Your product or service also must be desirable. However, if the prospect *doesn't* like you for any reason, you have little chance of closing the sale regardless of the appeal of your product or service.

So what makes you likable to a prospect? What makes any salesperson likable? The answer is so simple that you may not believe it at first:

People prefer talking to listening.

PEOPLE PREFER TALKING TO LISTENING

"When asked to identify the No. 1 problem of salespeople," according to an article published in the *Wall Street Journal*, "nearly half of 432 corporate buyers surveyed recently said salespeople are 'too talky.' Indeed the survey by a New York consulting firm suggests that an inability to communicate is souring many buyers on the salespeople who call on them."

Everyone — young and old, women and men, introverts and extroverts alike — prefers talking to listening. People want other people to *be quiet and let them talk*. People have a need to express their opinions and be heard, and they like this far better than they like to listen to anyone else talk.

If you doubt this, think about the people you personally enjoy the most. Aren't they people who listen? Think about the people whom you might cross the street to avoid. Aren't they so full of themselves they bombard you with their news, their opinions, and their concerns? People who never let you get a word in edgewise?

If you still doubt this, think about this: You're having a conversation with a friend on a street corner after a meeting. Your friend hasn't said much, and has indicated several times she will need to leave soon because she's tired and wants to get to bed early.

Then you ask her about something in her life that is particularly important to her. She lights up. She begins to tell you...and she tells you more...and then she *really* tells you how strongly she feels about it. Thoughts of home and sleep are temporarily forgotten. Your friend is on a roll. You stand there talking (that is, listening to her) for a good twenty minutes more.

If you *still* have doubts, think about this: Has anyone ever complained about a person who *listens* too much?

Well, the "open secret" to getting your prospects to like you is: *simply listen to them.* That's all. If you listen to them, they will like you. They will like you regardless of your personality or theirs. They will like you regardless of whether you and they have nothing in common or everything in common, but disagree on all of it. That's testimony to the power of listening.

The More You Listen, the More Your Prospects Will Like You

Put yourself in your prospects' shoes for a moment. What do you really think is going on in their minds when you're making your sales presentation? Do you think they hang on your every word?

Not likely. They are thinking about the new budget cut, or the problems on the production line, or what they're going to do as soon as you leave.

What does it take to be a top, professional salesperson? Among other things, it takes the ability to use simple phrases like:

- "Wow."
- "Really?"
- "You're kidding!"
- "That's great."
- "How'd you do it?"
- "What happened then?"
- "Tell me more."

You can test this concept and observe the results for yourself. The next time you're talking with a co-worker, friend, or family member, try remaining quiet, and using some of these phrases.

Say "Really?" or "How'd you do it?" or "Tell me more," and see what happens. When you use comments like these to indicate you're really listening and are truly interested in what someone has to say, what do you suppose that person's reaction will be? Negative? Of course not. The person will love it. And you probably won't have said five words.

To observe the other side of this coin, you might try this experiment. Corner someone at a party and start telling him about your business, your philosophy, your hobby, and your children's accomplishments. Every time he tries to add something to the conversation, interrupt and continue your discourse. What do you think his response will be? Positive? Probably not. He will probably be thinking, "This is the biggest bore I've ever met in my life."

Your prospects are no different than any other people. Like everyone else, your prospects prefer talking to listening and prefer listeners to people who talk too much. So the more you listen, the more your prospects will like you.

The more your prospects like you, the more willing they will be to buy whatever product or service you sell.

BECOMING A BETTER LISTENER

Your prospects will have to feel you are *really* listening to them, not just waiting patiently until they're finished. Listening well requires that you be genuinely interested in the person, or, at the very least, you must acquire skill in listening.

How difficult is it to become a better listener? It isn't difficult at all, and you certainly don't have to alter your personality in any way. It simply takes acquiring and using certain skills, and *awareness* — awareness of the importance of this skill to your success as a salesperson. You must have an understanding that acquiring this skill will increase the amount of money you earn. On each sales call you must demonstrate to your prospect that you are actively listening.

Tiny Lint, a mentor and true sales professional, showed me that successful sales is a procedure, not a random event. When he first started with my company, I tried to have him earn money as soon as possible. I'd have him set up appointments, then I'd go out and sell them. Then we would share the commission.

Tiny had gotten himself into a sales slump, and asked me to go out with him on a presentation and give him my evaluation. I was flattered because he had so much experience. At the appointment, I noticed he was preoccupied with selling a health insurance program, although the prospect was detailing his concern about work injuries putting him out of action. If Tiny had listened, he would have seen that his prospect was a prime candidate for disability insurance. Ultimately, there was no sale.

Outside, Tiny asked for my views. "You weren't tuned in to what the prospect was saying," I offered. "He was interested in disability insurance. You were so tied in with what you were going to say next, you didn't listen."

"Roy, you're right," Tiny admitted easily. "I forgot. Listening is a very important part of selling. A good salesperson is a good listener. A great salesperson is a great listener."

"Tiny," I asked him, "why did you ask me along?"

"I could have struggled for weeks trying to find out what I was doing wrong. You were able to spot what I was missing in just one call. Look at the money you saved me."

LISTENING WITH YOUR BODY

When you are genuinely interested in what your prospect has to say, your facial expression and body language will convey it.

How? Look directly at the prospect. You might lean slightly forward as you respond appropriately with phrases such as, "Really?" or "Then what happened?" Your facial expression, whether one of interest, concern, or amusement, will indicate to your prospect you're following what he or she is telling you — and you can't fake facial expressions.

Keep in mind that your facial expressions and body language will give you away if you *aren't* actively listening. (It may be worth your while to invest some time in books or videotapes about body language and what different postures or mannerisms convey. You would learn, for example, *not* to listen to a prospect with your arms and legs crossed, which indicates, "I don't believe you," or "I don't want to hear this.")

CLARIFYING WHAT YOU HEAR

Active listeners ask questions to help clarify a fact or opinion
the prospect has expressed. Offer supportive comments, such as
"Yes," "I see," or "Uh-huh," and when your prospect is
telling you his or her specific needs or problems — information
vital to your sales presentation later in the conversation — take
notes.

WHAT NOT TO DO

Don't frequently glance at your watch. Don't interrupt your
prospect in the middle of a sentence or thought. Don't maintain
an expressionless face. Don't ask a question about something
your prospect has already covered thoroughly. Don't sit still
and maintain silence. (You will find some very specific, step-by-
step procedures on listening to and drawing out prospects in the
next chapter, "The Art of Asking Questions.")

WHY BE A GOOD LISTENER?

The fact that the more your prospects like you, the more willing
they will be to buy from you should be enough reason to motivate the professional salesperson to be a good listener, but there
are other excellent reasons to be a good listener, as well.

GATHERING INFORMATION

To help you fill your prospect's need or solve his or her problem, you need to gather information that will help you offer
accurate, on-target solutions. To gather information, you have
to listen. When you don't listen, you'll miss opportunities to
learn important facts and opinions. Consequently, you may
make offers that are based on inaccurate or incomplete information — and that are totally off. How much confidence can your
prospects have in you, or in your ability to truly understand
their unique problems or fill their unique needs, when it's
obvious you haven't heard what they've said?

LISTENING BUILDS TRUST

People buy your product or service not because they understand *it*, but because they feel *you* understand *them*. Listening builds trust. It demonstrates your sensitivity and understanding, and it helps you gain the important information you need in order to meet your prospects' needs.

Let me illustrate the difference between a poor listener (and therefore a do-nothing salesperson) and a good listener/good salesperson. First, the poor salesperson:

> *Salesperson:*   *Hi there, Sue. How's it going today?*
>
> *Prospect:*   *Not so good. We just discovered a hideous foul-up on the production line. I think we're going to have to trash everything that came off the line this whole week.*
>
> *Salesperson:*   *Yeah ... um ... yeah, great. Well now, let me show you this new product we just came out with. You're going to really love it!*

No matter how great the new product, and how precisely it may have fit the prospect's needs, do you think the salesperson made the sale? The prospect probably thought (if she thought about it consciously at all), "How can anyone as insensitive as that possible help me solve my problems?"

Now the good salesperson: This salesperson made a call on a high-powered busy executive. This executive was so busy that he quickly made it clear he didn't have time to talk with the salesperson, and he'd appreciate it if she'd make her presentation and be on her way...fast.

This salesperson was a professional. She began asking questions...and listening. She asked about the executive's business, how he'd achieved his current success, problems his business was facing and his goals for the future.

The more the executive talked, the more the skilled salesperson listened. Time passed quickly.

The executive even canceled a meeting he had scheduled, and went right on talking. The busy executive didn't have time to talk with a salesperson, but he had plenty of time to talk about the things that interested *him* with a person who sincerely listened. Do you suppose this salesperson made her sale?

With practice, you can learn to listen to what is said (and what is said between the lines, or implied) and make the prospect feel at ease. Here is a conversation between a salesperson and a prospect. "Listen" for information about the prospect.

Salesperson:	*Good morning, Mr. Jones. I'm Sarah Smith from XYZ Company. How is your day going so far?*
Prospect:	*Not bad, thanks. How about yours?*
Salesperson:	*Very good, thank you. I believe you mentioned that your daughter was in a play last week. How did it go?*
Prospect:	*Great. She remembered all her lines and came through like a trooper. It was a good play, too.*
Salesperson:	*When will she be acting again?*
Prospect:	*Pretty soon. She's already talking about doing summer stock after school is out.*
Salesperson:	*Summer stock?*
Prospect:	*Yes, there's a group that does plays in our church during the summer.*
Salesperson:	*That'll be a good experience for her. What's your son planning for the summer?*
Prospect:	*He's going to be a counselor at a tennis camp again. He really loves that game.*
Salesperson:	*With the children so busy, what about the family trip you and your wife wanted to take?*
Prospect:	*I don't think we'll be going in the summer. Maybe in the fall, when it's cooler.*
Salesperson:	*That will probably be a better time. I'd like to tell you about our new widget. However, in order for me to do the best job I possibly can for you, I need to ask you a couple of questions. Is that all right?*

DIALOGUE QUESTIONS

1. Was this a cold call?
2. What is the prospect's name?
3. How many children does the prospect have?
4. Approximately how old are the children?
5. What is one of the objectives for this call?

ANSWERS

1. No. The salesperson asked a personal question about the prospect's daughter. She must have talked to the prospect before.
2. Mr. Jones.
3. Two. The salesperson mentioned only a daughter and a son.
4. The children are probably teenagers. Summer stock and counseling at camp are the activities of adolescents, not young children or adults.
5. One of the objectives was to introduce the prospect to a new product, a new widget.

LISTENING AT HOME

A good salesperson is a good listener. A *great* salesperson is a *great* listener.

Everyone in your life will respond positively to you the more you listen. In fact, you can benefit greatly, in your personal life as well as professional life, if you practice on friends and family members. I suggest you acquire your new listening skills by consciously trying these methods with friends, your spouse, and your children. You will be amazed at how they respond to you what you learned.

You will learn how to apply your listening skill more specifically in the next chapter, as well as in Part Two.

THINGS TO REMEMBER

- People prefer talking to listening.
- The more you listen, the better your prospects will like you.
- People buy because they like you.
- A good salesperson is a good listener; a *great* salesperson is a *great* listener.

EXERCISES

Recall a time when you were the prospect, and a salesperson was a poor listener.

1. What was your reaction?

2. Did the salesperson make the sale? Why or why not?

7

THE ART OF ASKING QUESTIONS

How do you encourage your prospects to do the talking? The best technique for encouraging someone else to talk is to ask questions.

Think of a conversation as a game of catch. Every time you're talking, you've got the ball.

When you've got the ball, what's going on in your prospects' minds? Do they prefer listening to you, or doing the talking themselves? Do they like you more when *you* talk or when *they* talk? Are you gathering important information when *you're* talking or when *they're* talking?

As you can see, the conversation ball is a hot potato for you. The longer you hold the ball, the less your chances for making a successful sale. You want to give the conversation ball back to your prospect as quickly as possible.

How? Ask a question. Your prospect will answer, and thereby take the ball.

How long will your prospect hold the ball without tossing it back to you? That depends on the kinds of questions you ask.

Don't ask questions that can be answered by yes or no.

You:	*Did you play golf last week?*
Prospect:	*No.*
You:	*Are you having any problems with your present system?*
Prospect:	*Yes.*
You:	*Do you think the problem is the monitor?*
Prospect:	*No.*
You:	*Are you going to use it again?*
Prospect:	*No.*
You:	*Is that important to you?*
Prospect:	*No.*
You:	*Will Peterson get the job?*
Prospect:	*No.*

Clearly, this sounds more like an interrogation than a conversation. The prospect's yes or no response puts you constantly on the spot to devise a new question. Furthermore, it delivers no new information on which to base your next question. Your conversation lacks focus, and it won't take long before both of you are exhausted.

The previous examples are closed-ended questions. Closed-ended questions can be fully answered with a simple yes or no. They generally start with the phrases:

- "Is it...?"
- "Are you...?"
- "Will he...?"
- "Does it...?"
- "Have you...?"
- "Do you...?"
- "Has it...?"

As the name implies, closed-ended questions bring the topic of conversation to a quick close.

There *is* an important place for closed-ended questions, as I will explain later, but don't use this kind of question when your goal is to encourage your customer to open up and talk freely.

OPEN-ENDED QUESTIONS VS. CLOSED-ENDED QUESTIONS

Instead, use the open-ended question. Open-ended questions often begin with the words.

- "What...?"
- "Where...?"
- "When...?"
- "Who...?"
- "Why...?"
- "How...?"

Examples include:

- "*What* problems are you having with your present system?"
- "*Where* do you think the problem is?"
- "*When* will you be using it again?"
- "*Who* do you think will get the job?"
- "*Why* is that important to you?"
- "*How's* your golf game coming along?"

Notice that these open-ended questions cover the same topics as the closed-ended questions you read earlier, but these questions encourage your prospects to elaborate.

While open-ended questions usually begin with these words, any question that cannot be fully answered with a yes or no reply is open-ended. The following questions will also give you more than a yes or no answer.

- "Can you *explain* that?"
- "Can you *tell me* more?"
- "Would you please *elaborate*?"
- "Would you please *tell me* why?"

Your prospects will almost *have* to say more than just a few words in response to these open-ended questions. They will answer in their own words and own way. Open-ended questions avoid the atmosphere of a third-degree grilling. They tend to relax the prospect, and allow you to draw out the information

you need about how your product or service can help the
person.

Here is how a salesperson could use open-ended questions in a
conversation with a prospect:

Salesperson: *What's your favorite sport?*

Prospect: *Well, I guess I'd have to say tennis. I don't
get out to play as often as I'd like, but
when I do play, I find it completely relax-
ing.*

Salesperson: *How often do you play?*

Prospect: *I try to get out twice a week, but with my
busy schedule, it's not always possible. I'm
not very satisfied with my tennis club, so I
guess I'm not as motivated to get out as
often as I should.*

Salesperson: *What club do you belong to?*

Prospect: *The Green Hills Club, over on Thompson
Road. But I've been thinking about changing to the Forest Glade Club.*

Salesperson: *Why is that?*

Prospect: *Green Hills seems to be going downhill.
Membership is dropping off, and the
facilities just aren't being kept up as well
as they used to be. It's not as much fun
going there anymore. Most of my friends
have already switched to Forest Glade,
and I guess I'd better quit putting it off
and get my membership changed too,
before the 15th.*

Salesperson: *Why the 15th?*

Prospect: *That's the last day to sign up for the next
tournament at Forest Glade. I'd really like
to play in that tournament.*

As you can see, the open-ended question keeps the conversation ball in your prospect's hands much more effectively. Open-
ended questions encourage your prospects to give more expan-
sive replies. You receive new information, and you can base
your next questions very comfortably and naturally on your new
information. The following are more examples.

CLOSED-ENDED QUESTIONS

- *"Is this feature* important to you?"
- *"Are you* having any problems with your present office storage systems?"
- *"Will anyone else* be using this equipment?"
- *"Have you* tried doing it this way?"

OPEN-ENDED QUESTIONS

- *"How* do you feel about office automation?"
- *"When* will the decision be made?"
- *"Why* do you think that happened?"
- *"Where* will your new plant be located?"
- *"How* is that working out for you?"

In most cases, a closed-ended question can be rephrased to turn it into an open-ended question. For example:

CLOSED-ENDED QUESTIONS

1. "Is anyone else involved in this buying decision?"
2. "Do you think that will work?"
3. "Will you need delivery soon?"
4. "Are you having problems with the service you're using now?"
5. "Is this working for you?"
6. "You think the quality is excellent, right?"
7. "Do you think this should be changed?"

REPHRASED AS OPEN-ENDED QUESTIONS

1. "Who else will be involved in this buying decision?"
2. "How well do you think that will work?"
3. "How soon will you need delivery?"
4. "What problems are you having with the service you're using now?"

5. "How is this working for you?"

6. "What is your opinion about the quality?"

7. "What are your thoughts about changing this?"

Your own awareness of the effectiveness of open-ended questions and your ability to phrase questions to make them open-ended can play a major role in your selling success. Carefully phrasing your questions and making sure they're open-ended encourages your prospects to talk. The more they talk, the more they'll like you, and the more willing they will be to buy your product or service. Thus, your skill in turning closed-ended questions into open-ended questions is important.

CONTROLLING THE FOCUS OF CONVERSATIONS

You will gain two other important benefits when you let your prospects do the talking.

* The only time you know what your prospects are thinking is when they're talking.

* The only time you can control the focus of your prospects' attention is when they're talking.

Take a moment to think about the last time you listened to a speech, a sermon, or a classroom lecture. While the speaker was talking, did he or she have any idea what was going on in your head? Probably not. While the speaker was talking, did your thoughts stay riveted on every word being said, or did your mind sometimes wander off?

Now let's suppose the speaker singled you out and asked you a direct, open-ended question — a question that encouraged you to express your thoughts and opinions freely. While you were answering the question, would your thoughts be wandering off onto unrelated subjects? You'd be focused, right? And while you were talking, who would have control over the focus of attention? The speaker is in control, because he or she asked a specific question to focus your thoughts on a specific topic.

The very same dynamic is at work on every sales call you make. When *you're* doing the talking, your prospect's mind may be wandering off in a thousand directions. You have no idea what his or her thoughts may be, but when your *prospects* are talk-

ing, you know what they're thinking. Only when they're talking
can you "control" their thinking — not their actual thoughts,
of course, but the *focus* of those thoughts. Your open-ended
questions control the *subject* of discussion. As long as your
prospects keep talking, their attention remains focused on
specific topics.

"Act, don't react" is crucial advice for the professional salesperson. When you ask a question, you are taking action. You
are demonstrating leadership and taking control of the conversation. When your prospects answer your questions, they react
— they follow your lead.

FACT-FINDING QUESTIONS AND FEELING-FINDING QUESTIONS

Sir Laurence Olivier once advised, "You have to have the
humility to prepare and the self-confidence to bring it off." The
best salespeople in the business prepare a list of standard qualification questions to be used on every sales call. In addition to
the standard queries, they design specific questions that relate
directly to the prospect being called on.

Your goal in making a sales call is to be of service — to help
your prospect fill a need or solve a problem. You need to gather
background information that will allow you to offer accurate,
effective solutions. You need to learn basic facts, and you also
need to learn your prospects' attitudes and opinions — the
kinds of things that are important to them.

To uncover these two types of information, you must ask two
different types of open-ended questions: *fact-finding* questions
and *feeling-finding* questions.

FACT-FINDING QUESTIONS

As the name implies, fact-finding questions are asked to uncover basic, concrete facts — the "hard" data. Their purpose is
to help you qualify the prospect and direct your presentation to
fit the particular needs of the buyer.

Fact-finding questions should be simple, easy to answer, and
designed to relax the prospect. You want to avoid giving your
prospects the feeling that they're getting the "third degree."

Yet, at the same time. these questions should be designed to provide valuable information to help you properly qualify your prospects. and to guide your presentation to fit their needs.

Here are some examples of open-ended, fact-finding questions:
- "Who else is involved in this buying decision?"
- "How will this product (or service) be used?"
- "What product (or service) do you use now?"
- "When will you need this system to be operational?"
- "Where will your product be displayed?"
- "What are your size restrictions?"
- "What exact specifications will be required?"

FEELING-FINDING QUESTIONS

Facts alone, however, are rarely enough. You also need to uncover your prospect's feelings — their attitudes and opinions, the things that are important to them, their emotions and motivations for buying whatever product or service you sell.

To gather this information, ask open-ended, feeling-finding questions. Here are some examples:
- "How do you feel about that?"
- "Why is that important to you?"
- "What do you like most about your present system?"
- "Would it be fair to ask what you like least about your present system?"
- "What would you think about doing it this way?"
- "Why are you considering that change?"
- "What is your opinion about that?"

Again, think of the specific product or service you sell. What kinds of feeling-finding questions would be useful in your own selling situations to help you uncover your prospect's feelings, attitudes and opinions?

Be aware of one potential trap when you are asking open-ended questions, whether fact-finding or feeling-finding questions. In the following conversation, see if you can discover what happened.

Salesperson:	What do you think of that? Great idea, right?
Prospect:	Yeah, sure is.
Salesperson:	Where do you do your jogging? In the park?
Prospect:	Yes.
Salesperson:	What's the best day for you? Thursday?
Prospect:	Yes, Thursday.

In each example, the salesperson has asked a good, open-ended question. However, before the prospect could reply, the salesperson quickly added a second, closed-ended question. The prospect will most likely respond to the second question in each pair, since it was the last one asked, and the answer is going to be the undesirable yes or no, or at best a brief reply. Something else happened, too. The salesperson, in effect, answered his or her own question. Where does that leave the prospect? With little to say. Worse, it signals that the salesperson doesn't really have much interest in the prospect's actual response. It's a common tendency when someone is first learning to ask open-ended questions to follow an open-ended question with a closed-ended one. It's something of a nervous habit, a "conversation filler." But it works against your real objective, so watch for it and teach yourself to avoid it.

THE FRIENDLY, SILENT, QUESTIONING STARE

One thing you can do to stop yourself from this tendency is to pause after your open-ended question, and look at your prospect, waiting for a response. This is called the Friendly, Silent, Questioning Stare, or FSQS technique. It was developed by my friend, Jack Berman, of the Berman Institute of Agreeable Selling. Here is how it works:

Let's say you have just asked your prospect a good open-ended question. After asking that question, stop, remain silent, and look at your prospect with warmth and genuine interest. This kind of stare is *friendly*. You care about that person. It is *silent*. You are waiting for the person to respond. It is *questioning*. Something about your intention will cause your face to register a questioning expression. While it is not actually a *stare* (as your gaze is not rude, penetrating, or threatening), you do look at your prospect openly and receptively, waiting to hear what he or she will say.

THE REFLECTIVE QUESTION

An additional conversational technique, the *reflective question*, will encourage your prospect to continue talking on the same subject. Here's how it works:

> *Prospect:*   *I played golf every Saturday until I broke my rib.*
>
> *Salesperson:*   *Broke your rib?*
>
> *Prospect:*   *I've wasted my entire week getting records in order for the tax audit.*
>
> *Salesperson:*   *Tax audit?*
>
> *Prospect:*   *I'm leaving in the morning for New York.*
>
> *Salesperson:*   *New York?*

As you can see, a reflective question simply repeats a few key words from the speaker's last statement. When you use the reflective question, your prospects will sense your interest. They know you're listening, and will feel encouraged to continue talking about the same subject, filling in with even more detail. The conversational ball will be in their court that much longer.

A word of caution: Use the reflective question sparingly, or you'll sound like an echo.

THE CLOSED-ENDED QUESTION

As I mentioned earlier, closed-ended questions — questions that can be fully answered with a simple yes or no reply — don't work well when you want to encourage your prospect to do the talking. There are times, however, when closed-ended questions *can* be used as an extremely effective conversational tool.

- "May I call you on Friday?"
- "Is this the correct size?"
- "Is quality important to you?"

Suppose you have done an outstanding job of encouraging your prospect to do the talking...so outstanding, in fact, that your prospect is going on a rather long a time about a skiing vacation in Aspen, a recent surgery, or any other topic that has caught that person's interest, but is getting far from your goal of helping that person solve a problem or fill a need. Although you have done a wonderful job of listening, it is time to change the subject and return to the objective of your sales call.

At your first opportunity to courteously get a word in edgewise, ask a closed-ended question. Your prospect will respond with the expected yes or no, and then it's your turn to talk again. Now you have regained control of the conversation. Immediately ask an open-ended question that will get the conversation back on track — on the subject *you* want to discuss.

Again, your questions help you focus the conversation. In the sample dialogue below, notice how the salesperson's closed-ended question brings one topic of conversation to an end. Then the salesperson asks an open-ended question to introduce his or her new topic of conversation.

Prospect:	*And we had fresh powder for skiing almost every day. And the food! You can't imagine the fantastic restaurants in Aspen.*
Salesperson:	*So you had two full weeks of skiing in Aspen, right?*
Prospect:	*Yes.*
Salesperson:	*I really envy you that trip. It sounds wonderful. Mr. Jones, you mentioned earlier that you are having problems with collating on your present copy machine. Could you tell me more about that?*

Be sure to acknowledge the first conversational topic before going on to the next one or you'll sound rude. For example, don't do this:

Prospect:	*You can't imagine the fantastic restaurants in Aspen.*
Salesperson:	*So you had two full weeks of skiing in Aspen, right?*
Prospect:	*Yes.*

> *Salesperson:*   *Mr. Jones, you mentioned earlier that you are having problems with collating on your present copy machine. Can you tell me more about that?*

Unless you acknowledge what your prospect has just said with the sentence, ''I really envy you that trip,'' or ''Your trip sounds wonderful,'' you will give the impression of being uncaring and discourteous.

Are these techniques manipulative? Quite the reverse. They provide your prospects with total freedom to express their thoughts and feelings completely. At no time do you ever suggest or imply what responses you want your prospects to give, and at no time do you ever suggest or imply that their responses are right or wrong.

THE DIRECTIVE QUESTION

There is one kind of question, however, that *is* manipulative, and you may at some point have been advised to use it in sales. This is the *directive question*, where the salesperson directs the prospect to the desired answer. This technique not only annoys the prospect, it can backfire on the salesperson. Here's an example:

> *Manipulative*   *If I could show you how to do what you're*
> *Salesperson:*   *doing now for less money and time, that would interest you, wouldn't it?*
>
> *Prospect:*   *Well ... yes ... I guess so.*

However, the more sophisticated prospect might reply.

> *Prospect:*   *Ah, listen buddy, no thanks. I've got to get back to work now. So long.*

I do not recommend the traditional directive question. I do, however, recommend that you turn this kind of question into a closed-ended, feeling-finding question.

> *Straightforward*   *If I could show you how to do what*
> *Salesperson:*   *you're now doing for less money and time, would that interest you?*
>
> *Prospect:*   *Yes, actually, it would.*

To transform the directive question into the closed-ended, feeling-finding question above, replace the words:

"That would interest you, wouldn't it?"

With:

"Would that interest you?"

However, even with this transformation the prospect can only say yes or no to this version of the question.

These techniques — the open-ended and closed-ended fact-finding and feeling-finding questions; the friendly, silent, questioning stare and the reflective question — allow you to maintain control of the conversation, and to keep attention focused on the subjects of importance to you. These techniques allow the conversation to focus on subjects that will help you do the most effective job of solving your prospects' problems or filling their needs.

To help fix these different kinds of questions more firmly in your mind, see if you can identify each kind of question below:

1. "How many locations do you now serve?"
2. "How do you feel about the new price hike?"
3. "Union problems?"
4. "Is that a picture of your family?"
5. "When do you want it delivered?"

PRACTICING THE ART OF ASKING QUESTIONS

These methods for drawing people out and encouraging them to talk about themselves can be an invaluable, social asset. You can use open-ended, fact-finding and feeling-finding questions to stimulate wonderful conversations with everyone, from friends and family members to people you meet in the checkout line. Remember: The more you listen, the more people will like you.

Try practicing these conversational techniques not only while calling on prospects, but also while chatting with co-workers or in conversation around the dinner table. The more you practice, the smoother and more comfortable these techniques will be for you.

- Pretend the conversation is a game of catch, and the object is for the other person to have the ball. Each time you're talking, you've got the ball. Try to get rid of the ball as quickly as possible with open-ended questions. These questions often start with the words: *Who, What, Why, When, Where,* and *How.*

- Ask closed-ended questions, those starting with *"Will you...?" "Did you...?" "Does it...?" "Are you...?" "Is it...?"* and so on. Then watch the ball come right back to you — fast. Question four above, *"Is that a picture of your family?"* is an example of a closed-ended, fact-finding question.

- Ask open-ended, fact-finding questions. Notice the kinds of information these questions help you uncover. Questions one and five above, *"How many locations do you now serve?"* and *"When do you want it delivered?"* are examples of open-ended, fact-finding questions.

- Ask open-ended, feeling-finding questions. Notice the different kind of information you receive. Notice how the feeling-tone of the conversation shifts as well. Question two above, *"How do you feel about the new price hike?"* is an example of an open-ended, feeling-finding question.

- Try using the Friendly, Silent, Questioning Stare technique and the reflective question. Notice the encouragement these techniques give the other person to continue talking on the same subject. Question three above, *"Union problems?"* is an example of the reflective question.

- Try changing the subject of conversation. First, use a closed-ended question to terminate one topic, then an open-ended question to introduce a new one. How well does this work for you?

THINGS TO REMEMBER

+ Let your prospects do the talking. They will like you more.

+ Let your prospects do the talking. You can gather important information that will allow you to serve their needs more precisely.

+ Ask open-ended questions instead of closed-ended questions.

+ Ask fact-finding and feeling-finding questions.

+ Use the Friendly, Silent, Questioning Stare.

+ Use reflective questions, sparingly.

+ To change the subject of conversation, use a closed-ended question followed by an open-ended question.exercises

---

EXERCISES

1. Develop a *fact-finding question* that you might ask to interest a prospect in your product or service.

2. Develop a *feeling-finding question* that you might ask to interest a prospect in your product or service.

3. What is the purpose of using:
   a. Open-ended questions?

   b. Reflective questions?

   c. Directive questions?

   d. Closed-ended questions?

8

THE SIX BUYING MOTIVES

People buy for their own reasons People don't buy for your reasons, or your company's reasons. People buy your product or service for their own reasons, every time. Their reasons may not necessarily be sensible, intelligent, or even rational, but they are *their* reasons.

People have six motives for buying any product or service.

- ◆ Desire for Gain — $
- ◆ Fear of Loss — $
- ◆ Comfort and Convenience
- ◆ Security and Protection
- ◆ Pride of Ownership
- ◆ Satisfaction of Emotion

The Six Buying Motives are not presented in any special order. No one motive is any more important than any other. However. at least one of these motives — and often more than one — applies to every purchase, every time.

DESIRE FOR GAIN — $

The first Buying Motive usually means desire for financial gain. Desire for Gain might prompt a company to buy an expensive computer system, an advertising campaign, or newer, more efficient production equipment. As a result of any one of these purchases, the company expects to earn more profits.

Desire for Gain might prompt an individual to buy the services of a Certified Financial Planner in order to gain more profits from personal investments, or to invest in real estate or T-Bills in hopes of financial gain. You may have been motivated by the desire for financial gain when you bought this book. You expect to gain increased selling skills that will help you earn more money.

Further examples of purchases stimulated by Desire for Gain would be a money market account, a college education, an apartment building, a cattle ranch, raffle tickets, or stock in a company with predictable, stable growth.

FEAR OF LOSS — $

The next Buying Motive usually refers to fear of financial loss. Fear of Loss may prompt a company to hire the services of guard dogs to patrol the warehouse at night, or to subscribe to a computerized market data service to stay informed about the competition. Fear of Loss may prompt a jewelry store owner to install bars on all easily accessible doors and windows of the store. It may cause a manufacturer to purchase product liability insurance as protection against loss through lawsuits caused by product malfunctions.

An individual motivated by Fear of Loss may make such purchases as dead-bolt locks, yard lights, any type of insurance, burglar alarms, a safety deposit box, a safe, various kinds of locks, a security guard service, or a bonded messenger service.

COMFORT AND CONVENIENCE

Think about your own workplace for a moment. What items has your company purchased in order to provide comfort and convenience for employees? Depending on the company's size and budget, you may be enjoying such comforts and conveniences as an employee lounge, pleasant interior decorating, a temporary help service, parking facilities, secretarial services, a copy machine, an elevator, vending machines, a lunchroom, and readily available, hot coffee.

What items might you have purchased primarily for your own comfort and convenience at home? These might include an electric can opener, an easy chair, a CD player, an air conditioner, a computer, an electric blanket, down pillows, and a microwave oven.

SECURITY AND PROTECTION

Many purchases are motivated by the desire to avoid physical harm, either to ourselves, our loved ones, or our property.

For example, a company doesn't want to change vendors because they feel secure their present supplier will be there to take care of their future needs. A company may install an impressive drainage system on its grounds in order to protect against physical damage from floods, use sturdy shipping cartons and cushioned packing materials so its product can be shipped without damage, or protect its trade secrets stored in computer memory with a trained field staff and a security system that monitors the flow of vital information.

An individual, on the other hand, may buy a can of Mace or karate lessons, home exercise equipment, a smoke alarm, a plastic car cover, or a raincoat. Other examples might be an annual physical examination, a bodyguard, vitamin supplements, back-up computer disks, a chain-link fence, fireproof filing cabinets, new brakes for the car, the services of a professional safety manager, or a bedside telephone.

PRIDE OF OWNERSHIP

Why does a person buy a luxury car, a yacht, or an elegant home? What motivates a person to amass a collection of antique thimbles, fill a greenhouse with exotic plants, or buy an original work of art? Why does a company spend money on exterior landscaping or an interior decorating service? Why does an executive buy an expensive, polished brass nameplate for the door?

Although some of these purchases may be hard to justify logically, these are simple things we are proud to own. There is a bit of the "label mentality" in most of us. Many of us willingly pay an added premium to wear clothing with an exclusive label, drive a "prestige" car, or even use "name" office equipment.

Examples of purchases motivated by Pride of Ownership might include jewelry, purebred animals, a sports car, high-fashion clothing, designer furniture. or membership in a country club. Take a moment to think about your own recent purchases. What purchases have you made that were motivated primarily by the pride you feel in owning them?

SATISFACTION OF EMOTION

Why do we send flowers to someone we love? Often it's because we want to make our loved one happy. In other cases, however, that purchase could be motivated by a desire to gain approval, appreciation, or love in return. Why does someone throw a lavish, expensive party? Why does a friend willingly pick up a tab for lunch? Why do we buy cologne, manicures, or tickets to a charity ball? These purchases make us feel good about ourselves We all want to gain approval and love. We all want to avoid disappointment and disapproval.

I am referring here to the specific emotions associated with love and ego. These feelings can include: wanting to give joy, delight, comfort, or safety to loved ones; seeking approval, appreciation, and love from others; fearing disapproval or rejection; seeking to impress, intimidate, or ingratiate oneself with others; wanting to look good, literally and figuratively; and being unwilling to look bad, literally and figuratively.

Examples of purchases motivated by Satisfaction of Emotion would be new tires on the family car, an unexpected gift for a friend, a family portrait, a hairpiece, employee gifts at holiday time, new furniture for the employee lounge, cosmetic surgery, or new clothing for a special party.

PEOPLE BUY EMOTIONALLY, NOT LOGICALLY

Every one of these Buying Motives is emotional, not logical. I cannot emphasize this point strongly enough: People buy emotionally, not logically. In order to sell effectively, you must fix the idea firmly in your mind that *everyone* buys for emotional reasons. They buy because emotionally, they desire financial gain or fear financial loss. Emotionally, they want comfort and convenience, or security and protection. Emotionally, they want to feel pride of ownership or to satisfy the needs of love and ego. Sometimes people are aware of their underlying emotional motivations, but much of the time they are only vaguely aware of their motives. The underlying Buying Motives affect personal purchases and company purchases alike, since it is a human being, after all, who makes the decision to buy a product or service for a company.

Different people will have different motives for the same kind of purchase. Suppose, for example, that you see three different people walk into a pet store, and half an hour later each walks out with a St. Bernard. Out of curiosity, you ask the first person why she bought the dog. "I live alone," she says, "and I have to admit I get lonely. I expect Bernardo here will give me companionship, affection, and love. Look at that! He's licking my hand already."

You ask the next person who emerges from the store why he bought the dog, and he says, "A St. Bernard is a breed I've always wanted to own. This particular fellow has an exceptionally fine pedigree. Would you like to see his papers?"

The third person says, "There have been a lot of burglaries in my neighborhood lately, even in the daytime. My wife and I are gone all day, so our apartment is a perfect target. Burglars are going to think twice about breaking in when they see a guard dog this size."

The first person bought the dog for affection — Satisfaction of Emotion. The second person's motive was the dog's lineage — Pride of Ownership. The third person's was the dog's size — Fear of Loss and/or Security and Protection. There could be additional motives: a dog breeder, for example, could have bought a pedigreed female St. Bernard because of her fertility and lineage — Desire for Gain. Conceivably, an Alpine mountaineer also could have bought the dog, with brandy cask attached, for Comfort and Convenience.

It is also true that *more than one motive can apply to the same purchase.* Suppose you are a construction contractor, talking with a woman who's considering remodeling her kitchen. You are selling her on the idea of doing the remodeling and on hiring you for the job. But what is her dominant Buying Motive? The remodeled kitchen would add value to her home — Desire for Gain. The current kitchen is so outdated that her home may be difficult to sell — Fear of Loss. The remodeled kitchen would provide much more comfortable and convenient work space — Comfort and Convenience. The current wiring, plumbing, and appliances are old and unreliable; remodeling now could prevent damage from electrical fires and plumbing leaks — Security and Protection. The woman can take personal pride in the remodeled kitchen and be proud to show it to friends — Pride of Ownership. She can also gain personal satisfaction and the appreciation of family members who will enjoy the new beauty and convenience — Satisfaction of Emotion. Any one or any combination of the Six Buying Motives could apply.

In order to sell the woman the remodeling job, you need to know her dominant Buying Motives — *the emotions that underlie her decision* — because you will want to appeal to those motives in your sales presentation.

Appealing to your prospects' dominant Buying Motives — appealing to their emotions — is what selling is all about. One group of salespeople, advertising copywriters, know this very well. Recently I saw an ad for Cadillac which illustrates this point beautifully. It said:

JUST FOR YOU

All these years you've been doing for others. Summer camp. Orthodontist. Ballet lessons. Tuition. Now it's time to do something for you. The two of you. A beautiful, new Cadillac. And it's all you hoped it would be, in comfort, ride, and luxury.

Isn't it time you did something just for you?
See your Cadillac dealer soon. Best of all...it's a Cadillac...

Since a Cadillac is an expensive car, you would think the potential buyer would calculate the logical reasons for buying such a substantial purchase. But does this ad appeal to logic, reason, or intelligence? Not at all. It's a direct appeal to emotion. Do you suppose that ad was effective in persuading people to buy?

Here is another ad, also for Cadillac, which ran in *Time* magazine. The picture shows an attractive man getting into a Cadillac as the sun sets over the PanAm building in New York. The ad said:

THE CADILLAC HOUR

It's time to head home. Time to discover anew how accommodating your Cadillac can be. As you slide in and adjust the plush power seats, you feel the tensions of the day begin to ease. The quiet surrounds you. Push a button, and the stereo radio seeks out music to match your mood. Stop for weekend supplies, and the available new electronic level control activates automatically, to maintain a smooth, level ride. Merge into the freeway, and you appreciate those special Cadillac conveniences available, as your Cadillac remembers to turn on it's lights with the approach of dusk.

*The Cadillac Hour. In some ways,
it's the best time of the day.*

Another example is an ad for Jaguar, which appeared in *Town and Country* magazine. It shows a beautiful Jaguar parked in front of a luxurious home, which looks like it could be in Palm Springs. The ad says:

Frankly, we doubt that you'll buy a Jaguar because of its fuel economy.

Here are two compelling facts. You'll get 14 miles per gallon from Park Avenue to Wall Street. And 20 miles per gallon from Beverly Hills to Palm Springs.

Or how about this ad in a recent issue of *New Yorker* magazine. The photograph shows the front of a new Mercedes with emphasis on the world famous emblem. The ad simply reads:

Don't Die Wondering.

Do you suppose the people who wrote these ads know what motivates people to buy their cars?

You bet they did.

Everyone buys emotionally. I don't mean only "emotional" people, I mean *everyone*, from the opera diva to the college professor. People buy for their own reasons, no matter what product or service you sell. For example, suppose you're selling real estate, and you're stressing proximity to the bus line, stable subsoil, or the renowned school system. However, if your prospect really wants to take pride in a prestigious address, you won't be nearly as successful as you could be if you addressed the appropriate Buying Motives. Or, suppose you're selling cars, and you're stressing automatic transmissions or electronic ignitions. If your prospect wants comfort, to take pride in the car's "name," and to satisfy her ego, you won't be nearly as successful as you could be.

PEOPLE WON'T TELL YOU THEIR BUYING MOTIVES

People do not, however, readily *admit* their dominant Buying Motives. If you sat down and asked your prospect his or her dominant Buying Motives for a recent purchase, he or she wouldn't, or couldn't, tell you. Psychologists report, even over a long period of time, most of their patients seem reluctant or unable to reveal their dominant motives for any of their actions. Why? One reason is that *our motives often overlap*.

Suppose you just purchased a new jacket. What was your dominant motive in making that purchase? Maybe you bought the jacket for comfort; you expect it to keep you warm. You might have bought it simply because it has a style or label that you're proud to wear or show your friends. Maybe you bought it because the color makes your eyes look bluer, or it makes you look taller and thinner, or in some way it makes you feel good about yourself — it gives you emotional satisfaction. Maybe you bought the jacket for all three reasons merged together: it's comfortable, you're proud to own it, and it makes you feel good about yourself.

The primary reason people don't readily admit their Buying Motives is because it would make them feel too exposed.

Psychologists tell us people feel vulnerable admitting, sometimes even to themselves, what they care about, desire, or fear on a deep emotion level. Who wants to admit that we bought a jacket because it makes our eyes look bluer? People would think we were conceited. Who wants to admit that we bought a jacket as a status symbol — that it has the ''right'' label, and we feel proud to own it? We don't like to admit these things. The Six Buying Motives are real, but if we openly admit our real reasons for making a purchase, other people might laugh. We tend to hide our real reasons, because we just don't want to feel that vulnerable.

Well, your prospects are no different. They are not going to tell you or anyone that the real reason they want to buy the copy machine you're selling is because it has a prestigious name. Who wants to admit to that kind of vanity? They are not going to tell you or anyone that the real reason they want to contract your interior decorating service is because a well-decorated office will make them feel more important and appear more successful to others. Who wants to admit to that kind of vanity? Your prospects are not going to tell you or anyone that the real reason they're interested in your computer system is because they're scared stiff that without it, their competitors will beat their socks off, they will lose their clients, or perhaps even see their whole business go down the drain. Who wants to admit to that kind of fear?

Don't expect your prospects to be totally forthright and honest about the real reasons that motivate them to buy. No one is really honest about these things.

APPEALING TO THE DOMINANT BUYING MOTIVE

Once you know all Six Buying Motives, however, you can appeal to them all, and see which provoke your prospects' strongest responses.

For example, suppose you describe a benefit of your product or service that appeals to Comfort and Convenience, and you see your prospect rise about three feet out of the chair. That tells you to keep returning to that motive throughout the remainder of your presentation. You will use your prospects' reactions to help you keep your presentations focused on the areas that are most important to each individual prospect.

However, don't stop when you've uncovered just one motive that is important to your prospect. As you know by now, more than one Buying Motive may apply, and the motive you have not yet uncovered may turn out to be the most important of all. Continue asking good, open-ended, feeling-finding questions to get additional reactions.

For example, suppose you have already discovered that profit — Desire for Gain — is extremely important to your prospect. You can start exploring other areas by asking questions like: "How would your company feel about you if you were to solve the problem by ... ?" This tells you whether being a "hero" is important to this person. If so, another motivation is ego — Satisfaction of Emotion. You might also ask: "How important is security to you?" and you would find out how the person feels about Security and Protection. As your presentation unfolds, you will emphasize the areas that you find are important to your prospect. You will learn more specifically how to use these questions to draw out your prospects' dominant Buying Motives, when you learn about the Feature/Benefit/Reaction Sequence in "Step Five: Fill the Need."

Several years ago, I read an article about an executive with a major car manufacturer in Detroit. He had been looking for a residential lot in Grosse Pointe Farms, Michigan — a very elegant, affluent community. The real estate salesperson who was showing him various lots found out this executive really liked trees, especially oak trees.

In the article, the executive recalled, "The realtor showed me this lot, and I fell in love with it. It was exactly what I was looking for. When he told me the price, I almost had a heart attack. It was about twice as much as the limit I'd set myself for the purchase. And the realtor said, 'Yes, but look at all those oak trees. There's one ... there's two ... there's three ... there's four ... five ... six ... there's *seven* of the most beautiful oak trees you'll ever find in the world.' " The executive said, "Every time I objected to the price, the salesperson started counting those oak trees. Finally, I *paid* the exorbitant price ... for those seven oak trees. And the realtor threw in the lot for free."

Do you suppose the realtor was aware of what was important to that executive? You bet he was: Pride of Ownership of oak trees. He geared his presentation to stressing what was most important to that prospect, and made the sale.

Remember the Electric Association and the energy crunch? If you recall, they found that the same salespeople who were most successful in convincing their customers to use *more* electricity were also most successful in convincing the same customers to use *less*. Why? Because although the objective has completely reversed, the procedure remained exactly the same. The salespeople were still appealing to the customers to do things for their *own* reasons, not for the utility companies' reasons.

EMOTION VERSUS LOGIC

World Class Selling is designed to be an ethical way to sell. Some people might argue that appealing to emotions rather than to logic is manipulative — that addressing people's emotions when they don't realize it is "hitting below the belt." In my view, professional salespeople don't manipulate in any way, and appealing to the emotions is no exception.

Why is it not manipulative?

THE HISTORICAL PRECEDENT: First, if you think about it, the art and science of persuading, leading, or inspiring others depends entirely on an appeal to the emotions, and always has. Think of Churchill, rallying the spirit of the English during World War II: "We have nothing to fear but fear itself" is an appeal to emotion. Think of Martin Luther King, rallying thousands of civil rights activists: "I have a dream" is an appeal to emotion. Think of Lincoln at Gettysburg, commemorating the dead and rallying further commitment to the Civil War: also an appeal to emotion. Think of Roosevelt, asking Congress to enter World War II: "a day of infamy" is an appeal to the emotions. Think of King Harry in Shakespeare's *Henry V*, urging his outnumbered band of soldiers on to victory at Agincourt: his "For God, for Harry, and for England!" speech, one of the most powerful in English literature, is certainly an appeal to emotion.

Leaders and orators, in history and in fiction, appeal to emotions because emotions *move* people, and *moving* people — to choices, to actions, to join in a common cause — is what leadership and persuasion is all about.

So the question becomes: What *kind* of emotions do leaders — and salespeople — appeal to? Although appealing to base and negative emotions does work with some people some of the time, it is not what you do in the Track Selling System.™ As a professional salesperson, you are seeking ways to solve your prospects' problems or fill their needs, not make them do what *you* want them to do.

PERSUADING IS NOT PRESSURING: In the Track Selling System,™ you do not attempt to influence or change your prospects' emotions in any way. For example, you don't say: "You really want to make your wife happy, don't you?" Instead, you pay close attention to the emotions your prospects already have and attempt to give them what they want.

> Salesperson: *The bed and breakfast inn I recommend has a special dining room and play area for children and a charming, breakfast nook for parents overlooking the flower garden. This inn seems to particularly appeal to women, maybe for these reasons.*
>
> Prospect: *Really?*
>
> Salesperson: *How do you think your wife would feel about having breakfast away from the kids, who'd be happily playing on the swings after their hot cereal, while she'll be having croissants and coffee with you, surrounded by all those daffodils?*
>
> Prospect: *She'd love it.*

PEOPLE HAVE STRONG FEELINGS OF THEIR OWN: People have strong, genuine, deeply felt emotions to start with. When they buy anything, including things they buy on their own initiative that no one is trying to "sell" them, they buy for emotional reasons. You couldn't change that even if you wanted to. Since your job is to help your customers fill their needs or solve their problems, look to their emotions — their Buying Motives — to tell you how you can serve them best. It's as simple as that.

PEOPLE BUY EMOTIONALLY,
THEN JUSTIFY THEIR PURCHASES LOGICALLY

As a professional salesperson, your goal is to help the prospect buy now and *wear well*. It is important to keep the phrase "wear well" firmly in mind, because after the sale has been made, another psychological principle comes into play:

People buy emotionally, then justify their decisions logically.

This means that once the sale has been made, people stop responding emotionally and begin concentrating on the sound, practical, rational, business reasons why the purchase was made. Later on, if asked why they bought, most people will not even remember their emotional motives. They sincerely believe that they bought the product or service for straightforward, logical reasons. If you ask, they will list these logical reasons for you.

For example, a couple will buy a home for emotional reasons: it's charming and looks "just right;" it has a prestigious address; socially prominent people live in the neighborhood. However, once the contract has been signed, the couple will justify their decision logically: the home is a good value; it is bound to appreciate; it is near good schools; it is an excellent investment.

People buy emotionally, then justify their decisions logically. *Therefore, you must provide your prospects with logical as well as emotional reasons why your product or service will benefit them.* And the logical reasons must be valid.

What would happen, for example, if you sold someone an advanced computer software package — the best available — and a top-of-the-line computer storage system, and the prospect woke up a two o'clock in the morning and realized, "Hey, I don't even *own* a computer!"

That sale is not going to wear very well.

Of course I am overstating the case to make a point, but remember your main goal as a professional salesperson is to provide genuine, beneficial service. Your sale should help you build an ongoing relationship that turns a prospect into a longtime customer. As a professional salesperson, everything you do, you will do with honesty and integrity. Honesty is the best "method" a salesperson can use. It builds trust and rapport, and leads to successful sales. You will discover your prospects' needs and problems honestly: by asking directly, in fact-finding and feeling-finding questions. You will discover your prospects' dominant Buying Motives honestly: by noticing which motives they respond to most strongly, and focusing on the benefits of your product or service that will satisfy those motives. You will also provide your prospects with good, logical reasons to justify their purchases — the same good, logical reasons that persuaded you in the first place that your specific product or service can fill their needs or solve their problems.

USING THE SIX BUYING MOTIVES IN YOUR PERSONAL LIFE

Knowing that people buy for their own personal, emotional reasons can be just as helpful in your personal life as it is in your sales career.

For example, if you want a raise, would you walk into your boss's office and give *your* reasons for wanting it: "I have house payments, car payments, and three kids in braces — I need that extra income!"? Hardly. You will be much more effective and successful if you appeal to your *boss's* reasons — your *boss's* Desire for Gain, Fear of Loss, Satisfaction of Emotion, or any of the other Six Buying Motives that might apply.

If you want your children to do better in school, you had better appeal to *their* reasons instead of *your* reasons. This is basic human nature, and it is the kind of knowledge that can be helping you achieve your goals in every facet of your life — not just selling.

THINGS TO REMEMBER

* People buy emotionally, not logically.
* People buy for one or more of the Six Buying Motives:
    * Desire for Gain — $
    * Fear of Loss — $
    * Comfort and Convenience
    * Security and Protection
    * Pride of Ownership
    * Satisfaction of Emotion
* Different people will have different motives for the same purchase
* More than one motive can apply to the same purchase.
* You will need to know your prospects' dominant Buying Motives, so you can appeal to those motives in your sales presentations.
* People don't admit their dominant Buying Motives because it would make them feel too vulnerable.
* Buying Motives often overlap.
* People buy emotionally, then justify their decisions logically.

EXERCISES

1. Imagine that you are the head of a company. Put yourself in the prospect's place and read the sample responses below to find out how a potential purchase might fulfill the motive of:

    a. Desire for Gain — $: "Renting a truck delivery service at $_____ per month allows my firm to operate at less than if it operated its own fleet."

    b. Fear of Loss — $: "By providing crucial, financial information quickly for the corporate and local offices, this new automated marketing system would keep me from missing prospects who are ready to buy. Because it would keep me from missing my market share, it would ensure that we didn't lose profits."

     c. Comfort and Convenience: "A temporary help service that provides dependable office workers and is available when I need them lets me relax and know I can serve my customers with reliability and ease."

     d. Security and Protection: "Having access to a computer storage system that is backed by a trained field-service group, together with a security system that monitors the flow of vital information, allows me to rest assured that this investment will be well protected."

     e. Pride of Ownership: "Installing a robotic assembly line will establish my company's leadership in the field."

     f. Satisfaction of Emotion: "This tire company offers the emotional satisfaction of maximum safety for me and my family."

2.   Now describe how the Six Buying Motives would appeal to you as the buyer of your own product or service.

     a. Desire for Gain — $:

     b. Fear of Loss — $:

     c. Comfort and Convenience:

     d. Security and Protection:

     e. Pride of Ownership:

     f. Satisfaction of Emotion:

3.   As a salesperson, how do you determine which Buying Motives are important to a prospect?

4.   In past sales that you've made, what were some of the most typical Buying Motives that influenced your prospects to buy?

9

GUIDING YOUR PROSPECTS THROUGH THE FIVE BUYING DECISIONS

Before we begin the Seven Steps of the Track Selling System,™ let's take another look at the Five Buying Decisions that you learned about in Chapter Two. As you recall, before your prospect buys your product or service, they make the Five Buying Decisions, in precise, psychological order. This is the buyer's "hidden agenda."

However, even though your prospects are following a precise pattern of decisions, they may not be aware this pattern exists.

You know it exists, so you can gear your presentations to help your prospects move smoothly through the Five Buying Decisions. This will make your presentation more effective and successful.

DECISION ONE: THE SALESPERSON

As you recall, your prospects' first Buying Decision will be about you, the salesperson. Do they like you? Do they think you have integrity and good judgment?

Think about your own Buying Decisions. Have you ever been faced with the decision of making a purchase in one of two stores? In one store the clerks are friendly and courteous, and they call you by name. In the other store, the clerks are surly.

They often converse among themselves, are annoyed when you ask a question, and make you feel as though you've imposed when you ask them to ring up the sale.

Well, your prospects are no different from you. If you've got the only game in town, people will buy from you whether they like you or not. However, they probably *do* have a choice of another salesperson, who represents the same or a competing product, whom they can buy from. The more they like you, the more willing they'll be to buy from you.

By now, of course, you know the simple secret of helping your prospects make this first Buying Decision positively: Let *them* do the talking. You know this isn't a matter of employing any tricks or altering your personality in any way. You simply ask your prospects good, open-ended questions to keep the conversational ball in their court, and listen intently and sincerely to what they have to say.

You will learn the Track Selling System's™ proven, step-by-step process for helping your prospects make the first Buying Decision positively in Chapter Ten: "Step One: Approach," Chapter Eleven: "Step Two: Qualification," and Chapter Twelve: "Step Three: Agreement on Need."

DECISION TWO: THE COMPANY

After your prospects have made a positive decision about you, their next decision will be about your company. Is it honest? Will it back its commitments? Does it have a good reputation? Does it have the capacity to perform as promised?

Think for a moment how you make your own purchases. Suppose that you are going into the store to buy a $1.98 can of spot remover. This is a relatively insignificant purchase. Nevertheless, does the manufacturer's integrity and degree of competence even fleetingly cross your mind? Do you wonder if the glowing claims on the label are true? These two questions focus on the *company* — whether that company really cares that its product satisfies customers, or is simply out to collect that $1.98 and tough luck to you if the product is worthless. If there were two brands of spot remover on the shelf, one manufactured by a company whose name you know and trust, and the other unknown, which would you probably buy? You would be making this buying decision based primarily on your comparative feeling about these two companies.

Here is a more expensive example. Suppose you were going to hire a contractor to construct your $300,000 home. Would the degree of competence and integrity of that contracting firm cross your mind? Of course it would. You would most likely spend a great deal of time checking the contractor's references, finding out how well that company had performed for its clients in the past. If you found that the company didn't enjoy a good reputation and didn't honor its commitments, would you still be interested in hiring the contracting firm?

Of course not. Well, your prospects are no different from you. They too make Buying Decisions about your company, and these decisions are both real and highly influential.

How might you use this knowledge to increase your sales? Let's suppose that you're a salesperson in a shoe store, waiting on a customer who has just tried on two pairs of shoes from different manufacturers. Both pairs fit perfectly and both pairs are identically priced. Your customer likes the color and style of each pair equally well and is trying to decide which pair to buy.

Now suppose that you indicate the pair of shoes on the left and say, "I'm really glad to see you're trying on a pair of Walker Brothers shoes. That company has been in business for over fifty years. We've been carrying Walker shoes here for almost twenty-five years, and in all that time we've never heard a single complaint about them. Walker is totally committed to quality craftsmanship." Do you think that kind of information would influence your customer's decision about which shoes to buy?

Taking this concept one step further, have you ever been in a selling situation in which your competitors have a product or service very similar to yours? Perhaps the competitive product or service performs just as well as yours and is even priced the same. If you were to give your prospect honest, accurate information about the integrity and competence of your company, would that information give you the "edge" and help your prospect make the decision to buy your product or service instead of your competitor's? I have found that in all selling situations, *if you take time to help your prospects make a positive decision about your company*, and your competition neglects this important area, *it will directly increase your sales.*

In the same way, a negative decision about your company can adversely affect your selling process. Your goal as a professional salesperson is to help the prospect buy now and wear well. If you cannot assure that person that your company has integrity and competence — if, in reality, your company does not honor its commitments or for some reason doesn't perform as promised — would it be easy to persuade the prospect to buy now? If you *did* make the sale in such a case, is it likely that it would wear well?

To a prospect, every employee represents the company. Several years ago, Singapore Airlines hired Max Sacks International to train their telephone reservation agents. We recommended to management that they equip each reservation agent with a mirror on their desk and the word ''Smile'' on the mirror so that the agents could see themselves smile when they answered the phone. The sound of the smiling voice carried over the telephone.

Why was this important? In any company, no matter how small or large, every employee plays a role in selling the company's image and service. Airline agents selling to travel agents and corporate executives are part of the *outside* sales force. Mechanics, pilots, and secretaries are part of the *inside* sales force. In effect, every company employee in some way sells or unsells the company.

You will learn the Track Selling System™ procedure for helping your prospects make the second Buying Decision positively in Chapter Thirteen: ''Step Four: Sell the Company.''

DECISION THREE: PRODUCT OR SERVICE

After your prospects have made positive decisions about you and your company, their next Buying Decision will be about your product or service. Does it fill a genuine need? Does it solve a genuine problem?

Remember that each of these decisions is made on the basis of your prospect's ''hidden agenda.'' Your prospects will not ask you if your product or service will fill a need or solve a problem. In fact, your prospects may not be aware that a problem or need exists. They may be perfectly happy with things just the way they are.

Fortunately, you now know how to discover what problems or needs exist. Let your prospects do the talking so you can gather important information that will allow you to fill their needs precisely. Ask open-ended questions to encourage your prospects to express their thoughts and opinions freely.

To illustrate this procedure, imagine you work for a company that sells various brands of computer hardware and software to businesses. As a consultant and salesperson, your job is to assess the needs of your clients and recommend specific products to meet those needs. In the following example, you are calling on Ms. Simpson, the operations manager for a small manufacturing company.

Salesperson: *What computer system do you use now?*

Prospect: *We don't use computers at all.*

Salesperson: *What would be your main use for a computer system?*

Prospect: *Primarily for handling bookkeeping and billing functions, but we may want to expand the system later to do additional tasks.*

Salesperson: *How do your employees feel about your present bookkeeping and billing system?*

Prospect: *Frankly, the employees in this department are bored doing tedious, repetitive tasks. Turnover is high.*

Salesperson: *What other problems are you having with your present system?*

Prospect: *Well, to tell you the truth, there have been frequent billing errors, and they cause problems with customer relations.*

Salesperson: *What is your budget situation?*

Prospect: *We haven't set a budget yet.*

During this time you are not offering any solutions. You are simply asking questions and gathering information that will allow you to pinpoint this prospect's problems and needs.

A genuine need exists. You have listened carefully and understand the problems and needs she faces. You can now show her how your products will solve her problems and fill her needs precisely.

If you want to find our how important this information is to your prospect's own Buying Motives, you could continue by asking questions designed to elicit a reaction, such as:

- "How would your employees feel if you set up a system that would free them from these tedious, repetitive tasks?"
- "How would it affect your profits if you could lower your turnover rate in the bookkeeping department?"
- "How much more time would you have if you didn't have to deal with all those unhappy customers because of billing errors?"
- "How do you feel about being able to accomplish all of this for less than you expected to pay?"

Although I have oversimplified this example, it does illustrate the point that by asking good, open-ended questions, you can encourage your prospects to give you every shred of information you need to know. You can also show your prospects how your product or service solves their problems or fills their needs precisely.

You will learn the detailed Track Selling System™ procedure for helping your prospects make the third Buying Decision positively in Chapter Fifteen: "Step Five: Fill the Need."

DECISION FOUR: PRICE

The fourth Buying Decision in your prospect's "hidden agenda" is the price of the product or service you sell. Note that this Buying Decision is number four, not number one. Many salespeople believe that their prospect's Buying Decision is based primarily on price, but this is not so.

People don't buy price. They buy value.

SUMMARIZING VALUE

Consider the old adage: "You get what you pay for." Or: "You can't spend a little and get a lot." Or: "If the price sounds too good to be true, it probably is." Your prospects won't object to a high price if they feel they are receiving *good value* for the money.

Therefore, when you quote a price, you will want to first summarize what the prospect will receive for that money to remind him or her of the value of that purchase. I strongly recommend that you memorize and use the following statement:

> *For your* [summary of features], *the price is* [quote the price].

For example, you might say:

- "*For your* initial order of five gross of snap fasteners, size MM, in black, *the price is* $2,900."
- "*For your* hot-air balloon ride of one hour for four people, *the price is* $200."
- "*For your* car insurance on two automobiles, including the liability, collision, and uninsured motorist coverages, *the price is* $430."

AVOID "COST"

Also, when you quote the price, I strongly suggest that you avoid the word ôcost.ö It has a negative impact. Instead, use words like *investment, fee, price*, and *annual premium* — anything but the word "cost."

You will learn the precise Track Selling System™ procedure for quoting the price in Chapter Fifteen: "Step Five: Fill the Need."

WHEN YOUR PRODUCT OR SERVICE IS EXPENSIVE

Many salespeople believe that if their product or service is expensive, it is more difficult to sell, or that people balk at high-priced items. This is not necessarily true. It may not be fair, but people do equate high price with high value. People expect to get what they pay for. Your product's or service's higher price can actually draw business to you.

For example, a number of years ago one of the leading American car manufacturers prepared to introduce a new, luxury model by conducting a survey. They showed interior and exterior photographs of the car to hundreds of people and asked them what they thought the price of that car would be. The average price named in the survey was $18,000.

Before conducting the survey, the manufacturer established the price of the car at $8,500. The survey told the manufacturer that the price was too *low* — that they had better raise the price of that car if they wanted people to buy. So they did and put their car on the market for $12,500. As I said, that was many years ago; today the car would be several times that.

People expect to get what they pay for. If you're selling an extremely low-priced item, compared with others of it kind, you may find that that low price is an actual disadvantage. There is no need for you to be apologetic to your prospects if your product or service is high priced. Your prospects may tell you that your price is too high — it's their responsibility to their company to buy as low as possible — but they won't want to sacrifice value for low price.

The English writer John Ruskin once wrote:

> *"It is unwise to pay too much, but it is worse to pay too little. When you pay too much, you lose a little money, that is all. When you pay too little, you sometimes lose everything, because the thing you bought was incapable of doing the thing you bought it to do. The common law of business balance prohibits paying a little, and getting a lot. It cannot be done. If you deal with the lowest bidder, it is well to add something for the risk you run, and if you do that, you will have enough to pay for something better."*

DECISION FIVE: TIME

At this point, your customer has made four of the Five Buying Decisions. Your prospect has decided that you are a decent, likable person with integrity and good judgment. Your company sounds honest and capable. Your product or service fills a genuine need or solves a genuine problem, and the price is fair in terms of value received.

The only thing left to decide is *when* to buy. When that's all that's left to decide, it's time to ask for the order.

Can you see how closing the sale can be, and should be, the logical conclusion to a well-given presentation? This is the exact time to close the sale. After your prospect has decided positively about you, your company, your product or service and the price, the only logical decision left is when to buy.

Yet, if you will recall, surveys show that 62 percent of the time, just when the salesperson should be closing the sale, he or she never asks for the order. Is it any wonder that just 20 percent of salespeople make 80 percent of all sales?

FEAR OF REJECTION

One reason this happens is that many salespeople fear rejection. If they don't ask for the order, how can the prospect possibly say no? However, if these salespeople would just say, ''Will you buy?'' they would be very successful. I'm sure that in the first few months I was selling insurance, many of the people I called on thought I was some kind of good-will ambassador, just laying the groundwork for the *real* salesperson, who would be out later to ask for the order. I *sold* my prospects; I just didn't ask them to *buy*. It finally dawned on me that if I was going to earn my livelihood from commissions, I'd better start asking people to buy, and I did. I found they *did* buy.

Most sales interviews are terminated by the prospects, not by the salesperson. The salesperson goes on and on, and the prospects finally have to say, ''That sounds great. Where do I sign up?'' or ''I want to think it over,'' or ''I want to get another price.'' The prospects *have* to terminate the interview. If they didn't they would expect the salesperson to move in with them forever, dreading the moment of having to ask for the order.

In actual fact, the fear of rejection is groundless. When a prospect says, ''I don't want to buy your product,'' or ''I don't want to do business with you,'' that is not a personal rejection of the salesperson, only of a business decision. The prospects don't even know the salespeople personally, so how can they reject them?

Children understand this. When you tell them no, they know it doesn't mean you don't love them anymore. It just means no. Children, like the 38 percent of salespeople who *do* ask for the order, persist in asking, ask in various ways, and are quite successful in getting what they want.

Confusion

Besides the fear of rejection, there is another factor why 62 percent of salespeople don't ask for the order. Many of them are just plain confused. They aren't sure exactly when to close the sale and they aren't sure exactly how. Because they aren't sure exactly when and how it's done, it is more comfortable for them to just skip that minor step, and walk off without making a sale.

And why *wouldn't* salespeople be confused? If you ask an experienced salesperson: "How will I know when to close a sale?" this is what often happens:

Salesperson:	*Um ... you'll just know.*
You:	*How will I know?*
Salesperson:	*Well, I really can't explain it; it's just something you'll feel.*
You:	*How will I know when I feel it?*
Salesperson:	*Well, I really can't explain that either, but, uh, you'll learn.*
You:	*How will I learn?*
Salesperson:	[Giving you a jovial pat on the back.] *You'll learn by closing too early and too often.*

Now I ask you, what kind of help is that?

My grandfather once told me, "You can no more teach what you don't know than you can go back to where you ain't been." Many companies train their new salespeople by sending them out with experienced ones. The rookies watch the experienced salespeople in action, and then are told, "There. That's all there is to it. Just do it like I did."

That type of selling is not a transferable skill. You have to know *when* to ask for the order, and you have to know *how*. There *is* a right time to ask for the order: when the other four Buying Decisions have been made positively, and the only logical decision left is *when* to buy. If salespeople asked for the order just once, think how their success rate would change. How many would move out of the low-producing, ineffective 80 percent?

NOW IS THE TIME TO "TAKE UP THE COLLECTION"

When your prospect has made all other Buying Decisions positively, it is time to ask for the order. Or, as Mark Twain would say, it is time to "take up the collection." This famous humorist went to church one Sunday and heard a missionary speak. In describing the sermon, Twain convincingly emphasized the importance of knowing when to stop. He wrote:

> *"He was the most eloquent orator I ever listened to. He painted the benighted condition of the heathen so clearly, that my deepest passion was aroused. I resolved to break a lifelong habit, and contribute a dollar to teach the gospel to my benighted brethren. As the speaker proceeded, I decided to make it five dollars. And then, ten. Finally, I knew it to be my duty to give to the cause all the cash I had with me — twenty dollars. The pleading of the orator wrought upon me still further, and I decided not only to give all the cash I had with me, but to borrow twenty dollars from my friend, who sat at my side. That was the time to take up the collection.*
>
> *However, the speaker proceeded, and I finally dropped off to sleep. When the usher awoke me with the collection plate, I not only refused to contribute, but I'm ashamed to state, that I actually stole fifteen cents."*

Now is the time to take up the collection. When the prospect has made all other Buying Decisions positively, and the only remaining decision is when to buy, it is time to ask for the order.

You will learn the step-by-step Track Selling System™ procedure for exactly how to ask for the order, not just once but five times, in Chapter Fifteen: "Step Six: Act of Commitment."

STEPPING TOWARD SUCCESS

Up to this point we have briefly touched on many skills of the professional salesperson, including: writing down the objectives for your sales calls; letting your prospects do the talking; asking open-ended, feeling-finding and fact-finding questions; and appealing to your prospect's Six Buying Motives. You are also aware of the Five Buying Decisions, which your prospects will make in a precise, psychological order, and the Six Buying Motives that cause everyone to buy. Now it is time to put this skill and information together. Turn to Part Two of this book to learn the precise, step-by-step process of the Track Selling System™ that will put you on the road to successful selling.

THINGS TO REMEMBER

- Each prospect makes the Five Buying Decisions, in precise, psychological order, before buying whatever product or service you sell. The decisions are about:
    1. Salesperson
        a. Integrity
        b. Judgment
    2. Company
    3. Product or Service
    4. Price
    5. Time

- People don't buy price; they buy value.

- A high-priced item is not a barrier to successful sales.

- Prospects who say no are rejecting a business decision, not the salesperson.

PART 2

THE SEVEN STEPS OF TRACK SELLING

There are Seven Steps in the Track Selling System™ that parallel the Five Buying Decisions:

1. Approach — First Decision: Salesperson
2. Qualification — First Decision: Salesperson
3. Agreement on Need — First Decision: Salesperson
4. Sell the Company — Second Decision: Company
5. Fill the Need — Third and Fourth Decisions: Product or Service and Price
6. Act of Commitment — Fifth Decision: Time
7. Cement the Sale

These steps help your prospects make each of the Five Buying Decisions positively.

You will find that these Seven Steps make sense. They lead you from one to the next easily and logically. As you understand them and apply them to your own selling, you will feel the confidence that peak performers feel. Having an exact procedure to follow on every sales call will make you more effective and successful. Knowing exactly what to do without doubt or hesitation will also give you added self-assurance.

The Seven-Step procedure has been field-tested and it works. Although it is structured, it is not canned. You will find it completely adaptable to your own personality, the different personalities of your prospects, and the specific product or service you sell. In every step, you will be of service to your prospects with complete integrity, using persuasion, not pressure.

Before beginning, here is a capsule preview of the Seven Steps.

STEP ONE: APPROACH: Your prospects' first Buying Decision is about you, the salesperson. Do they like you? Do you have integrity and good judgment? Step One is designed to help your prospects make this decision positively. People buy because they like you.

STEP TWO: QUALIFICATION: This is your information-gathering period. In Step Two, you will qualify the person as a genuine prospect and uncover the problems or needs that exist. They will determine if you are honest, have integrity and know what you are talking about.

STEP THREE: AGREEMENT ON NEED: You will summarize for your prospect the information you gathered in Step One and Step Two to verify and clarify these facts. You will be demonstrating your understanding of your prospects' unique problems and needs. Your prospects buy not because they understand your product or service, but because *you* understand *them*.

STEP FOUR: SELL THE COMPANY: Your prospects' second Buying Decision is about your company. Does it operate with integrity? Does it have the competence and capability to perform as promised? In Step Four, you will supply your prospects with the information they need to make this decision positively.

STEP FIVE: FILL THE NEED: Your prospects' next two Buying Decisions are about the product or service you sell and the price. In Step Five, you will show your prospects how your product or service solves their problems or fills their needs precisely and the *value* they will receive for their purchase price.

STEP SIX: ACT OF COMMITMENT: The only Buying Decision left is when to buy. Now is the time to ask for the order or the act of commitment. In Step Six, you will ask for that order — five times, if necessary — without applying any pressure.

STEP SEVEN: CEMENT THE SALE: People buy emotionally, then justify their Buying Decisions logically. In Step Seven you will "cement" in your prospects' minds the *logical* reasons that made their purchasing decisions wise, sound and intelligent so that your sales will wear well.

To be effective, these Seven Steps must be followed in *precise order.* Your prospects' Five Buying Decisions are made in precise, psychological order. The Seven Steps are designed to carry your prospect smoothly through this series of decisions in that same precise, psychological order.

Imagine a ship approaching a canal with seven locks. The ship first tries to navigate Lock Four, then Lock Six, then Lock Three, and so on. That is fairly hard to imagine because a ship cannot get from one lock to another without passing through the locks in between. To attempt to do otherwise would result in a battered and beaten ship.

The Seven Steps don't work well out of order, either. They don't often produce a sale and can result in a confused, frustrated, self-doubting salesperson. However, when used in order, the Seven Steps lead you logically to a successful sale.

A very important point to remember here is the sales cycle. Remember, as discussed in Chapter Four, selling is selling is selling. The one major difference in selling is the sales cycle. The Seven Steps may occur on one call, or several calls over a long period of time. The process works regardless of your sales cycle, and the Seven Steps of Track Selling™ work in telephone sales as well as face to face calls.

I hope you enjoy learning these steps. Visualize the prospect having an invisible sign reading, "What will it do for me?" (You will learn more about this in Chapter 14: "Step Five: Fill the Need.") For now, *you* are the prospect. Relate your own experience to the new learning wherever you can. Apply the new learning to your past and future experience. You may be stepping tentatively now, but you'll be walking and running by the time you are done with this book.

10

STEP ONE: APPROACH

Approach is just what it sounds like: Getting to know the prospect. Introducing yourself and establishing rapport. In fact, the first two steps of the Track Selling System™ — Approach and Qualification — are so important that they determine your success — or failure — later on in closing the sale.

THE INTRODUCTION

The introduction is how you introduce yourself when you first make a sales call. It is your opportunity to create a good first impression, and you create the first impression in this business situation exactly the same way you would in your personal life.

Psychologists tell us people make a lasting impression on others in the first three to five minutes of their meeting. Therefore, whatever you do in the first three to five minutes you meet your prospect will have a lasting effect on your entire business relationship! Research findings also indicate that we ''communicate'' many facts about ourselves — and how we feel about others — predominantly by nonverbal means. Specifically, although we may be talking with someone, only seven percent of the communication the other person receives is actually by what we *say*. 38 percent is communicated by our tone of voice and 55 percent by our facial expressions and body language.

When you enter a prospect's office, you can be sure that he or she has many business problems — and considers most of them higher priority than talking to a salesperson. To hold your prospect's attention and interest, your approach has to be creative.

THE FIVE ELEMENTS OF INTRODUCTION

What does this mean for you? Conduct yourself as a warm, friendly person — the kind of person your prospect would enjoy having as a friend. Enter your prospect's office with an air of confidence and friendliness. Use a warm, genuine smile that shows you are sincerely interested in the other person. A smile is truly the universal sign of friendship. Call your prospect by name. Maintain eye contact and offer a warm, firm handshake. Greet your prospect and introduce yourself in your own words, but make sure your introduction includes the following five aspects:

1. Greeting your prospect ("Good morning," "Hello," and so on)
2. Calling your prospect by name
3. Giving your own name
4. Identifying your company
5. Asking an open-ended. rapport-building question

"Good morning, Mr. Smith. I'm Alice Jones of the Truitt Company. How is your day going so far?"

You might think introducing yourself is so automatic and natural in a business situation that I shouldn't have to mention it. I have been out with several salespeople on several calls who forgot to introduce themselves. me. or their boss.

This procedure is simple, logical. and no different from the way you would handle an initial meeting with any other friend.

THE HANDSHAKE

As you introduce yourself. offer a warm, firm handshake. It's a sincere gesture of friendship in any language. Should you shake hands when you and/or your prospects are women? In today's business world women expect to be treated exactly as men are, neither deferred to nor patronized. So whether you are a man or a woman, you should offer a warm, firm handshake regardless of your prospect's gender.

THE BUSINESS CARD

Offer your business card to your prospect immediately after this introduction period. Have your card conveniently at hand when you go into the meeting, so you don't have to fumble around for it and create a distraction for both you and your prospect. Searching your pockets or purse for a lost card will brand you as an amateur. By offering your card now, at this early point in the sales call, you will help put your prospect at ease. While your prospect is talking with you, he or she might forget your name or your company's name. Your card will be a handy, reference source to refresh your prospect's memory.

Should you ask your prospect for a card in return at this point? In many cases, your prospect will automatically give you a card when you give yours. If this doesn't happen, and you see business cards on display on your prospect's desk, it is certainly appropriate to ask for one.

If your prospect doesn't offer you a card, and you don't see any on display, think twice before asking for one. Why? Suppose the prospect doesn't *have* any business cards. The prospect who is temporarily out of cards may feel embarrassed, and the prospect who doesn't have business cards at all may feel down-right unimportant. It isn't worth the risk.

"NO COFFEE, THANKS."

Politely decline an offer of coffee, beverages, or a cigarette. Drinks spill on paperwork and ashes fall on expensive desks and carpets. Although it is a little thing, use a breath freshener just before you meet the prospect. Little things like these can add up and make a difference.

BUILDING RAPPORT

Peak sales performance in Step One: Approach depends greatly on how effectively you build rapport with your prospect. There's no way around it — as professional salespeople, *we're in the people business*. People skills make product knowledge and technical knowledge pay off.

SEVEN WAYS TO IMPROVE YOUR PEOPLE SKILLS

Here are some techniques that you can use to establish rapport with your prospects and improve your people skills. You will learn more about these techniques in Chapter 20: "You're in the People Business."

- Smile.
- Develop a genuine interest in others.
- Talk in terms of the other person's interests.
- Use the other person's name.
- Give compliments.
- Listen.
- Make the other person feel important.

PERSONAL AND BUSINESS RAPPORT

There are two types of rapport that you can generate: personal and business. Which has the higher priority in a sale? When the situation calls for it, open the presentation with personal rapport.

What do you do when a busy prospect skips over your personal greeting and prefers getting down to business? Respond to what the potential buyer wants. If business comes first, deal with personal rapport later.

EVERYONE BENEFITS FROM RAPPORT

Establishing rapport is not just for the benefit of the salesperson. According to market research, today's corporate buyers seek rapport with the salespeople who call on them. They want to do business with someone they like and trust. Thus your skill at building harmonious relationships with your prospects will make it much easier for you to make more sales.

SELLING YOURSELF

By building rapport in Step One: Approach, you are selling yourself — helping your prospects decide they like you. How? I'm sure you know the answer by now:

Let your prospects do the talking.

The more your prospects talk, the more they'll like you.

This technique may sound too simple to be true, yet you will find it unbelievably successful, no matter what your personality, your prospect's personality, or the specific product or service you sell. People buy because they *like* you, and the more your prospects talk, the more they will like you.

THROW THE BALL:
OPEN-ENDED AND CLOSED-ENDED QUESTIONS

When speaking with prospects in Step One: Approach, pretend that the conversation is a game of catch and that the object of the game is to have your prospect carry the ball. Every time you're talking, *you've* got the ball. The object is to try to get rid of it as quickly as possible by asking open-ended questions. These questions often start with the words: *Who, What, Why, When, Where* and *How*.

To refresh your memory, here are examples of open-ended and close-ended questions.

Closed: *"Will you be taking a vacation this year?"*

Open: *"Where will you be vacationing this year?"*

Closed: *"Are you glad about that?"*

Open: *"How do you feel about that?"*

Closed: *"Did you work before joining this company?"*

Open: *"Where did you work before doing this?"*

Closed: *"Is your son's team doing well this season?"*

Open: *"How is your son's team doing this season?"*

Closed: *"Do you recommend Joe's Restaurant?"*

Open: *"What restaurants do you recommend?"*

Closed: *"Is your Collie in obedience class?"*

Open: *"How's your Collie doing in obedience class?"*

Closed: *"Do you enjoy fly fishing?"*

Open: *"What kind of fishing do you enjoy most?"*

Closed: *"Do you see yourself doing this in five years?"*

Open: *"What do you see yourself doing five years from now?"*

It may be helpful to spend a few minutes re-reading Chapter Seven: "The Art of Asking Questions."

THROWING THE BALL WITH ESTABLISHED CUSTOMERS

With long-established prospects, you already know many facts about what is going on in their personal lives. You will find it natural and completely comfortable to ask your initial, open-ended questions based on information you have received on previous calls.

+ "How did your daughter do in that soccer match?"
+ "Which car did you decide to buy?"
+ "How's Jack doing with his new braces?"
+ "When will you be moving into your new home?"
+ "How did your fishing trip go?"

These personal, open-ended questions are helping you achieve multiple goals. You are not only encouraging your prospect to do the talking, you are also establishing warm, genuine rapport.

Questions like these illustrate to your prospects that you have really listened to what they have told you before. You are demonstrating that you care about these people, not just as business prospects but as fellow human beings. You are establishing yourself as a friend.

THROWING THE BALL WITH NEW PROSPECTS

What about calls you make on new prospects — cold calls — in which you have no prior information about the prospect's personal life? These situations present a greater challenge, but there are guidelines you can use to help you develop your rapport-building questions. For example, be alert to your surroundings. You may be able to base your initial, open-ended questions on something you see or a mood your prospect projects.

- "With this magnificent view, how do you manage to get any work done?"
- "With your hectic schedule, what do you do for relaxation when you get away from here?
- "I see by your photographs that you like to ski. How long have you been skiing?"
- "How did you do [whatever the prospect takes pride in]? I know it takes good judgment and hard work."

You may want to give a sincere, honest compliment, and then ask a question based on that subject.

- "Your secretary certainly is efficient. How long has he or she been working for you?"
- "You've got the perfect location for your plant. How did you select this location?"
- "Your title is impressive. What responsibilities does your job entail?"

MIXING PERSONAL AND BUSINESS RAPPORT

You may find it helpful to prepare some general questions in advance about non-controversial current events, local entertainment, sports events, and so on. On the other hand, you may need to make your first questions business-oriented, then switch to personal subjects as soon as your prospect gives you some information to base these questions on.

Of course, it goes without saying that your questions should not be *too* personal or on subjects that could be considered insensitive or in bad taste. For example, you would definitely not ask such questions as: "How old are you?" "How much do you earn?" or "Why are you getting a divorce?" You wouldn't ask questions like these of a friend, so you certainly wouldn't show such insensitivity to your prospects.

Use questions that are in good taste and that encourage your customers to talk about themselves, their hobbies, career histories or future ambitions, personal goals, families, vacations, opinions, and so on.

PHRASES EVERYONE LIKES TO HEAR

Once your prospects begin talking, respond with the phrases everyone likes to hear:

+ "Wow!"
+ "Really?"
+ "You're kidding!"
+ "That's great."
+ "How'd you do it?"
+ "What happened then?"
+ "Tell me more."

This is the time to use every conversational skill you have: open-ended, fact-finding and feeling-finding questions; reflective questions; and the Friendly, Silent, Questioning Stare.

ESTABLISHING RAPPORT: WHAT TO DO AND WHAT NOT TO DO

Take a look at this sample dialogue between a salesperson and a new prospect.

> *Salesperson:*   *Good morning, sir.*
>
> *Prospect:*   *I'm Charles Smith. Have a seat. Would you like some coffee or tea?*
>
> *Salesperson:*   *Uh, yeah, thanks.* [Reaches for the cup of coffee and spills it; looks awkward and embarrassed.] *I, uh, I know you're going to be interested in our office automation system. I'm sure you've heard of ABC Office Automation?*
>
> *Prospect:*   *Yes, I have. By the way, do you have a business card?*

Salesperson: *Oh, yes.* [Hands prospect a business card.]

Prospect: [Reading.] *Frank Gardner.* [Looking up.] *Are you any relation to Harry Gardner of Criterion High-Tech?*

Salesperson: *Uh, no, no relation. Mr. Smith, our office automation is state-of-the-art and definitely meets your needs. Our company has taken top awards on the efficiency of our system. ABC Automation is one of the five fastest-growing companies in this field.*

Prospect: *Well, we've been looking at office automation, but so far we didn't find one we could use.*

Salesperson: *You'd have to go far to beat the quality of our product and service.*

Prospect: [Politely.] *I'm sure that's so.* [Phone rings.] *I'm sorry, but my schedule has gotten pretty hectic. Why don't you leave your materials and price list, and, uh, we'll get back together another time.*

Now let's look at a more effective way of establishing rapport.

Salesperson: [Entering prospect's office and extending hand.] *Good morning, Mr. Smith. I'm Frank Gardner of ABC Automation.* [Shakes hands; then gives prospect his business card.]

Prospect: *Pleased to meet you. Have a seat. Would you like some coffee or tea?*

Salesperson: *No thanks, I'm trying to cut down. Your receptionist and staff are very courteous. They made me feel welcome.*

Prospect: *Glad to hear it.*

Salesperson: [Sitting down and looking around.] *Your office decor is in good taste and also has a comfortable feel to it. It all goes along with the excellent reputation of your company.*

Prospect: *Tell me, are you related to Harry Gardner of Criterion High-Tech?*

Salesperson:	*No, I'm afraid not ... but if it'll help me get the order, I might discover I am!*
Prospect:	[Laughs.]
Salesperson:	*I see in the Times that your company is growing rapidly and maintaining its reputation for quality. What are your plans for handling the increased loads for your office staff?*
Prospect:	*We are looking for help.*
Salesperson:	*Mr. Smith, I'd like to tell you about ABC Office Automation. However, for me to do the best job I possible can for you, I need to ask you a couple of questions. Is that all right?*

Notice how Frank was effective in establishing his presence and rapport with Mr. Smith. Frank imparted respect for his prospect by using his name. He showed caring for the executive by extending his hand first, then his business card. Frank sincerely complimented Mr. Smith on his employees and the decor of his office. Frank also made Mr. Smith feel important by saying he had read about the firm's growth in the *Times*, and he acknowledged the firm's reputation for quality. He conveyed his desire to serve the company's needs by asking how Mr. Smith planned to meet increased office loads.

These seven interpersonal techniques are field tested. You can count on them to make your rapport-building effective.

THE SALES CYCLE OF RAPPORT-BUILDING

How long should the rapport-building portion of your sales presentation last? There is no hard-and-fast rule about the length of time you should devote to this vitally important step. You will need to use your own good judgment and be adaptable to the individual selling situations you meet.

WITH NEW PROSPECTS

The *sales cycle* of the specific product or service you sell will have a major influence on the amount of time you spend building rapport. As you recall, the sales cycle is the time between your first contact with your prospect and the time your sale is transacted. If the sales cycle of your product or service is short, it may be possible for you to walk into your prospect's office and emerge half an hour later having closed the sale. In cases like these, it is still necessary for you to spend a sufficient amount of time establishing warm rapport.

On the other hand, the product or service you sell may be exceptionally complex and/or expensive. The normal sales cycle may stretch on for months, even years, before your sale is transacted. In cases like these your prospects are facing serious buying decisions, and will need to develop a great deal of trust in your integrity and good judgment before they decide to buy from you. You may find yourself making call after call on a single prospect without moving beyond Step One: Approach and Step Two: Qualification. My advice is to let your own good judgment be your guide. Take as much time as required to build warm, genuine rapport.

Admittedly, there may be times when the prospect may at first see you as an unfortunate nuisance, even when you are there by appointment. This may not have to do with you at all, but with the prospect's previous negative experiences with salespeople, or with his or her own immediate circumstances. While you can't control the circumstances that affect your prospect, you *can* show respect and sensitivity by asking, ''Can you spare the time now or shall we make another appointment?''

WITH ESTABLISHED CUSTOMERS

How about the time devoted to rapport-building on the calls you make on long-time clients? These people may have known you for years. They already like you; they are already aware of your integrity and good judgment. Can you skip Step One of the sales process with these long-established friends.

No, you cannot. Every prospect or customer you call on, in every sales call you make, is making a decision about you, the salesperson. This includes your long-established customers. You can't take their friendship for granted. You can't leave this important Buying Decision to chance. In the introduction portion of Step One: Approach, you create a good first impression; in the rapport-building portion, you let your prospects do the talking. The more they talk, the more they will like you —

and the more they like you, the more willing they will be to buy the product or service you sell.

If you put into practice only this much of what you learn in *World Class Selling*, you will be amazed at your increased success as a professional salesperson.

SAMPLE DIALOGUE FOR STEP ONE: APPROACH

Gerri, a professional salesperson, is about to approach her prospect, Dick. She is returning the call he made to her office earlier, in response to a newspaper ad.

> *Prospect:*   [Answering telephone] *Hello?*
>
> *Salesperson:*   *Hello, this is Gerri, from Happiness is Hawaii Tours. I understand someone telephoned earlier to talk about a vacation in Hawaii for the Jacobson family. Is this Mr. Jacobson?*
>
> *Prospect:*   *Yes, it is.*
>
> *Salesperson:*   *Mr. Jacobson, how can I help you with your vacation planning?*
>
> *Prospect:*   *Call me Dick, Gerri. We don't know very much about Hawaii, but we saw your ad in the paper and it sounded tempting. I'd love to take my family somewhere special like Hawaii, if it isn't too expensive. How much are your Hawaiian tours?*

Notice that after her introduction, Gerri doesn't say much at all. She lets her prospect do the talking. Watch for this "quiet salesperson" approach as you follow this ongoing conversation in future chapters.

MAKING A GOOD FIRST IMPRESSION

First impressions make all the difference, so when you first meet a prospect, connect with this person. Maintain eye contact. Introduce yourself and anyone who is with you. Extend your hand for a handshake, and make sure the grasp is firm. Keep your business card handy to present to the prospect. Even over the telephone, you can make your prospect feel cared about. It makes all the difference.

Remember: People don't care how much you know until they know how much you care.

THINGS TO REMEMBER

* Your major goal in Step One: Approach, is to help your prospects make a positive decision about you, the salesperson.

* Introduce yourself, and include these five elements:

    1. Greeting your prospect

    2. Calling your prospect by name

    3. Giving your own name

    4. Identifying your company

    5. Asking an open-ended, rapport-building question

* Build rapport, using these seven interpersonal techniques:

    1. Smile.

    2. Develop a genuine interest in people.

    3. Talk in terms of the other person's interests.

    4. Use the other person's name.

    5. Give compliments.

    6. Listen.

    7. Make the other person feel important.

* To sell yourself, let your prospects do the talking.

EXERCISES

1. What interpersonal techniques do you currently use to establish rapport with your prospects?

2. Begin to prepare a written plan for a real sales presentation that you can use on one of your own sales calls. (You are beginning your written plan with Step One: Approach. By the time you complete Step Seven: Cement the Sale, you will have a written plan that covers all seven steps of the Track Selling System.™)

   To make this exercise more effective, choose an existing prospect or a customer who is a prospect for additional products or services, on whom you actually plan to make a sales call in the near future.

   Identify your objectives for that sales call. Then put them in writing on a separate sheet of paper, or in the blanks below.

WRITTEN OBJECTIVES FOR THE SALES CALL

Prospect's name:

Prospect's title:

Kind of business:

Specific objectives for this sales call:

3. Next, prepare a written plan for Step One: Approach for this anticipated sales call.

   In the first part, "Introduction," write the exact words that you will use as you enter that meeting and introduce yourself to your prospect. Remember, the five elements that should be included in your introduction are: a greeting, calling your prospect by name, giving your own name, identifying your company, and asking an open-ended, rapport-building question.

   In the second part, "Rapport-Building," write three open-ended questions that you could use to encourage your specific prospect to begin talking freely. Prepare a sheet as follows, or fill in the blanks.

Written Plan for Step One: Approach

a. Introduction:

b. Rapport-Building (three open-ended questions):
   1)

   2)

   3)

11

STEP TWO: QUALIFICATION

In Step Two: Qualification, you help your prospects determine exactly what they need. Then you gear the rest of your presentation to meeting those needs. Remember: A professional salesperson is a giver, not a taker.

How will you know what your prospect needs? By drawing out the right answers. And how will you do that? By asking the right questions. Peak performers prepare a list of questions before they make a presentation to the prospect.

Step Two: Qualification builds upon your successes in Step One: Approach. You continue to build rapport with your prospect. You maintain your role as a warm, likable person — the kind of person your prospect would enjoy having as a friend. You continue helping your prospect make a positive decision about you, the salesperson. In the back of their minds, your prospects are still considering whether you are likable and have integrity and good judgment.

THE FIRST THREE QUALIFICATION QUESTIONS

The Qualification step gives you the opportunity to gather vital information. There are three basic pieces of information that must be answered at the outset if a sale is to take place:

+ Need
+ Authority
+ Budget

IS THERE A NEED?

Does the prospect genuinely need your product or service? If the answer is yes, you have the right and responsibility to sell. If the answer is no, the responsible action is to let the sale go.

In this step, you determine whether this person or organization has a need for the product or service you sell, how the product or service would be used, the existing problems or needs your product or service could alleviate, and what aspects of your product or service would be most important to this particular prospect.

WHO HAS THE AUTHORITY?

Is the person to whom you are speaking the one who can say yes and carry that decision through into action?

When calling on new prospects or making cold calls, one of the first things you want to discover is whether the person you are talking with is the decision-maker — the person with the authority to make the purchase. Suppose that you inadvertently make your presentation to someone who is not the real decision-maker. One of two things could happen.

1. You will have to make that presentation all over again to the real decision-maker.

This means that your current presentation is a waste of time for both you and your prospect.

2. The person with whom you are speaking will relay your information to the decision-maker.

This first employee whom you talked to probably does not have your high degree of sales skill, your same thorough knowledge of your product or service, or your sincere convictions. Furthermore, this person is most likely not familiar with the Five Buying Decisions and would not present the material to the decision-maker in a way that parallels the order of those decisions. This person is also most likely not familiar with the Six

Buying Motives and doesn't know how to appeal to the decision-maker's dominant Buying Motives.

Moreover, why should he or she want to? *You* are the one who is motivated to sell the product or service, not the person who is relaying your message. If you inadvertently fail to present to the real decision-maker, I guarantee your sale will be "lost in the translation."

How do you find out if you are speaking with the decision-maker? All you have to do is ask. For example:

- "What other people will be involved in this purchasing decision?"
- "Who else do you feel should be in on this meeting?"
- "Who else shares this purchasing responsibility with you?"
- "What is the decision-making process at your company?"

What if you find that the person you are talking to is not the decision-maker? Ask, "Who *does* make the buying decisions?", then set up an appointment with that person. You may not achieve the objective you had in mind for this sales call; however, in light of this new information, you reset your objective, and your "act of commitment" becomes the appointment with the new prospect.

BUDGET

Can the prospect afford to buy your product or service? Are there genuine price considerations, or is cost just an objection that must be met later on? Often, prospects balk at price when what they really mean is that one of the Five Buying Decisions has not been addressed to their satisfaction. On the other hand, if there truly is no funding for your product or service, it is best to know that sooner than later.

QUESTIONS TO KEEP YOUR PROSPECT TALKING

To find all this out, you have to know what your prospect is thinking. How? By gathering information. And how do you do that? By keeping your prospect talking.

It isn't difficult to encourage your prospect to continue to talk freely. Remember the questions you learned about in Chapter Seven: "The Art of Asking Questions." Just ask the right questions. In Step Two: Qualification, you will put what you learned into practice.

Here is a quick recap of the different kinds of questions a professional salesperson uses:

1. The open-ended question: Within this category, there is the open-ended, *fact-finding* question, which is designed to uncover facts; and the open-ended, *feeling-finding* question, which is designed to uncover opinions and/or attitudes.

2. The reflective question: Use this to encourage the prospect to talk by reflecting back a key word or phrase the prospect has said.

3. The directive question: Use this to guide the prospect toward the response you want — a yes or no response — to move both parties to a quick understanding.

In Step Two: Qualification, you will use all three kinds of questions. For the most part, however, you will use the open-ended, fact-finding question and the open-ended, feeling-finding question. In Step One: Approach, your questions were focused on personal topics. In Step Two, your focus will shift to business-oriented topics.

Incidentally, if you have not yet practiced the questioning techniques from Chapter Seven, I recommend that you do so now. You might also want to re-read that chapter.

MAKING THE TRANSITION

How do you move smoothly from Step One: Approach to Step Two: Qualification? Fortunately, we have developed a method that has stood the test of time for thousands of Track Selling System™ graduates. The following statement will make the transition for you:

"[Prospect's name], *I would like to tell you about our* [name of your product or service]; *however, in order for me to do the best job I possibly can for you, I need to ask you a couple of questions. Is that all right?*"

This statement is so important that you should memorize it. It is one of the few statements in the Track Selling System™ that I will ask you to memorize. Read it over as many times as required to commit it to memory. When you are ready, write this transition statement from memory in the space provided below.

After making this transition statement, you will ask open-ended questions to help you qualify whether this person is a genuine prospect, and to help you uncover specific problems or needs. During this portion of your sales presentation, you are offering no solutions at all, simply encouraging your prospect to talk freely and give you the information you need for your own specific, selling situation.

As your prospect talks, *listen*. Take note of the important information you are receiving. In the later steps of your presentation, you will use this information to offer on-target solutions that solve your prospect's problems or fill his or her needs.

GENERAL AND SPECIFIC, OPEN-ENDED QUESTIONS

An open-ended question permits prospects to answer in as many words as they choose. These questions can be used to provide you with general information, which will lead you to an outline of your prospect's needs.

Open-ended questions are started easily with the words:
- "What?"
- "Why?"
- "When?"
- "Where?"
- "Who?"
- "How?"

For example:
- "*What* is the real problem in office automation?"
- "*Why* is an automated office system important to you?"

- *"When* did you first notice the problem in your inventory reporting?"
- *"Where* did you turn for help?"
- *"Who* makes the final decision on budget?"
- *"How* is that important to you?"

For example, a salesperson could ask for the prospect's views on a specific aspect of company operations:

Salesperson: *Tell me about the on-the-job training*
                programs you supervise.

Prospect: *I supervise the quality-control programs of*
                our computer.

Open-ended questions come to your rescue when you are not acquainted with a person or you need more input on what is required. While there are no standard questions that will fit all your Qualification requirements, there are some general and specific questions that you could develop to uncover what you need to know in your own selling situations.

For example, if you were selling the services of temporary employees, you would need to learn when your prospect normally has the busiest season, so you would know when your temporary help would probably be requested. So you would ask: "What is your busiest season?" You might find yourself incorporating that same basic question on almost every sales call you make with new prospects. In the same selling situation, other important questions might be:

- "What positions would you be most apt to fill with temporary employees?"

By this question, you would learn what types of workers this prospect needs and whether your company has workers with those skills.

- "How many temporary workers do you think you might need at one time?"

By this question, you would learn the size of this prospect's need and know if your company can handle a request of this size.

- "How much advance notice would you be able to give when these temporary employees are needed?"

By this question, you would learn the timing required and know if your company can meet needs within this time frame.

  ♦ "What is your normal rate of pay for workers in this category?"

By this question, you would learn whether your own rates will sound reasonable to this customer.

OPEN-ENDED, FACT-FINDING QUESTIONS

This kind of question provides the input that qualifies your prospects and helps you design your presentation to fit their specific needs. In addition, it helps establish rapport and reinforce a positive buying decision about you, the salesperson. I recommend that you start your qualification with a fact-finding, open-ended question. Ask your prospects about relevant, factual information and encourage answers in their own words. It relaxes them and allows you to draw information from the person much more easily.

ASKING GENERAL, OPEN-ENDED, FACT-FINDING QUESTIONS: Here is the *general approach.*

  ♦ "What kind of product delivery system do you have?"
  ♦ "What is the decision-making process in your company?"
  ♦ "What are your company's plans for integrating a computerized system to upgrade the accounting and manufacturing areas?"
  ♦ "In what volume do you ship your machinery parts?"
  ♦ "How price-sensitive are the digital measuring instruments?"
  ♦ "Who would be involved in using the software?"
  ♦ "What do you think about implementing automated plant maintenance procedures?"
  ♦ "What are your budget considerations?"

ASKING SPECIFIC, OPEN-ENDED, FACT-FINDING QUESTIONS: The following questions are more detailed and bring forth more detailed answers. They illustrate the *specific approach*.

- "What demographics are you appealing to with your housing development?"
- "How large of an office will you require for your telemarketers?"
- "What time frame in installing and operating automated sales reporting procedures best meets your requirements?"

OPEN-ENDED, FEELING-FINDING QUESTIONS

You will also want to discover your prospect's attitudes and opinions, what aspects of your product or service are most important to this person, and what will motivate him or her to buy. To find this out, you ask open-ended, feeling-finding questions.

ASKING GENERAL, OPEN-ENDED, FEELING-FINDING QUESTIONS: To continue with the temporary employee example, you might ask the following *general* questions:

- "How is your present system of handling work overloads working for you?"

By this question you would find out what problems your prospect is now experiencing.

- "How would your employees feel about you if you could relieve them of their seasonal work overload?"

By this question you would find out whether this prospect would enjoy being a hero.

- "How would it affect your company's bottom line if you could handle peak demands more effectively?"

By this question you would find out how important Desire for Gain is to this prospect.

Other general, feeling-finding questions might include:

- "How do you feel about the noise factor in the amplifiers?"
- "What do you think you need to get the job done?"

ASKING SPECIFIC OPEN-ENDED, FEELING-FINDING QUESTIONS: You can also ask *specific*, feeling-finding questions to elicit the details of how your prospect feels:

- ''How do you feel about air compressor oil with thermal stability for your machinery?''
- ''How does it make you feel not to hear clearly on a long-distance phone call to an important client?''
- ''What do you think about equipment inventory at distant plants being automatically filed and maintained on a central system at your corporate headquarters?''

MOST AND LEAST

The following two questions can be extremely valuable. They can help you zero in on exactly what problems or needs exist, and exactly what is important to each, individual prospect. Again, I suggest you memorize these two questions:

1. ''May I ask what you like most about ...?''
2. ''Would it be fair to ask what you like least about ...?''

For example:

- ''May I ask what you like most about your present laser-testing equipment?''
- ''Would it be fair to ask what you like least about your laser-testing equipment?''

Or, suppose that your prospect is now using your competitor's product or service. Asking these two questions could reveal exactly what your prospect liked most and least about that competitive product or service. Later in your presentation, you could use this vital information to emphasize how your own product or service provides exactly what this prospect likes best, and how it can reduce or eliminate the exact things he or she likes least.

Even when a competitive product or service is not involved, your prospect may be currently handling things in ways that are advantageous and disadvantageous. Again, later in your presentation you could show how your own product or service can improve on the advantages, and reduce or eliminate the disadvantages.

In short, knowing exactly what your prospect likes and dislikes can help you focus your presentation later on the areas of most importance to each individual prospect.

FINDING THE BENEFITS

Perhaps the product or service you sell offers unique benefits — benefits not available in any other product or service of its type or not easily found in your area. In Step Two: Qualification, you can ask questions that will let you know how your prospect feels about these unique benefits.

For example, suppose that your product is machinery used on the production line, and that its benefit is that it offers safety devices not available on any other machinery of its type. Although you will not be mentioning these safety devices until later in your presentation, you can find out, now, how your prospect will feel about these safety features. You might ask:

- "How frequently do your employees have accidents caused by equipment malfunction?"
- "How would it affect your employee morale, if these accidents could be cut by 50 percent?"

If you were selling insurance, you may know that your policy offers coverage not available anywhere else. So you might ask:

- "What coverage do you have now for business interruption?"
- "What would happen to your company if a loss of this type occurred?"

If your bank is the only one in the immediate vicinity that offers the convenience of Saturday banking hours, you might ask:

- "How important would it be to be able to go to the bank on Saturdays?"

If your company is the only local manufacturer of a specific product, enabling you to provide quick delivery of urgent orders, you might ask:

- "How might it help your customer relations if you could get these parts — whenever you needed them — in a few hours?"

Questions like these help you uncover problems and discover how your prospect would feel if the problem could be solved. These questions also lay important groundwork. Your product or service offers unique benefits, and you are finding out how important these unique benefits might be to your prospect. When the prospect shows a high level of interest, that's your cue to make a mental note to emphasize these unique benefits as your presentation unfolds.

DEVELOPING YOUR OWN QUESTIONS

What you are learning in the Track Selling System™ is a procedure for your sales presentation — not a canned speech. Therefore, the questions you ask in the Qualification step will be your own, based on whatever information you need to gather during your own specific, selling situations. Your goal is to qualify your prospect as a genuine, prospective buyer, to uncover the problems or needs that exist, and to find out the precise ways in which your product or service can be valuable to your prospect.

Here is a ''starter list'' of the kinds of questions you might want to ask:

- ''How do you feel about ...?''
- ''What do you think ...?''
- ''Do you think it would be better if ...?''
- ''What would you suggest ...?''
- ''What is your opinion about ...?''
- ''Why is ... important to you?''
- ''What would be your reaction to ...?''
- ''What would happen if ...?''
- ''What do you think is a better way to do ...?''
- ''Where do we start ...?''
- ''What do you think the real problem is?''
- ''What do you think you need to get the job done?''
- ''What is your biggest worry about ...?''
- ''Could you tell me more about ...?''
- ''How important is ... to you?''
- ''Could you give me an example of ...?''

- ◆ "What difference would it make if ...?"
- ◆ "How has ... affected you personally?"

And don't forget these important two questions:

- ◆ "May I ask what you like most about ...?"
- ◆ "Would it be fair to ask what you like least about ...?"

You may develop a standard list of questions you can use over and over again, on sales call after sales call. Refer to the Sample Qualification Form in the forms section of the book. However, you will need to design additional questions, which you will gear to the situation you face on each specific sales call. Remember to have definite qualification questions *in writing* before going on your sales call. Base additional questions on the facts and feelings that your prospect expresses as your presentation unfolds.

As you know, everyone buys for his or her very own reasons. Your goal in the Qualification step is to uncover the dominant reasons each individual prospect has for buying the product or service you sell. Remember: in this step you will be gathering information only. You will be offering no solutions at all.

REFLECTIVE QUESTIONS

Reflective questions are used to encourage the prospect to talk — to give valuable information — by reflecting back a key word the prospect has said.

Suppose your prospect is in the market for your product or service and expresses a concern:

Prospect: *I'm concerned about your company's reliability.*

Salesperson: *Reliability?*

Repeating the word, reliability, informs the prospect that you are paying attention to his or her concerns. Therefore, he or she feels encouraged to continue:

Prospect: *We were having our products shipped for many years. Then they started taking us for granted. They were late in delivering our goods to our customers, and that created*

> *hard feelings with some of our better*
> *customers.*

When the salesperson repeated the word, reliability, that communicated the essence of the prospect's concern. The reflective technique is important because it encourages the other person to talk, and provides you with input and insight on what that person needs or wants. It lets the prospect know you are listening, indicates that you really care about the prospect's needs, and shows that you are really interested in helping.

DIRECTIVE QUESTIONS

Directive questions are used to avoid rambling answers. They are used to guide the prospect toward the desired, specific piece of information — usually a straight yes or no. This time-saving technique moves both parties to an understanding as quickly as possible. For example:

- "Is a money-back guarantee on our product important to you?"

Unfortunately, some salespeople use directive questions to manipulate other people or put words in their mouths. That's why the directive question sometimes has a negative connotation. For example, the salesperson says: "If I could show you a way to increase productivity and at the same time save you money, that would be something you would be interested in, wouldn't you?" In this case, the salesperson is manipulating the person to the answer he or she wants.

So be careful when using the directive question. Use it to focus the prospect to a yes or no answer, but don't try to manipulate the answer.

USING THE THREE KINDS OF QUESTIONS

Let's now observe how a salesperson applies these three kinds of questions — open-ended, reflective and directive — to qualify the prospect.

The salesperson is talking to the president of an electronics manufacturing company. The president is aggressive and interested in using communication technology in her sales efforts.

> Prospect: *I'm looking for a communication system to quickly contact prospects and customers across the country.*

The salesperson replies with an open-ended, fact-finding question:

> Salesperson: *What are some of the things that are important to you in a communications system?*
>
> Prospect: *A system that is flexible, allows for multiple lines, and has a clear, conference-call sound. A system that is reliable and holds up under heavy use.*

Notice the use of the reflective question:

> Salesperson: *Heavy use?*
>
> Prospect: *We had some bad experiences with phone systems. Poor line quality, breakdowns, important clients who couldn't get through to us. We couldn't afford downtime for repairs. We get into lots of conference calls with many of our customers from across the country and, in some cases, from Europe. Sometimes lines get disconnected, customers get disgusted — it's a bad scene! A good, reliable communication system is a must if I'm going to expand my business.*

Now, the directive question:

> Salesperson: *Would you like a communication system that's fiber-optic, state-of-the-art, has the best sound you can find today, and has the flexibility and reliability you need to grow?*
>
> Prospect: *You got it!*

TAKING NOTES

As you ask your open-ended questions, you will be receiving a great deal of information from your prospect. Some of it may be quite complex. Take notes, if appropriate, to help you remember what you've learned. It may be wise to first ask: "Do you mind if I take notes?'' In most cases, your prospects will be complimented by the fact that you are taking notes. It demonstrates that you feel their comments are important and adds to your credibility. Keep your note-taking as brief and inconspicuous as possible, so it doesn't create a distraction.

Also, use discretion when your prospect tells you confidential material. For highly sensitive information, you might want to stop your note-taking momentarily and simply remember the information until after the sales call, when you can jot down a few brief notes. Note-taking is exceptionally important when your sales involve multiple calls on the same prospect.

Before going into your next meeting with that person, review the notes you have taken so you will remember the information you have already received. Your prospect will love it, for example, when you jotted down that he planned to go on a fishing trip and three months later you ask him if he enjoyed his fishing trip. You can also use these notes to help you devise new questions that will help you gather even more information.

KEEPING CURRENT

At your next meeting, take time to review with your prospect the ground you have already covered. Then ask this all-important question:

- ''Has anything changed?''

Why is this question so important? Think how often things *do* change in the business world. Monthly? Weekly? In some businesses, things change daily. You may continue working under the assumption that one set of circumstances still exists, when in reality the whole scene has undergone a sudden shift. When you offer solutions, how accurate will they be, based on outdated conditions? On multiple calls, review with your customer the information you have received up to that point. Then ask: ''Has anything changed?''

DON'T STINT ON QUALIFICATION

How much time should you spend on the Qualification step? As much time as required in order to gather the information you need. If the sales cycle of your product or service is exceptionally short, it might be possible to discover what you need to know by asking just a few, well-chosen questions. If the sales cycle of your product or service is long, however, you may make many calls on one prospect without ever moving beyond Step One: Approach and Step Two: Qualification — establishing rapport and uncovering problems or needs.

How important are these first two steps in the sales procedure? *Seventy-five percent* of the success of your sale will depend on how well you perform in the Approach and Qualification steps. You are helping your prospects decide that they like you, that you have integrity and good judgment and that you understand the problems and needs they face.

Steps One and Two are unique within the Track Selling System.™ Besides the fact that 75 percent of the success of your sale depends on these first two steps, they often overlap. You can ask personal questions in the Approach step, then business-related questions in the Qualification step, then shift back to personal questions again. Your conversation may go back and forth between personal and business questions many times during the first part of your sales call. These are the *only* two steps within the Track Selling System™ that are interchangeable.

In both steps you maintain your role as a friendly, likable person — the kind of person your prospect would enjoy having as a friend. In both steps, you let your prospects do the talking, telling you about their personal lives and their business problems and needs. In both steps, the more your prospects talk, the more they like you. The more they like you, the more apt they will be to buy whatever product or service you sell, which is *why* these two steps affect 75 percent of your sales success.

WHEN THERE ARE PROBLEMS

I have promised you that the Track Selling System™ can adapt to any situation you meet on your sales calls. Let me show you how this works.

WHEN THERE'S "NO MONEY NOW"

Suppose that you walk into a meeting expecting to make a sale. In the process of asking your qualifying questions, you discover the prospect has a genuine need for the product or service you sell, but no budget available to buy it for at least six months.

What do you do? You simply change the goal of the call. You work towards getting an act of commitment, a "next step" toward making a successful sale. You will attempt to set a definite appointment time to come back and talk with the prospect when the purchasing budget becomes available. Your goal, as you recall, is to make a sale now or get an act of commitment now. In this situation you simply shift your goal to getting the act of commitment, but your basic sales procedure remains exactly the same.

When you attend that next meeting, you will review with your prospect the information you have already learned. Then ask, "Has anything changed?" Over six months' time, you can expect that some changes will have occurred.

"WHAT'S THE PRICE?"

Suppose that you are qualifying your prospect — finding out what problems or needs exist — and suddenly your prospect asks: "What's the price? How much is your product or service going to cost me?"

First of all, you know that your prospect makes a series of Five Buying Decisions, in precise, psychological order. Secondly, you know that the Track Selling System™ is designed to carry your prospect through the Five Buying Decisions, in the same precise order. This question about the price is definitely out of order.

What do you do now? Ask your prospect if he or she would mind delaying that question just a bit, since there is important information you will need to know before you can answer it accurately. *Act*, don't react, in this situation. Maintain control. Assure your prospect that you *will* answer that question.

Before you answer the question about the price, make sure you have first addressed yourself to the prospect's buying decisions that precede the decision on price: the decisions about you, your company, and the product or service you sell. *Then* talk about price.

You can use a form of the transition statement you learned to move smoothly from Approach to Qualification in this dilemma.

> "[Prospect's name], *I would like to tell you about our* [product or service]. *However, in order for me to do the best job I possibly can for you, I need to ask you a couple of questions. Is that all right?*"

You can use a variation of this statement to delay answering your prospect's question on price until it fits into the proper place in your presentation. You might say:

* "Bill, I'm glad you asked me that. Price is certainly an important consideration, and I'll discuss that very thoroughly with you in just a minute, but in order for me to do the best job I possibly can for you, I need to ask you a couple more questions. Is that all right?"

And then you would go right back to asking questions that will keep your prospect's attention focused on the topics *you* want to discuss — questions that keep your presentation flowing in proper order.

* "Frank, I would like to tell you about Max Sacks International's sales training program. However, in order for me to do the best job I possible can for you, I need to ask you a couple of questions. Is that all right?"

And if the prospect answers yes, then address the three considerations — Need, Authority to Buy, and Budget.

* "What are some of your concerns with a sales training program?"
* "What will be the decision-making process?"
* "What is your budgetary situation?

"SORRY, LATER ..."

Suppose you have scheduled a meeting with a prospect, but when you walk into the room the prospect says, "Gosh, I'm sorry , but I'm terribly busy right now. Just drop off one of your brochures, and I'll get back to you." Your response? Use a different variation of the same sentence:

* "Mr. Jones, I can appreciate that. However, in order for me to do the best job I possibly can for you, I need to ask you a couple of questions. Is that all right?

Then you dig right in, asking good, open-ended questions that encourage this prospect to talk freely. You may want to make your first questions business-oriented, then shift to personal questions as quickly as you can. And guess what? You have moved right into Steps One and Two of your sales procedure: establishing warm rapport, qualifying the prospect, and finding out what problems or needs exist.

There may be times when your prospects really *are* busy, and you are going to have to respect that. In most cases, however, no matter how busy your prospects are, they have plenty of time to talk about what *they* want to talk about, with a person who sincerely listens.

USE ONLY THE STEPS YOU NEED

Suppose that your goal on a sales call is simply to qualify a prospect and uncover the problems or needs that exist. Your product or service requires a long sales cycle and you know it is unreasonable to expect to make a sale after just one call on that prospect.

What do you do in your first sales call? You *don't* try to go through all seven steps of the Track Selling System,™ nor do you try to fit in as many steps as you can in the time allotted. You only go through the first two steps: Approach and Qualification. You will cover the other steps in subsequent calls.

On any given sales call, *use only as many of the steps,* in precise order, *as are required to help you achieve your objectives* for that particular sales call.

What if, after you proceed through the Approach and Qualification steps with a prospect, you schedule another meeting for a later date? At the next meeting do you begin your presentation at Step Three: Agreement on Need? Absolutely not. You go right back to the beginning — Approach and Qualification — and work forward from there.

Why? Because your prospect makes a series of Five Buying Decisions, in precise, psychological order, *on every sales call you make.* The Track Selling System™ is designed to carry your prospect smoothly through these decisions, helping the person make a positive decision on each. Even if you've called on a prospect many times, you begin your presentation with Step

One: Approach. You again ask open-ended, personal questions based on information you have learned from the previous call. Take the time to establish rapport. You are *reminding the prospect that he or she likes you.*

Then you continue with Step Two: Qualification. You review the information you have gathered on the first call, ask if anything has changed, and ask questions that help you uncover more of the important information you need to know if you are to serve this person's needs. You are *reminding the prospect of your integrity and good judgment.* Remember: 75 percent of the success of your sale depends on how well you perform in these first two steps. This is true whether you are making your very first call or the twentieth call on a prospect.

SKIPPING THE FIRST STEP

Occasionally it may make sense for you to skip Step One: Approach and go directly to Step Two: Qualification. Don't begin by skipping Step One, of course, but what if your prospect makes it clear he or she wants to skip the amenities and get right down to business?

Do what the *prospect* wants. If the prospect wants to talk business first, do it. Afterwards, you can turn to establishing rapport. You can do this because Step One and Step Two, and only Step One and Step Two, are interchangeable.

Whichever step comes first, be sure to fully complete both Steps One and Two. You must first take care of selling yourself and qualifying the prospect before you can move on to Step Three: Agreement on Need.

Tony DiMaggio, a sales professional and top producer for Idea Man in San Jose, California, told me, "The Track Selling System™ helped me to understand that I didn't have to go in there and make small talk in the beginning of my call. I could get down to the business reason I'm there, and then five or ten minutes later build personal rapport. It helped me to understand that I didn't have to do Approach and Qualification in any particular order, as long as I completed them before going on to Agreement on Need."

SAMPLE DIALOGUE FOR
STEP TWO: QUALIFICATION

In the previous chapter the last question the prospect, Dick, asked the salesperson, Gerri, was: "How much are your Hawaiian tours?" In the following dialogue, notice how Gerri uses the memorized Approach/Qualification transition statement to delay answering him until the proper moment in her sales presentation. Also notice her use of open-ended, feeling-finding and fact-finding questions, and her use of the reflective question. ("Back East?" and "Mexico?") In addition, notice that Gerri asks the valuable question, "What did you like best about ...?" Finally, while Gerri is qualifying Dick in this conversation, she is also gathering information about what is important to him.

As you follow this conversation, notice what *you* think is most important to this prospect in terms of his need for a travel service. What do you think are his dominant buying motives?

Salesperson:	*Well, Dick, we have a variety of pricing, depending on the time of the year and the number of islands you visit. In order to get the best possible price I can for you, I need to ask you a couple of questions. Is that all right?*
Prospect:	*Sure, go ahead.*
Salesperson:	*How many of the members of your family would be going on vacation with you?*
Prospect:	*My wife and I and our two teenage daughters for sure. I'd like to take my son, who's in college back East, if we could work out the timing so he could come along.*
Salesperson:	*Back East?*
Prospect:	*He goes to Boston College, and he seems to love the school. But, in his letters he keeps complaining about the nasty, cold weather, which he's not used to after growing up in Los Angeles. It's hard to get grown kids to go on vacation with you, unless you find something that really interests them.*
Salesperson:	*Um hmmm.*

Prospect:	*I just have the feeling that the hot sun in Hawaii might be just the thing that interests him after a winter in Boston.*
Salesperson:	*So you're thinking this would be a winter vacation, Dick?*
Prospect:	*I know that it's probably difficult to get into some of the places in Hawaii over Christmas, but I think it's our only chance of having a last family vacation. Our son is home from college December 15th until January 15th. If it's possible to do anything on those dates, I think we can take the whole family along.*
Salesperson:	*What islands were you thinking about visiting, Dick?*
Prospect:	*We've never been to Hawaii. We hear a lot of good things about Maui, although I suppose the kids would want to go to Honolulu. It seems pretty touristy, but I think they would like to say they had been to some of those famous landmarks. Which islands do you recommend, Gerri?*
Salesperson:	*Well, probably the most important thing is to find out what you want in a vacation. There are different activities available on each of the islands, so I need to find out how you want to spend time while you're on your vacation. What activities does your family most enjoy on a vacation?*
Prospect:	*Well, the girls like lying on the beach, and hopefully, meeting boys. My son is a real snorkel and scuba-diving enthusiast, so I think he would enjoy a place where he would have access to some coral reefs and tropical fish. My wife and I like a combination of activities. I enjoy deep sea fishing, but she's not very interested in that. I would like to be able to do that, but still have some time with her to take some tours of native cultures.*
Salesperson:	*Um hmmm.*

Prospect: We went to Mexico once, before the children were born, and we really enjoyed that.

Salesperson: Mexico, hmmm? What did you like best about that vacation?

Prospect: It seems like it must have been one of our favorite vacations, because we have pages of pictures in our scrapbook. Just learning about another culture was fascinating — so much history in a place like that. The tour wasn't so heavily scheduled that we felt like we had to be on a bus or looking at scenery every minute.

Salesperson: [Laughs appreciatively.]

Prospect: I also liked not having to make all the plans, and having to be responsible for what we were not supposed to miss, and what to stay away from because it was a tourist trap. How does it work at Happiness is Hawaii Tours? Is it heavily structured, or do you have some time on your own?

Salesperson: We price our package tours several ways. We can include a tour package where you have activities planned for the whole time you're gone. Or, we can build in a tour that is partly on your own, then hooks up with some of our specific tours that fit in with your family's needs. Let's look at your children's interests separately from yours and your wife's, so we can plan a vacation that will be memorable for everybody in the family.

Prospect: That sure would be nice to have a vacation where we didn't feel like we were doing everything for the kids. Or vice versa.

Salesperson: You said your daughters were teenagers. Exactly how old are they, since the beginning of the teens and the end of the teens generally have interests in different activities?

Prospect:	*My youngest daughter is thirteen, and our oldest daughter is seventeen. And that's true; sometimes they have very different interests.*
Salesperson:	*If your thirteen-year-old could come away from that vacation with one memory, what do you think it would be?*
Prospect:	*Boy, that's a good question. I think she's really interested in understanding how she fits in the world and understanding how living in Los Angeles might be different than living in Hawaii. Maybe she'd like to spend some time where she could look at some of the customs and some of the history of the particular part of the world.*
Salesperson:	*How about your seventeen-year-old?*
Prospect:	*Like I said, she's interested in looking at boys, and trying to be rescued so she doesn't have to go to college or get a job. I don't know. She's not much of a modern woman, and my wife and I discuss that a lot. I think some supervised beach activities with other kids her own age would have a lot of appeal.*
Salesperson:	*How about you and your wife? What special memories would you like to take away from this vacation?*
Prospect:	*Like I said, I've wanted to take my family on an exciting vacation for a long time. We've gone to Disneyland, and we've gone back to visit relatives. But we've never done anything as a family that we've wanted to go back to, year after year. I'd kind of like to start a family tradition, so that we'd get the family together every winter to go to Hawaii. We thought about taking the kids with us to Mexico, but my wife reminded me that she didn't enjoy all the restrictions about drinking the water, and she thought about the problem of the kids doing the same. I'd like Hawaii to be*

*something that could become an annual
tradition.*

Salesperson: *I'd like to ask you just a couple more
questions, so that I can help make sure that
this could be the best vacation of your life.
What do you and your wife and family like
to do for activities in the evening, when
you're on vacation?*

Prospect: *I hadn't thought about that. I realize that
sometimes I don't plan for that and don't
end up planning for the fancy dinners and
things that the family seems to want to go
to when we get away from our home town.
My wife likes to be taken out to dinner
when she's on vacation, and go someplace
with food she might not be able to find
easily in a restaurant in Los Angeles. The
kids are pretty happy to go along, as long
as it's a fun atmosphere and it's not stuffy
— with a white linen tablecloth and
dressed-up waiters.*

Salesperson: *You said that the departure dates that
would be ideal for you would be sometime
in that space during your son's vacation,
between December 15th and January 15th.
Is that correct?*

Prospect: *Yes. I don't believe that my daughters have
that much vacation, but I'm pretty sure I
could check on that now. Just a minute.
[After a pause]. According to their school
schedule, they're available after December
18th, and they have to be back to school on
January 5th.*

Salesperson: *So which would fit best for you, Dick? One
week or two weeks?*

Prospect: *If we can put together the rest of the
details to fit, my ideal choice would be to
have two full weeks. Sometimes it takes
part of a week for me to slow down and
realize I'm on vacation. I hate to think I'd*

> *have to go home in a few days when I finally relax.*

Salesperson: *What kind of budget have you put aside for your family vacation this year, Dick?*

Prospect: *Well, it's pretty important for me to bring this whole family together, but it has been a little bit of a strain on the budget putting my son in college. I think this might be the time to dig into that special savings account. I think if we could do the whole vacation for under $5,000, I would be pretty happy.*

Salesperson: *Now, would you visualize your son leaving directly from Boston, or coming back to Los Angeles to join you?*

Prospect: *I think some of that would depend on the differences in the costs of the flights. I know that if we could put something together for Hawaii, he'd probably want to spend every minute he could in the sun.*

THE LOGICAL CONCLUSION

About 75 percent of the sale is determined in the first two steps, Approach and Qualification. If the prospect likes and trusts you, and if you know what their needs and wants are, then closing the sale should be the logical conclusion to a well-given presentation.

THINGS TO REMEMBER

- Your goal in Step Two: Qualification is to qualify your prospect and discover the exact problems or needs that exist.

- You will accomplish this goal by asking open-ended questions that encourage your prospect to express both facts and feelings freely.

- Using the Approach/Qualification transition statement helps you move smoothly from Step One to Step Two.

- On all subsequent sales calls after reviewing information previously covered, remember to ask: ''Has anything changed?''

- If the prospect asks you about the price at this early stage, don't answer directly. Instead, use the Approach/Qualification transition statement to delay answering until the proper point in your sales presentation.

- Start at the beginning with the Approach and Qualification steps in every sales call you make. Sometimes, however, you can reverse the order of Step One and Step Two.

EXERCISES

1. What is the difference between a general and a specific fact-finding question?

2. What do general and specific fact-finding questions accomplish?

3   What is the difference between a general and a specific feeling-finding question?

4.   What do general and specific feeling-finding questions accomplish?

5.   Think about the specific product or service you sell. What types of information do you need to know from a prospect in order to discover what problems exist and how well your own product or service will help solve those problems?

6.   What are some of the questions that you might ask a prospect in selling your own product or service?

      a. General fact-finding questions:

      b. Specific fact-finding questions:

      c. General feeling-finding questions:

      d. Specific feeling-finding questions:

7.   What would you do if your prospect wanted to "skip the small talk" and get down to business?

8.   How would you handle a prospect who says "just give me a brochure and the price?"

9.   In the previous chapter, you began preparing a written plan for a real sales presentation that you may have coming up with an actual prospect.

    a. Re-read that written plan now.

    b. Next, either in the following space or on a new sheet of paper labeled "Step Two: Qualification," write the recommended transition statement that you will use to move from Approach to Qualification.

    c. Then write several open-ended questions that you might use for the prospect you have selected.

WRITTEN PLAN FOR STEP TWO: QUALIFICATION

"[Prospect's name], *I would like to tell you about our* [product or service]; *however, in order for me to do the best job I possibly can for you, I need to ask you a couple of questions. Is that all right?*"

Write the above transition statement below:

Write several open-ended questions:

12

STEP THREE: AGREEMENT ON NEED

I n Step One and Step Two of the Track Selling System,™ you introduced yourself to your prospect, established warm rapport, and gathered important information that will allow you to serve your prospect's needs.

If your sales cycle is short, you may have accomplished this in a single call. If your sales cycle is long, you have probably made multiple calls on the same prospect before reaching the point where you feel you have gathered all the information you need. You are now ready to move into Step Three: Agreement on Need.

The Agreement on Need is this simple:

- Summarize all the input you have received so far from your prospect in Step One: Approach and Step Two: Qualification.

Your summary might go something like this:

- As I understand it, you're looking for a video conferencing system that interconnects your home office with company managers and distributors across the country. You want this system to be interactive, with all parties able to talk with and view each other, at a price that fits your budget, and with first-rate technical backup. Is that correct?

Many salespeople overlook Step Three: Agreement on Need and hastily move to Step Five: Fill the Need. This is a mistake. If you don't fully understand your prospects' needs, they will assume you are not really interested in serving them. By summarizing the input you've received in Step One and Step Two, you communicate that you're tuned in to them — you care about their problems and you're both working together to fill their needs. Agreement on Need clears up the communication process, which is what selling is all about.

How can you more easily understand your prospects' needs and help them understand their *own* needs better? *Take the time to communicate sincerely that you want to be of service.* If most salespeople took the time to evaluate their selling techniques, including what they *don't* say to prospects, they would give more effective presentations and see that win-win relationships with their prospects make it easier for both parties to understand the prospect's requirements.

YOU ARE THE STAR

In Step Three: Agreement on Need, *you*, not your prospect, are the star of the show. Now it is *your* turn to take center stage and do most of the talking. In this step, you will demonstrate that you are a serious, professional sales counselor — one who uses persuasion, not pressure.

USING WHAT YOU FOUND OUT IN STEP TWO

Earlier in your presentation, your qualifying questions helped you uncover your prospect's exact problems. They helped you know:

- What this prospect wants or needs
- How your product or service might be used
- What aspects of your product or service are most important to this prospect and the benefits he or she expects to receive with the purchase

THE CAPSULE SUMMARY

Now it is time to put together all the information you received and present it to your prospect in a capsule summary form, using the following statement:

- *"As I understand it, you are looking for something that will* [summarize the important information you gathered in Steps One and Two: Approach and Qualification]. *Is that correct?"*

What do you include in the summary statement? That depends on the specific information you have gathered. It will be different on every sales call you make.

Here are several sample summaries to illustrate this step:

- *"As I understand it, you are looking for* equipment that will handle the sizes you are now filling and make pours accurately so they will meet with the Weights and Measures Department standards. The equipment must be easily serviced and handle the quantity of production you need in your operation. *Is that correct?"*

- *"As I understand it, you are looking for* an exceptionally fine-grained clay that can be wheel-thrown and fired at cone ten. *Is that correct?"*

- *"As I understand it, you are looking for* a brochure that will describe your product in simple language, easily understood by someone with no technical background at all. You want to feature the cost-cutting benefits your product provides, plus its ease of use. The brochure is to be a two-fold and include an order form for direct response. You want the proof delivered to you by March 31st, at the very latest, for your approval of copy and layout. *Is that correct?"*

- *"As I understand it, you are looking for* an electronic system to control your building's complete heating, cooling, and lighting systems, provide your employees with consistent comfort, and cut your energy bills by a minimum of 20%. *Is that correct?"*

This statement is so important that you should memorize the key words. Read it over as many times as necessary to commit them to memory. When you are ready, write the key words from memory in the space provided.

WHAT THE CAPSULE
SUMMARY CAN DO FOR YOU

What happens when you summarize the input from your prospect? You communicate that you are tuned in to that person and you care about his or her problems. Moreover, it communicates that the two of you are working together as a team — the essence of *World Class Selling*.

Why say, "*As I understand it, you are looking for ...*"? This statement gives you the opportunity to verify the information you have received, make sure that you heard correctly and have the facts straight, and make sure that you and your prospect are operating on the same wave length.

Why ask, "*Is that correct?*" This question gives your prospect the opportunity to clarify any misunderstandings that may exist. Perhaps you missed an important point. Perhaps the prospect inadvertently made a misstatement, omitted an important fact, or failed to explain something fully. By asking, "*Is that correct?*" you give your prospect the chance to speak up and correct any disagreements that may exist.

In addition, this capsule summary statement demonstrates to your prospect that you have *listened* — you understand his or her problems or needs. As you know very well by now, your prospects buy your product or service not so much because they understand *it*, but because they feel that *you* understand *them*.

Once you have verified and clarified your information, your statement shows that you truly understand what your prospect wants and needs. From this point on in your sales presentation you will know that you and your prospect are working in complete accords, each dedicated to achieving the same important goals.

SAMPLE DIALOGUE FOR
STEP THREE: AGREEMENT ON NEED

Remember the dialogue between Gerri, of Happiness Is Hawaii Tours, and her prospect, Dick, in the last chapter? By this time, you have as much information about Dick's specific ideas, plans, goals, and needs as Gerri has.

Re-read the conversation in Chapter Eleven. If you were Gerri, what would you say to Dick in Step Three: Agreement on Need? In the space below or on a separate piece of paper, write your version of the Agreement on Need statement.

As I understand it, you are looking for:

Is that correct?

Now compare *your* Agreement on Need statement for Dick's family with Gerri's version.

> *Salesperson:*   *Then, as I understand it, you're looking for a vacation package which would allow for a variety of activities — ones that would allow you to go deep-sea fishing while your son goes snorkeling. Your younger daughter could do some touring on her own, while your older daughter enjoys the beach. Your wife could go on some pre-planned tours alone, or with you. And also build in some free time. All this would be put into a total package that would not exceed $5,000, including air fare. Is that correct?*
>
> *Prospect:*   *Yes, that sounds like a dream vacation.*

The Delighted Smile

I hope you amazed yourself by your ability to spot Dick's concerns and needs, and summarize them accurately in this exercise, even before you read the Agreement on Need portion of our sample dialogue.

If your Agreement on Need statement is on target, your prospect will tell you so. The response might be, "Hey, yeah. That's *exactly* what I'm looking for." You will probably see a big, delighted smile spread across your prospect's face. People love to be understood, to have someone "get" them. How many times in the past do you suppose this prospect has run across a salesperson who listened to what he or she said and showed real understanding? How do you suppose it makes people feel to have you care so much about them that you can repeat back to them a succinct version of everything they have just said they wanted and needed. It makes them feel delighted and makes *you* very likable. It is this kind of professional sales presentation that can make you a standout salesperson and keep you in the upper, top-producing twenty percent.

When your prospect indicates that the two of you are in complete agreement on the needs or problems that exist — that you know exactly what that person wants or needs to buy — you are ready to move directly into Step Four of the Track Selling System.™

WHEN THE PROSPECT AGREES BUT THERE IS NO NEED

What happens when you summarize your Agreement on Need statement as follows?

> Salesperson: *As I understand it you're looking for a transportation company that can provide you overnight service from San Francisco to Vancouver with an air-cushion ride truck and then provide service from your warehouse in Vancouver to other points throughout Canada with an automatic tracking service and competitive pricing. Is that correct?*
>
> Prospect: *Yes, that's what I am now getting from my present transportation company.*

What does this tell you? This tells you that you have not spent enough time in Approach and Qualification to identify needs that the prospect is not getting from his present transportation company. The Agreement on Need step is your green light to proceed with your presentation or your red light to stop your presentation and go back into Qualification to uncover needs the prospect is not getting from the present supplier.

WHEN THE PROSPECT DOESN'T AGREE

What happens if you make your Agreement on Need statement and the prospect does not agree? When you ask, ''Is that correct?'' and the prospect says, no?

Obviously, this is just fine. One of the reasons you asked, ''Is that correct?'' is so you can verify your understanding of the prospect's situation. Therefore, you listen to the prospect to allow him or her to clarify the facts.

After this clarification, you review the Agreement on Need statement a second time, with the needed clarifications. If the prospect says no a second time, you just repeat this procedure again. You continue to clarify the information until you and the prospect are both in complete accord about his or her needs.

The following flow-chart illustrates this procedure:

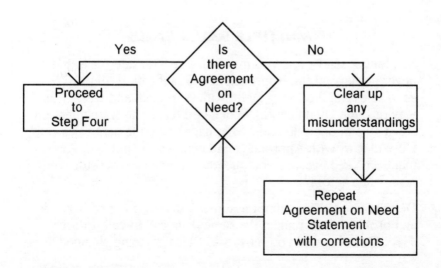

Suppose that you omitted Step Three: Agreement on Need from your sales procedure. You continued your presentation, assuming you clearly understood what your prospect needed, but your assumption was wrong. Could this misunderstanding have a direct effect on the success of your sale?

Consider your own sales history. On sales calls you have made in the past, have you taken the time to establish agreement with your prospects on exactly what they wanted or needed? If you did not, did you ever assume that your prospect wanted one thing, when in reality he or she may have wanted or needed something quite different? Could that misunderstanding have cost you some sales?

As a professional salesperson, you cannot afford to assume that you have heard correctly, remember every important fact, or even that your prospects have expressed themselves thoroughly, clearly, and with total accuracy. You cannot assume that you've pinpointed your prospects' problems and needs exactly. Instead, give your prospect a capsule summary of the important information you have gathered. Verify that your information and conclusions are correct. Give your prospect the opportunity to clarify any misunderstandings that may exist. Demonstrate that you have listened and that you truly understand.

Once you and your prospect have reached complete agreement on exactly what that person wants or needs, the two of you can proceed as a team — as partners — working in unity to achieve your common goals.

MULTIPLE SALES CALLS

In a longer sales cycle you may make several sales calls and never go beyond the Approach and Qualification Steps. On *each* sales call, you start again with Approach and work your way through Qualification. When you reach the Agreement on Need step in one sales call, what happens in the next sales call? Do you start with Approach and Qualification but skip Agreement on Need because you already provided the capsule summary once before?

Definitely not. You cannot assume that your prospect's needs and problems will remain the same from call to call. In Step Two: Qualification, you must ask, "Has anything changed?"

Similarly, in Step Three: Agreement on Need, you cannot assume that your prospect's situation will have remained the same since the Agreement on Need statement made during your last call.

Suppose, in a long sales cycle, you made two or three sales calls and covered the Approach and Qualification steps and, finally, the Agreement on Need step. You decide to put together a proposal for your next sales call. At this later meeting, re-establish rapport and do any additional qualification you need. Next, just to make sure, re-state the Agreement on Need, adding the sentence, "Has anything changed since our last meeting?" You might say:

- "Joe, in our last meeting, you were looking for a company video conferencing system that interconnects your home office with company managers and distributors across the country. You wanted this system to be interactive, with all the parties able to talk with and view each other, and at a price that fits your budget with first-rate technical backup. *Has anything changed since our last meeting?*"

Repeating the Agreement on Need statement helps you pin down whether *anything* — large or small — has changed since your last visit. If things have changed, you'll be better able to revise your presentation at this point. If you neglected to ask, "Has anything changed?" you could be in the middle of Step Six: Act of Commitment and the prospect could suddenly break in with "Oh, I'm sorry. I forgot to tell you. We just sold the company last week."

Things change frequently in business. Repeating the Agreement on Need statement, and then asking, "Has anything changed since our last meeting?" keeps you in control.

Staying on Track

There's one possible response that you should be prepared for, although it's not likely to occur very often. Suppose after you complete the Agreement on Need statement, the prospect breaks in and says, "Okay, where do I sign?"

Do you insist, "No, you can't do that now. I've got four more Track Selling System™ steps to cover."? Of course not. Instead, you write up the order, and *then* go through the last four steps. At almost any point in the Track Selling System,™ if the prospect asks to buy, go ahead and get the order, and then complete the rest of the steps in the sales procedure.

Why? Finishing the process ensures the customer stays sold, that your product or service wears well. There are no short cuts for the sales professional, even when the prospect buys "too early."

THE TRACK SELLING SYSTEM™ SO FAR

You have moved through three of the Seven Steps so far. In Step One you introduced yourself and established warm rapport. In Step Two you qualified your prospect. Now in Step Three, you made sure that you and your prospect were in complete agreement, working to achieve the same goals.

You are almost to the halfway point in the Track Selling System.™ Congratulations!

THINGS TO REMEMBER

- Make a capsule summary of the information you received in Step One: Approach and Step Two: Qualification.

- This lets you verify and clarify the information you have received, to make sure that you and your prospect are in complete accord.

- If your prospect doesn't agree when you ask, "Is that correct?" listen to his or her clarification, then make a revised Agreement on Need statement.

- The Agreement on Need is your green light to proceed or your red light to stop and go back to qualification.

EXERCISES

1. What advantages does the capsule summary technique
    have for:

    a. The prospect?

    b. The salesperson?

2. Prepare an Agreement of Need statement for the same
    prospect and sales call you have been writing about in the
    previous two chapters. You will have to use a little imagi-
    nation. Although you know the qualification questions you
    wrote down for Step Two, you have not heard the re-
    sponses your prospect will give. Try to imagine what facts
    and feelings your prospect might express when you ask
    those qualifying questions. On a separate page or in the
    blanks below develop an Agreement on Need statement.

WRITTEN PLAN FOR STEP THREE: AGREEMENT ON NEED

As I understand it, you are looking for:

Is that correct?

13

STEP FOUR: SELL THE COMPANY

Why "Sell the Company" now? You may think that Sell the Company doesn't make sense as the next step — that *Fill* the Need should, logically, follow *Agreement* on Need. After all, you have just finished reviewing with your prospects the problems and needs that exist. Wouldn't it be more logical at this point to follow through on that train of thought and show your prospect how your product or service solves those problems or fills those needs?

Remember the prospect's Five Buying Decisions? All prospects make a series of Five Buying Decisions — in precise, psychological order. We agreed that we must satisfy the prospect if we're going to get a commitment later on. So far, you have helped your prospect decide positively about you, the salesperson, through the Approach, Qualification and Agreement on Need steps of the Track Selling System.™ By now, your prospect most likely sees you as a friendly, likable person who has integrity and good judgment. This all addressed the prospect's *first* Buying Decision.

Now comes the prospect's *second* Buying Decision: about the company. The prospect makes this decision *before* deciding about the value of your product or service. There is little chance that you can Fill the Need with your company's product or service without satisfying the buyer's second Buying Decision.

REVIEWING YOUR ACCOMPLISHMENTS

At this point, let's review what your sales procedure has accomplished so far:

1. In Step One: Approach, you introduced yourself to your prospect and established warm rapport.

2. In Step Two: Qualification, you asked the right kinds of questions to help you uncover exactly what your prospect wants or needs to buy. You know the problems your prospect faces, what is important to the person and the things he or she likes most and least. You know the emotional motives that are most likely to prompt your prospect to buy.

3. In Step Three: Agreement on Need, you gave a capsule summary on the important information you gathered in Step Two. You asked, "Is that correct?" to verify and clarify the information you received. From this point forward in your presentation, you know that you and your prospect are working in complete accord, functioning as a team to achieve the same common goals. You are partners, engaged in *World Class Selling*.

STEPPING INTO STEP FOUR

As you begin Step Four: Sell the Company, you will maintain your role as a serious, professional sales counselor, one who uses persuasion, not pressure. As in Step Three, you will continue to be center stage.

In this step, you will help your prospect make a positive decision about your company. You *are* the company to your prospect. Your prospect wants to know — even if he or she never gives any indication that this is the case — whether your company operates with integrity, is capable of performing as you have promised, and will honor its commitments.

THE FIRST TRANSITION SENTENCE

Your communication about your company is usually based on the input you received from the prospect in the Approach and Qualification steps. To move smoothly into Step Four: Sell the

Company, first use the following transition sentences. The first one is a question:

- *"May I ask how much information you have about [your company's name]?"*

Your prospect may know a lot, very little, or nothing at all about your company. He or she may have strong positive feelings, neutral feelings, or perhaps even negative feelings about your company. This question, like the statements below, is so vitally important to the success of your sales presentation that you should memorize it.

- *"May I ask how much information you have about [your company's name]?"*

Why is the exact wording of this question so important? It is an open-ended question that encourages your prospects to freely express whatever facts and possible feelings they may currently have about your company. Whatever your prospects' knowledge or feelings are about your company, it is important that you give them the opportunity to express them. Here is how one salesperson does it:

> *Salesperson:*   *Mr. Prospect, if I were in your position I'm sure there would be some specific information I'd like to know about Company X. May I ask you how much information you have about Company X?*

YOUR PROSPECT'S RESPONSE

You have made the transition smoothly into the fourth step in your sales procedure by asking, "May I ask how much information you have about [your company's name]?" No matter what response you receive, you next state, "I understand. Let me quickly cover a couple of things I think would be important to me if I were in your position." You are now ready to supply your prospect with honest, accurate information to build trust in your company's ability to perform competently and with integrity.

What Does Your Prospect Already Know?

The facts you tell your prospect will depend on both your company itself and what your prospect already knows.

Lots of Information: It is possible that your prospect may know a great deal about your company.

For example:

> Prospect: *Well, I know that Allied is the largest manufacturer of ball bearings on the East Coast. My friend, Sam Jones, has been doing business with your company for years, and he is really satisfied with the service he's gotten.*

or even:

> Prospect: *I know everything there is to know about your Company X. My mother-in-law was married to Mr. Y from Company X for eleven years!*

This is just fine, in fact, it's great. But what do you say? You don't say, "Oh, that's great. I'm glad you already know a lot about us," or "Oh, that great. I'm glad you know what a good job we do." You say, *"I understand. Let me quickly cover a couple of things I think would be important to me if I were in your position."*

You then proceed to expand your prospect's knowledge of your company, telling the person important facts, statistics, credentials, or whatever else will fortify those positive feelings about your company.

Visual Aids: Psychologists say we receive information 77 percent through the eyes, fourteen percent through the ears, and nine percent through other senses. This tells you that you have to be a pretty good talker to sell with only a fourteen percent chance of having your story understood. However, by adding sight to hearing you increase the information received to 91 percent. Not only do people receive much more information by what they see and hear at the same time, their retention of that information is several times greater. So, top professionals use visual aids, such as charts, graphs, brochures, samples, slides, overheads and laptop computers. If you have visual aids, now is the perfect time to use them. However, keep in mind that you have just said, "Let me *quickly* cover a *couple* of things." You have promised to be quick and to cover only a couple of items. Honor your word, and keep your presentation short and to the point.

LITTLE OR NO INFORMATION: It is possible that your customer knows nothing at all about your company. He or she might respond:

> *Prospect:*   *Frankly, I don't know a thing about the Allied company. I just picked your name out of the Yellow Pages.*

A prospect may also be thinking things he or she isn't saying out loud:

> *Prospect:*   *I don't know who you are. I don't know your company's products. I don't know what your company stands for. I don't know your company's customers. I don't know your company's record. I don't know your company's reputation.*

CRITICAL INFORMATION: It is also possible that your prospect might express negative feelings about your company. In that case, it's even more important to encourage — even invite — that person to let you know. Expressing that information and possibly any accompanying feelings helps remove any subconscious barriers your prospect may have to you, your product or service, or your company. That person might say, for example:

> *Prospect:*   *Well, maybe I shouldn't mention this, but a couple of months ago I called your manufacturing rep for a quote. He said he'd get right back to me but no one ever returned my call.*

By now, you know that you don't immediately reply with:

- "Oh, I'm really sorry!"
- "That George; he really wasn't on top of it while his wife was recovering from surgery!"
- "I can't imagine how that happened. George is exceptionally good about calling people back. Could you have dialed the wrong number and gotten another company?"

Instead you simply say:

+ *"I understand."*

The prospect's negative feelings about your company are now out in the open and you have acknowledged them with "I understand."

RESPOND TO THE PROSPECT'S RESPONSE

This stage of your sales presentation is where you will deal with your prospect's response. In the above case, the prospect is obviously worried about receiving more neglectful treatment in future dealings with your company. So you will next state honest, accurate facts that will assure the prospect that this treatment will not be repeated. For example, you might say:

+ Sally, I know the rep who didn't return your call. He's no longer working for us. His replacement is highly qualified, capable, and conscientious. I know that won't happen *again.*

Or, if circumstances are different, you might say:

+ Sally, I'm sorry your phone call wasn't returned. I will look into it when I get back and *make whatever adjustments are necessary to see that this won't happen again.*

Again, you are standing out as a highly competent, likable, professional salesperson. When prospects express negative thoughts to the average salesperson, they are likely to expect an argument, or at the very least, defensiveness: "You're wrong," or "You must be mistaken," or "That couldn't have been *our* company." And when the salesperson is apologetic rather than defensive, that really doesn't help either. Prospects want acknowledgment that their salesperson has *heard* their complaint and a statement of intent to rectify the situation.

Your initial response, "I understand," negates all chance of argument. It aligns you on the prospect's side. You are expressing empathy, showing that you see things through that person's eyes and demonstrating that you really do understand. This "rebuttal" to any negative or outright hostile statements your prospects make must be completely non-argumentative. Simply state positive facts to support your own viewpoint.

By the way, this statement — "I understand" — is effective for handling *any* negative feelings your prospect expresses, at *any* point in your presentation, on *any* subject at all. You will find this technique equally effective for defusing potential verbal blow-ups in your personal life as well — in discussions with your spouse, your children, friends, or co-workers.

If the prospect says:

* "I don't know your company,"

You answer:

* "I understand. We've been in the area for a number of years."

This tells a prospect who is concerned about reliability that your company is reliable.

If the prospect asks:

* "What's your reputation?"

You answer:

* "We're recognized as a premier manufacturer in this community. We've established a fine reputation that makes a difference. Our company has made a commitment to keep you satisfied, and we have the training and experience to make our products work for you. Our company fine-tunes its operations to fit the unique desires of thousands of customers. We have a number of offices in this area and many more across the country, with a leading share of the market. Our support staff is in place to follow up with customers to keep them happy.

This tells a prospect who is concerned about reliability, flexibility, and convenience that your sale will wear well.

"I Understand"

Once your prospect tells you what he or she thinks about your company, what do you do? You say:

* "I understand. Let me quickly cover a couple of things I

Again, this statement is so important that you should memorize it, along with the earlier statement, *"May I ask how much information you have about [your company's name]?"* Read it over as many times as required to commit it to memory. When you are ready, write both statements, from memory, in the space provided.

Why is the exact wording so important? No matter what response your prospect gives — positive, negative, or neutral — you will find that your acknowledgment statement, "I understand," is completely comfortable, natural, and appropriate. If your prospect has paid your company excessive compliments, don't blush, squirm in your seat, or be tempted to add to the accolades. You simply say, "I understand." If your prospect knows little or nothing about your company, you won't be tempted to make any comments which might inadvertently make your prospect feel uneasy or ill-informed. You simply say, "I understand." And if the prospect expresses negative reactions to your company, you won't be tempted to become irritated or defensive. You simply say, "I understand."

The sentence, "Let me quickly cover a couple of things that I think would be important to me if I were in your position," accomplishes two important goals for you. First, you have provided yourself a perfect opening to give your prospect whatever additional information will be required to build trust in your company's integrity and ability to get the job done. In addition, the wording tells your prospects that you are seeing the situation through their eyes: the way you would if you were in their position. In short, you *understand.* As I've said several times before, your prospects buy from you not so much because they understand your product or service, but because they feel *you* understand *them.*

Throughout the Seven Steps of the Track Selling System™ you are being asked to memorize short questions or statements to include as part of your standard sales procedure. For the most part, these are transition statements that carry you smoothly

include as part of your standard sales procedure. For the most part, these are transition statements that carry you smoothly into the next step of the process. You will find that these questions and statements make good, logical sense and are therefore not at all difficult to memorize. Each fits comfortably into the situation without sounding stilting or forced. These memorized statements can add to your self-confidence, signaling in your own mind that you have moved from one step to the next in the sales procedure. These statements will also add to your confidence by focusing your attention on the goals and objectives you are working to achieve in a sales call.

Review the following transition sentences for a moment:

STEP TWO: QUALIFICATION

- "[Prospect's name], I would like to tell you about our [name of your product or service]; however, in order for me to do the best job I possibly can for you, I need to ask you a couple of questions. Is that all right?"

Optional statements:

- "May I ask what you like most about ...?"
- "Would it be fair to ask what you like least about ...?"
- "Has anything changed?"

STEP THREE: AGREEMENT ON NEED

- "As I understand it, you are looking for something that will [summary of important information you gathered in Step One: Approach and Step Two: Qualification]. Is that correct?"

STEP FOUR: SELL THE COMPANY

- "May I ask how much information you have about [your company's name]?"
- "I understand. Let me quickly cover a couple of things that I think would be important to me if I were in your position."

I cannot stress strongly enough that you use these memorized statements, *worded exactly as they are presented*, in the exact

I didn't grab these words out of thin air. They are the result of years of refining and honing and careful work done by thousands of successful salespeople for over 35 years. I tried one set of words, changed or refined them, saw how they worked in the field, compared the results with a previous version of the wording, and so on, until I found the best combination of words, in the best order.

The above statements are those that have proven the most successful in generating sales. They will give you the best results on your sales calls, and the best results on the bottom line. If you change the wording, you can diminish the effectiveness of your sales procedure, so don't change these statements in any way.

It won't take you long to memorize these short segments — and it won't take you long to appreciate the success you will achieve on your sales calls.

SELLING YOUR COMPANY

Now that you have said, "Let me quickly cover a couple of things I think would be important to me if I were in your position," you are ready to sell the company. In this step it is important to *sell*, not *tell*. Let me illustrate.

Your main objective in this fourth step is to help your prospects decide that your company has integrity and is able to perform as promised. You will do this by sharing honest, accurate facts about your company — facts that will instill confidence. Keep in mind that what you communicate to your prospects is influenced by what you have heard of their needs and concerns in the Approach and Qualification steps. You must supply your prospects with the answers if you're to sell the credibility and viability of your company.

Your replies to your prospect's spoken or unspoken questions must be in terms he or she wants to hear. To, "I don't know your company," you might respond, "I understand. Let me quickly cover a couple of things I think would be important to me if I were in your position. We have been supplying woodstoves to housing contractors in the Tri-City area since we were founded in 1979." To, "What's your reputation?" you might respond, "We are recognized as the most reliable supplier of woodstoves in this county." And so on.

When describing your company, you work with what you have — with what is true. Perhaps your company has been in business for over a hundred years. *Tell* the prospect that, but remember the invisible sign on your prospect's forehead: "What will it do for me?" You must also *sell* your prospect by pointing out the benefits that being in business for over a hundred years provides. You might say, "This means you will be dealing with a well-established firm, recognized throughout the industry as the leader in its field." (If indeed, that is true.)

On the other hand, perhaps your company is brand new. *Tell* the prospect that, then *sell* them by pointing out the benefits that feature provides: "Because we're new, we're enthusiastic. We're innovative. We're eager to provide you with the best service you have ever had." (If indeed, this is true.)

Is your office located nearby? Do you have branch offices in Duluth, Peoria, and Omaha? Is your manufacturing, shipping or servicing handled in a unique way? Do you have an impressive client list? Is your management exceptionally well qualified? Are your company policies straightforward? Is your company the largest, the fastest growing, or the best equipped to do the job?

Take the time to *tell* your prospect the honest, accurate facts about your company that would be most important to each specific prospect. Also take the time to *sell* your company, by pointing out the benefits that each of the features provides to that prospect.

You may also want to point out, if it is true, that you had the opportunity to work for many companies in this field, and you chose to sell for this particular company because ... and you proceed to tell the prospect why you chose it. You might say, "... first, because Allied is well established, has been in business for fifteen [or however many] years, and has an outstanding reputation, and secondly, because of the high quality of our ball bearings."

If you are or work for a manufacturer's representative, or a dealer or distributor for one or more manufacturers, your job is to sell your own company as well as that of the manufacturer of the product. For example, if you are or work for a dealer selling building materials, you would sell the prospect on the manufac-

turer: its experience, size, warranty, length of time in business.
You would also sell the prospect on your own local dealership:
its experience, size, warranty, length of time in business, and so
on.

RE-SELLING THE COMPANY

What about the calls you make on long-established clients?
These people may have been doing business with you for years.
They already know how long your company has been in busi-
ness. They know its policies and its track record for fair dealing.
Is it pointless to resell your company to these "old reliables?"

Definitely not. Take any customer for granted and you risk the
possibility of losing that customer. Remember: If you're not in
there selling *your* company, you can be sure there will be others
in there selling *theirs*. Always assume that you are countering
and balancing the input your clients are getting from your
competition. Believe me, your competition wants your client's
business every bit as much as you do — and will make strong
efforts to get it.

Your clients, no matter how well established, are making a
decision about your company on every sales call you make.
During your presentation those people may very well be sitting
there wondering if they should stay with your company, or
perhaps try buying from Jim Smith, who's been dropping by a
lot lately. Jim's company sounds intriguing, and he has been
leaving some enticing price lists.

You cannot assume anything, even the good will of a long-
established client. Take time on every sales call you make to sell
your company. Don't leave it to chance.

Of course, with a long-established client you handle this step in
a different way. You might say, for example, "Henry, you've
been with us for a long time. Let me recall for you some of
basic facts about the Allied company that have made us a good
choice and tell you some of the new developments we're
working on." Or you could share company news. Your company may have just won an award for sales, safety, or community service. Your company may have just hired new personnel
or adopted new policies or procedures that will make your
product or service better than ever. Perhaps your company has

added an important new client, developed a new product, added a new service, printed new brochures or catalog sheets, opened a new branch in Miami, expanded the shipping department, or installed a new software system. Share this news with your client, with the same enthusiasm you would share news with any other friend.

With a long-time client, it doesn't hurt to remind them of facts they already know about your company: you offer the best guarantees, the most up-to-date styles, have the best reputation for service, or any other information that is appropriate to the situation.

Your long-time clients probably won't *ask* for information about your company. It's your responsibility as a professional salesperson to supply this information without being asked.

The decision about your company is on your prospect's "hidden agenda." They may not even be aware they are making this decision. Yet if this decision is not made *positively*, regardless of how unconsciously it may be made, it will be difficult — if not impossible — to make the sale.

Think for a moment about how this hidden decision affects your own purchases, and you will agree how important it is. You would not, for example, buy a second car from a dealership that sold you a lemon in the past. You wouldn't have your car serviced at a repair shop that has earned a reputation for shoddy workmanship, fraud, or dishonesty. You wouldn't buy insurance from a company you know will ignore you when you submit your claim. You wouldn't buy an appliance from a manufacturer with a reputation for poor quality control whose equipment is known to break down frequently.

You buy from companies you trust, and your prospects are no different. Take time on every sales call for this very important step. Sell the company. You will be much more effective and successful when you do.

IF YOUR COMPANY IS HAVING PROBLEMS

What if you work for a company that has problems in its delivery, customer service, or in the quality of the product or service itself?

As I see it, there are essentially two routes open to you. One is to do your best to rectify the problems in the company by reporting the feedback you get from the field to your managers, as well as to the person or persons who may have caused the problem, and asking all concerned to change their procedures or behaviors. You will need to explain how the company's problems, or specific employee's actions, have caused customers problems, which reduces the number of sales you can bring in. Of course you will put your request for changed procedures and behaviors in terms of *their* interests, not yours. It is in the managers' and employees' best interests that adequate cash flows into the company on a regular basis, through your efforts and those of other salespeople. Don't put your request in terms of *your* interests, however; the managers and employees will be less concerned that you might be embarrassed in front of prospects or that your paycheck will shrink.

If the problem is a procedure that can be easily altered, or if it just one person's attitude or behavior and that person is willing to change, you can expect that your company will perform up to your (and your prospects') expectations in a relatively short time. If, however, the problem involves several interconnecting company procedures, or the behavior or attitude of many people, the problem may take a much longer time to be resolved. As a professional salesperson, you are honest with your prospects and always operate with the highest integrity. If you feel you cannot promise your prospects changes in the company by a reasonable length of time, as much as you might gain their admiration for personal integrity, your prospects are not as likely to buy from you. They will not buy until they have good reason to think your company will improve, and you may lose sales in the meantime.

This brings up the second route I see open to you as a professional salesperson. You can make plans to leave the company and find another one where your standards as a professional salesperson are matched by the company's competence, reliability, and courtesy. This is particularly important when the issue at stake is not merely one of negative employees or ineffective procedures, but rather involves high-level company policy. The professional salesperson, in my opinion, always first tries to bring the company up to the standards necessary to compete in today's business world. If that fails, he or she moves on to a company with higher standards.

I have been emphasizing what a professional salesperson might do. What would an *unprofessional* salesperson do? Well, that salesperson might make a few tries to change the company before getting discouraged, then resent the company *as well as* the prospects for their unwillingness to buy, and finally resort to twisting the truth, "buying time," and outright lying to prospects in order to get their business. This shady dealing, of course, does not stand up to scrutiny by the customers, since most of them will *see*, over time, that a company still has delivery problems, is discourteous, still makes shoddy materials, and so on. Then the salesperson seems as shoddy as the company, and will look like a liar to boot. It's just not worth it. If honesty had never been invented, it *should* have been invented as the best tool a salesperson ever had.

If you work for a problem company, do your very best to make changes where you can. If your prospects still have problems, go to work for a company you can be proud of. If you stay in the same field, of course, you may call on many of the same prospects as a representative of your new company. Your sales efforts while you were with your previous company will have convinced these people you are warm, likable, honest, and have good judgment. Because you laid careful groundwork in the past, your foot is already in the door.

SELLING A YOUNG COMPANY

Over the years some salespeople have expressed to me that they felt handicapped in the Sell the Company step because they worked for a new firm with a short history. In my experience that is *not* a handicap. This was brought home to me in a personal way when my associates and I started our Century Three Insurance Marketing firm in 1976. Out of approximately 1,800 life and health insurance companies in the United States, we sought out those we wanted to represent — carriers with first-class reputations for quality products and outstanding service to policy holders. We wanted our number-one carrier to be CNA, which had an outstanding portfolio of life, disability, and health insurance plans. This company was undergoing a reorganization, and for that and other reasons CNA's management was not taking on new General Agents. We weren't put off by this fact, however, and arranged a meeting with CNA's key managers.

Our "product" was our company's potential service to them — selling their policies to customers. However our "company" in this case was not actually Century Three (since we had formed only weeks before), but the experience, track record, and qualifications of the three of us who had started the company. We had a major job of "Selling the Company" — our experience — so they would take our "product" seriously. My colleagues and I put in several long days of discussion with CNA and provided a detailed projection of all we would accomplish. CNA's first Buying Decision was about the salesman — myself — and fortunately they decided positively; they liked me and believed I had integrity and good judgment. They decided positively about their second Buying Decision as well; they bought the "company" because of the experience, confidence, and competence of our management team. As a result, CNA awarded us a General Agency contract.

I had the same kind of "Sell the Company" experience with another carrier we wanted to represent, National Home Life of Malverne, Pennsylvania. I wanted this company to take us on as a General Agent for several reasons, including my admiration of its founder and chairman, Arthur DeMoss. Mr. DeMoss started National Home Life as a one-man operation from his kitchen table. He had reached potential customers primarily through direct mail, a very unusual step, and in a relatively short period of time, National Home Life became a multi-million-dollar organization. It was an amazing success story.

My first step was to call Arthur DeMoss directly. He acknowledged that he knew relatively little about his California operations and said he would have the appropriate regional vice president call me. In his telephone call and our subsequent face-to-face meeting, the California regional vice president seemed strangely uninterested in what Century Three could do for National Home Life, but instead focused on how long I had known Arthur DeMoss. In both conversations I steered the topic away from Mr. DeMoss, not mentioning that I'd only spoken to him once by telephone. The regional vice president said he would contact his superiors in Malverne and call me in a few days. Several weeks passed, with no word from the regional vice president. so I took the initiative again and called the senior vice president of National Home Life to ask for an appointment with him at their home office in Malverne. I asked him to advise Mr. DeMoss of my visit and see whether I might also meet with him during my stay.

Well, this assertive approach paid off. On a wintry day I hopped a jet to Pennsylvania and met with the senior vice president and other managers, discussing the objectives and background of our management team at Century Three. After the meeting the executives led me to Arthur DeMoss' office suite. He met me at the door with a warm smile and firm handshake. Although there was frost on his bay windows, the fire in the fireplace crackled and warmed the room. As we sat in his handsome leather chairs and talked, I realized I was in the presence of a man who personified dignity and integrity. I asked him about National Home Life's origins. He said, "Roy, it began on my kitchen table, as you know, years ago. My roots are still there. Part of my reason for going to direct mail was to contact the customer without a door-to-door hard sell. I wanted more than a soft sell; I wanted a *smart* sell, one that gave me customers that last."

"That last?"

"I have a growing business with customers who last, who stay with National Home Life for years. And I keep them with us by serving their needs first. Any company that thinks customers aren't important — well, they should try doing business without them! Treating both my customers and my employees with integrity — that's what makes National Home Life a success. That's what makes us a long-standing business."

Obviously, this was a salesperson who knew how to make a sale — tens of thousands of sales — "wear well."

I told him I noticed that his employees seemed proud to work there, and he said they believed in themselves and in fact deserved the credit for the company's success. "People with a positive attitude succeed," he said. Arthur DeMoss was the kind of executive who took pleasure in sharing credit with his employees. He got things done by working *with* his people, rather than working through them. In this way, he received more than enough reward, financially and emotionally.

Did I "Sell the Company" to Arthur DeMoss? You bet I did. Although Century Three had a short history, and was basically Roy Chitwood and Associates, collectively we had solid experience in insurance. Arthur DeMoss "bought" our small company that day, and we went on to become one of the top-producing general agencies for National Home Life.

A different kind of Sell the Company incident took place a few winters ago, when I took a flight to Minneapolis. I arrived in the Twin Cities about eleven at night. I stepped into the chilled air and told the taxi supervisor, "I want to go to the Decathlon Club" — a ten-minute drive from the airport. The supervisor relayed my request to a cab driver.

When the driver got out of the taxi to take my bags, his body language communicated that he was upset over a ten-minute fare at this time of night. I got in anyway and, from the back seat, called out, "The Decathlon Club, please. How are you doing, today?"

"What do ya mean, how am I doing? I'm a cab driver, ain't I? Where do ya wanna go?"

This seemed odd. I had already told him, "The Decathlon Club," I repeated. Then I tried again: "Cold weather you're having. Must be tough to be in traffic with all the snow."

"Are you talkin' to me?"

"Is there someone else in the cab?"

We were not, to say the least, hitting it off. He mumbled something I couldn't understand, and I replied, "Forget it. Please take me to the Decathlon Club."

When we arrived at the Club he hit the brakes, causing the cab to skid to a halt at the curb. He jumped out of the driver's seat and dumped my bags on the sidewalk. I paid him the fare with no tip. I'm sure he complained to his buddies that he was stiffed by a passenger on a ten-minute ride. I travel a lot, and I know cabbies have to sit for long hours at the airport to get a trip. Knowing this, I usually tip fifty percent of the fare, sometimes even one hundred percent. But this sourpuss flung my bags to the sidewalk, without the courtesy of carrying them inside. In my book, he earned a failing grade in Sell the Company.

But then there was the cab driver who sold his company with gold stars. The next day Saturday, I was scheduled to speak at 11:00 a.m. for a client in St. Paul, a trip of twenty to thirty minutes from the Decathlon Club, depending on the weather. I called a taxi to be at the Club at 9:30 a.m., and at 9:25 I walked

down to the lobby and saw through the glass entrance doors
that the cab was already waiting for me.

As I entered the cab, the driver said, "I hope I haven't inconve-
nienced you by arriving early." As I leaned back on my seat, we
started to chat. His name was Lloyd, he told me, and his wife
was Georgia. "She drives during the night, doesn't like to fight
traffic. I drive during the day. Where can I take you?"

I told him my destination.

"You're like me," he said. "Have to work today." Obviously
noticing my suit and briefcase, the cabby continued, "I used to
have one of those nine-to-five jobs. Didn't work weekends. The
company closed down — didn't want its employees to be
unionized. After nineteen years I was let go, out on the street.
So here I am, driving a cab."

"How do you like it, Lloyd?" I asked him.

"I love it," he replied.

As we neared St. Paul, I mentioned my cab experience of the
night before. Lloyd nodded his head. "That happens a lot.
Some drivers think the world owes them a living. We try hard
with our passengers. Our reputation gives us repeat business.
Lots of travelers call my cab company, let us know when
they're flying in, and we pick them up at the airport."

He handed me his business card that had his office and home
numbers. "My wife and I have beepers," he explained. "The
home number is in case you can't reach me through the dis-
patcher."

"When my old company shut down," Lloyd continued, "my
situation looked pretty dark, but it turned out to be a blessing.
Georgia and I love meeting people. Working for ourselves
offers us lots of business and personal rewards."

As I looked around his cab, it was clear that he knew the
importance of "Sell the Company." His cab was immaculate.
Even his and his wife's name signs on the dashboard were of
polished wood.

Since then, whenever I'm in Minneapolis, I turn to them for a
taxi. These days they use a mobile phone instead of a beeper
because it does a better job of serving their customers. Lloyd

and Georgia represent the best in a business that demands
service, courtesy, and a positive attitude.

SAMPLE DIALOGUE FOR STEP FOUR:
SELL THE COMPANY

In the following sample dialogue, notice how Gerri moves
smoothly into the Sell the Company step of the Track Selling
System.™ Notice also how she covers aspects of her company
that she knows will appeal to her prospect. Because Dick is
planning a family vacation, she stresses her company's experience with family vacations (rather than with, say, business trips
or conference junkets). She also finds a way to tie her
company's origins in with his son's need to get away from the
cold weather. She does this masterfully, and she is short and to
the point. Her whole presentation takes less than a minute.

> *Salesperson:* *Dick, I'm sure if I were in your position
> there would be some specific information
> that I would want to know about Happiness
> is Hawaii Tours. May I ask how much
> information you have about our company?*
>
> *Prospect:* *I know very little about you. I've been
> looking at your ads on and off for the past
> year, but this is the first time I've really
> investigated them. I don't know anybody
> who's gone on a trip with you.*
>
> *Salesperson:* *I understand. Let me quickly cover a
> couple of things that I think would be
> important to me if I were in your position.
> Happiness is Hawaii Tours has been
> planning family vacations in Hawaii for
> over 20 years. We started in the Northeast,
> where people like your son were happy to
> get away from the bad weather and get to
> Hawaii. As we've grown, we expanded and
> now have offices in San Francisco, Seattle,
> Los Angeles and Dallas. We have over 150
> travel agents in those cities, planning
> meetings for corporations such as Chevron
> USA, General Motors and also small or
> large family vacations, all on an annual
> basis. In fact, Happiness is Hawaii Tours*

sent more people to Maui last year than any other tour group, as reported in a recent issue of Travel and Leisure *magazine.*

ONCE THE COMPANY IS SOLD

In Step 4: Sell the Company, you have addressed the prospect's second Buying Decision: about your company. You have invited the prospect to express whatever he or she knows about your company — whether positive, neutral, or negative; you have tailored your company data to the prospect's needs that you determined in Step One: Approach and Step Two: Qualification, and verified in Step Three: Agreement on Need. You now know why a professional salesperson can't just leap from *Agreement* on Need to *Fill* the Need, no matter how logical that connection sounds.

Now you are ready to go ahead and Fill the Need in Step Five.

THINGS TO REMEMBER

+ In Step Four: Sell the Company, you help your prospect make a positive decision about your company.

+ Give your prospect the information he or she needs to be assured that your company operates competently and with integrity.

+ Sell the Company to long-time clients as well as to brand-new ones.

+ If your company has problems that cannot be rectified, consider finding a new company — one that you can be proud of and sell with confidence.

EXERCISES

1.   Suppose that you are selling your company to your pros-
     pect and your prospect has the concerns below (which he
     or she may or may not verbalize). Answer these concerns
     in a way that establishes your company's reputation and
     credibility. Also be sure to focus on those factors that
     distinguish your company from the competition.

     a. "I don't know your company."

     b. "I don't know your company's product."

     c. "I don't know your company's customers."

     d. "I don't know your company's record or reputation."

2.   How do you determine what information you will need to
     provide to your prospect to sell the company?

3.   Why is it important to sell the company to the prospect?

4.   Why is it advisable to *re*-sell your company to a long-
     standing customer?

5. In each step of the Track Selling System™ presented so
    far, I have asked you to prepare a written plan, with a
    specific prospect in mind, to use on an upcoming sales call.

    a. Take a moment to review your sales plans for Steps One
       through Three. Then, with that specific prospect and
       sales call in mind, write the following plan for Step Four
       on a separate sheet of paper, or fill in the blanks that
       follow.

    b. After writing the transition question and response, list
       five facts that would instill confidence in the competence
       and integrity of your company in this particular pros-
       pect.

WRITTEN PLAN FOR STEP FOUR: SELL THE COMPANY

Write your transition statement here:

("May I ask how much information you have about
[your company's name]? *I understand. Let me quickly
cover a couple of things I think would be important to
me if I were in your position.")*

FIVE CONFIDENCE-INSPIRING FACTS
ABOUT YOUR COMPANY:

a.

b.

c.

d.

e.

6.   What visual aids could you use to make your presentation
      more effective?

14

STEP FIVE: FILL THE NEED

In Step Five: Fill the Need, all the careful groundwork you have been laying will begin paying off for you. You will show your prospects precisely *how* your product or service solves their problems or fills their needs. Here is where you demonstrate your product or service. This can be accomplished with an actual product demonstration, slide presentation, presentation book, laptop computer, visual aids, or whatever you use to visually show what your product or service will do. In the previous chapter we talked about the importance of using visual aids. Do not make the mistake of thinking all you have to do is tell your prospects about your wonderful product or service. In Step Five: Fill the Need, you will help your prospects make positive decisions about your product or service as well as the price. How? By guiding them through a Feature/Benefit/Reaction procedure.

THE FEATURE/BENEFIT/REACTION SEQUENCE

All products and services have both *tangible features* and *intangible benefits.* When you describe a product or service's features and benefits and elicit the prospect's reaction, you can fine-tune your presentation to fill the prospect's needs precisely. That makes for a willing and satisfied prospect.

THE TANGIBLE FEATURES

The tangible features of a *product* are its concrete, physical characteristics, such as size, weight, shape, ingredients, color, and component parts — what the product actually is or does.

The tangible features of a *service* include how often the service is performed, the qualifications of the people performing that service, exactly what is included in the service, and so on.

THE INTANGIBLE BENEFITS

In contrast, *a benefit is something intangible that your prospect derives from a particular feature.* These are the advantages that come not from the actual product or service, but from the ways in which it enhances the prospect's sense of well being. A benefit answers the prospect's unspoken question, "What will it do for me?"

Feature (Tangible):	The product is compact.
Benefit (Intangible):	Your prospect can store it easily, saving room.
Feature (Tangible):	The product is portable.
Benefit (Intangible):	Your prospect can carry it, making his job easier.
Feature (Tangible):	The service is available on week ends.
Benefit (Intangible):	Your prospect doesn't have to rush. He or she can use your service on Saturdays, which saves time and stress.

One of the biggest myths in selling is that it's easier to sell people tangibles than intangibles. Most salespeople spend the majority of their sales presentation stressing the tangible, concrete features of the products or services they sell. They believe that it is easier to sell an automobile than to sell automobile insurance, easier to sell a swimming pool than to sell pool maintenance.

Over a million quarter-inch drills are sold in this country every year, but no one wants quarter-inch drills. They want quarter inch *holes*. They want the benefit they will derive from the quarter-inch drills.

The intangible aspects of your product or service appeal directly to the Six Buying Motives. *The intangible benefits — holes, not drills — prompt your prospects to buy.*

When people purchase a new luxury automobile, they're not buying transportation to get them back and forth to work. They're buying a name, ego satisfaction, security and protection. When people spend half a million dollars for a new home, they're not buying protection from the elements. They're buying an address, a lifestyle, and keeping up with the Jones's. In short, people buy benefits, not features.

PEOPLE BUY BENEFITS, NOT FEATURES

Because people buy benefits, not features, you will sell more effectively and successfully if you spend most of your sales presentation stressing the intangible benefits your product or service provides.

I advise my salespeople, *"Sell,* don't t*ell.* " When you describe the tangible features of your product or service, you're *telling.* You're giving honest, accurate information about what your product or service actually is or does. These facts add credibility to your presentation, and as you have learned, these facts, which appeal to logic, will be what your prospects will use to justify their buying decisions later and help ensure that your sales will wear well. These facts in themselves, however, do not motivate your prospects to buy or act now.

When you sell, however — when you describe the benefits — you are actually motivating your prospect to buy by appealing to your prospect's Buying Motives. When you sell, you help your prospect visualize why it is in his or her best interest to buy or act now.

TELLING THE TANGIBLE FEATURES: An insurance salesperson made the following statements to his prospect: "The policy term is one year," he said. "The policy has an 80% coinsurance clause. Liability limits are on a split-limit basis. The policy territory includes the United States and Canada. Losses caused by product withdrawal or recall are not covered."

In presenting the facts — the tangible features — the salesperson was *telling* not selling.

SELLING THE INTANGIBLE BENEFITS: In selling, he let the prospect know about the intangible benefits, which appeal to the prospect's Buying Motives.

"You'll gain peace of mind," he assured the prospect, "knowing your company will survive even if a large loss occurs."

"If a lawsuit is brought against you because of a covered loss," he continued, "the insurance company will defend you, thus freeing you of the time and worry involved in handling the legal details yourself."

"You may pay your premium in installments, thus conserving your valuable cash for other important uses."

"Should the need arise," he went on, "you'll have the security of knowing you can borrow against the accrued policy value."

And he concluded, "I'm always available to answer your questions, help you fill out forms, or assist in any way you need."

Now he was *selling*, not telling. Do you think his chances of selling were good? If you needed to buy insurance, would you be more sold by the features or the benefits?

"WHAT WILL IT DO FOR ME?"

Keep your sales presentation focused on the intangible benefits of your product or service — on selling, not telling. Imagine your prospect with a huge, invisible sign fastened to his or her forehead, which reads: "What will it do for me?"

WHAT WILL IT DO FOR ME?

Describing the features alone won't answer that question. Each time you name a feature, *you must also paint vivid, word pictures* to help your prospect visualize the benefits each feature provides.

Suppose, for example, that you are a bank officer talking with an elderly gentleman about your bank's direct deposit service.

> *Salesperson:*   *Each month, your Social Security check*
> *can be automatically mailed by the issuer*
> *directly to the bank, for immediate deposit*
> *in your account. Wouldn't that be useful to*
> *you?*
>
> *Prospect:*   [Indifferently.] *I guess so.*

What's wrong here? You've named a concrete, tangible feature
— what your bank's service actually does. The problem is that
you have told, but not sold. Your prospect is still sitting there,
waiting politely with no visible expression of interest or enthusiasm — still wearing that huge, invisible sign: "What will it do
for me?"

It's when you describe the *benefit* this feature provides that you
begin to sell.

How do you know *which* features and benefits are important to
your prospect? By his or her answers in Step One: Approach
and Step Two: Qualification. Those answers will help you find
out what he or she needs, how the product or service will be
used, and the prospect's area of concern.

Take, for example, a personal computer system. One feature is
that the personal computer system is modular. A benefit of this
feature is that the system can be upgraded in both size and
performance without loss of the original investment. (This
benefit appeals to the Buying Motive, Fear of Loss.)

To return to the elderly gentleman waiting to be sold about the
benefits of your bank's direct deposit service:

> *Salesperson:*   *This means you'll have no more worries*
> *about lost or stolen checks. Even if you are*
> *sick, away on vacation, or simply busy with*
> *other things, your check will be safely*
> *deposited in your account, ready to use*
> *when you need it. Your Social Security*
> *money will begin earning interest immedi-*
> *ately, and because the service is automatic,*
> *you won't have any more time-consuming*
> *trips to the bank. You won't have to wait in*
> *anymore bank lines. And you won't even*
> *need to fill out a deposit slip or lick a*
> *stamp.*

> *Prospect:*   [Sits up and shows definite signs of inter-
> est.]

Of course he does. Because you have just answered his ques-
tion, "What will it do for me?" by appealing to his Buying
Motives — possible Desire for Gain, Fear of Loss, Comfort and
Convenience, Security and Protection, and Satisfaction of
Emotion.

Eliciting the Reaction

To really sell this gentleman on your bank's service, you ask
him a question to get his *response* to this benefit.

> *Salesperson:* *How would you feel, Mr. Williams, know-*
> *ing that without having to go anywhere or*
> *do anything, every month you'd have your*
> *Social Security income already securely in*
> *your account, earning interest?*
>
> *Prospect:*   *Well, I'd like that.*

Uncovering Dominant Buying Motives
with the Feature/Benefit/Reaction Sequence

The Feature/Benefit/Reaction sequence is a powerful technique
for discovering which features and benefits of your product or
service are actually important to your prospect. Here's how it
works.

1. Describe a *feature.*

2. Paint a vivid, word picture of the *benefits* that feature
   provides.

3. Ask your prospect an open-ended, feeling-finding
   question tied to that benefit to get his or her *reaction.*

For example, this Feature/Benefit/Reaction sequence appeals to
the Buying Motive of Comfort and Convenience:

> *Feature:*   *The Retrofit company will install your*
> *solar panels with an alternate-power-*
> *source feature.*
>
> *Benefit:*   *This means that, after many rainy or*
> *cloudy days, for example, with the flip of a*

> *switch, you can draw electric power from storage batteries or the local power lines.*

Reaction: *How would you like knowing that you could never run out of power, no matter what kind of weather you had?*

Prospect: *I'd like it a lot. Running out of power during a rainy spell was one of the things I was wondering about.*

This sequence appeals to Fear of Loss:

Feature: *The Retrofit Company also backs its customized, solar panels with a long-term warranty.*

Benefit: *The warranty protects all components of your solar panel system for five years, so if anything ever goes wrong with them, we would replace them free of charge.*

Reaction: *How secure would you fell about your warranty being backed by one of the leading manufacturers of solar panels in America?*

Prospect: *I'd feel secure about that.*

HOW THE FEATURE/BENEFIT/REACTION SEQUENCE HELPS YOU SELL: The Feature/Benefit/Reaction technique helps you sell in several ways:

1. *It establishes your credibility* by demonstrating that your product or service does concrete things.

2. *The benefit helps your prospect visualize ways in which your product or service could make a difference in his or her life*, in keeping with that person's dominant Buying Motives and special needs and problems.

    For example, the following illustration appeals to the prospect's Desire for Gain and need to find ways to cut accounting costs by using technology rather than personnel.

    Salesperson: *You mentioned earlier that you're trying to increase your profits by automating your accounting operations.*

Feature: *With our customized accounting software
               you can complete and mail more invoices
               than you're doing now, with fewer people.*

Benefit: *You'll have accounting software that
               increases your accounting output, takes
               less time to do so, and will eliminate the
               need for several office workers. You will
               get more done and spend less money doing
               it.*

Reaction: *In what ways could you imagine this
               software affecting company profits, in
               terms of your accounting operation?*

Prospect: *We'd probably make three percent more a
               year after this was paid off, if we had three
               fewer people in accounting. We'd also
               increase our cash flow because of the
               faster turn-around time for sending in-
               voices.*

3.   The Feature/Benefit/Reaction sequence reveals your
     prospect's dominant Buying Motives.

     This is the third and most important result of the Feature/
     Benefit/Reaction sequence. Each feature that you mention
     will be related to one or more specific Buying Motives.
     Each time you ask a question that puts your prospect "in
     the picture" with a benefit, your prospect will respond —
     with words, facial expressions and body language. This
     response will verify that the benefit you just mentioned is
     important.

     Here are other examples related to each of the other
     Buying Motives.

BUYING MOTIVE: FEAR OF LOSS

Feature: *We've been in the temporary employee
               business for twenty years. We guarantee
               the quality of our personnel, or there is no
               charge.*

Benefit: *When you work with us, you will get com-
               petent workers who will maintain your
               company's high standards of productivity,*

thus keeping customers from buying elsewhere.

Reaction: *May I ask, in what ways might our service be of value when your company has to make critical decisions about increasing product output?*

Prospect: *Well, we could hire some of your workers in a pinch, to meet a deadline, but I must say, this isn't crucial to me right now.*

BUYING MOTIVE: COMFORT AND CONVENIENCE

Feature: *With an approved line of credit, you can phone in your request for a business loan and pick up your money the same day.*

Benefit: *This way you won't have the hassle of filling out complicated applications when time is short.*

Reaction: *May I ask, in what ways this quick, hassle-free loan service might help you cope with fast-growing customer demands for your product?*

Prospect: *Well, whenever the demand would start to rise quickly, we could borrow money to add more personnel or upgrade our equipment in time to meet that demand.*

BUYING MOTIVE: SECURITY AND PROTECTION

Feature: *You'll be doing business with one of the most conscientious stock brokerages in the state. Our brokers make certain you understand the ramifications of each investment before you buy.*

Benefit: *Thus you protect your investments by making informed decisions.*

Reaction: *How would your broker's attentiveness to your being highly informed help build your investment portfolio?*

Prospect: *Well, if I knew more about each stock I would make better decisions, and with your broker's advice, I would know which investments would be best for me.*

BUYING MOTIVE: PRIDE OF OWNERSHIP

Feature: *Our personal computer has received critical acclaim in Personal Computer and Computing magazines. Computing cited it as providing the most flexible applications and rated it as having the highest quality over all other models and brands in this class.*

Benefit: *You'd be using a computer that industry critics hold up as a model for quality and flexibility.*

Reaction: *How would it feel to operate a PC that is considered the standard in the business world?*

Prospect: *It would feel fine. But what I really want is a PC with a lot of memory.*

BUYING MOTIVE: SATISFACTION OF EMOTION

Feature: *Home Health Services provides competent health care right in your home.*

Benefit: *Home Health will train a member of your family to care for the patient when a doctor or nurse isn't available.*

Reaction: *How important is reliable health care to you and your family?*

Prospect: *It's important!*

Your prospect's response helps you verify whether or not that particular Buying Motive is important. As you can see in the examples, the first prospect is not particularly interested in the Fear of Loss motive for hiring temporary help. The other prospect's responses in these examples reflect varying degrees of interest.

DEGREES OF INTEREST

As mentioned earlier, you will know how important a particular Buying Motive is by what your prospect says, as well as the degree of emotional response that person shows. For example, your prospect may be *uninterested* (or even mildly annoyed), *somewhat interested*, or *enthusiastic*. An uninterested response indicates that your prospect doesn't care about that Buying Motive. Don't bring up any more features and benefits relating to that motive. A mildly annoyed response, which can occur occasionally, indicates that your prospect doesn't care about or even approve of that Buying Motive and may even be somewhat affronted that you'd think he or she would care about it. ("Who me, interested in other people's admiration? Who me, afraid of burglars breaking in?") Of course you don't attempt to appeal to that Buying Motive again.

Remember: Don't stop when you find enthusiasm for one dominant Buying Motive. Your prospect may have additional dominant motives.

BENEFITS OF THE FEATURE/BENEFIT/REACTION SEQUENCE

There are two other important results of the Feature/Benefit/ Reaction sequence. One is that, again, while you are asking your prospects to respond to a specific question, you are controlling the focus of their attention. You are focusing your prospects' attention on ways your product or service can potentially solve their problems or fill their needs.

The other is that the Feature/Benefit/Reaction sequence momentarily diffuses any anxiety your prospect may have about the cost. By the time you get to the fourth decision, price, you will have built a case for the many ways your product or service can do what your prospects needs, and thus, they will see the cost in terms of *value received*, rather than money out of pocket.

You will learn more about how to help prospects see the price in terms of value received in Chapter Fifteen: "Act of Commitment," as well as how to more specifically apply the Feature/ Benefit/Reaction sequence to the sales process in the remainder of this chapter.

WHY SEEK A REACTION?

The features that you assume will be important to a prospect may not have a high priority at all.

Several years ago, while I was working with a big, vinyl siding manufacturer, I accompanied a salesperson to the home of a prospect. The salesperson was going through his presentation, calling out the features and benefits.

"The vinyl siding is a solid color, clear through," he stated. "So you'll never have to paint your house again."

The prospect sat there, unmoved.

"This means," the salesperson persisted, "no expensive paints to buy each year, no ladders to climb, and no fumes to recover from."

No response from the prospect.

Relentlessly, the salesperson repeated the features and benefits. The prospect was clearly losing interest. What was the salesperson doing wrong?

Finally, the prospect solved the riddle by saying glumly, "I don't know what I'll do in the summer, now that I can't paint my house."

Clearly, to him not having to paint his house each year was *not* a benefit.

Had the salesperson asked him, "How important is it to that you don't have to paint your house again?" the prospect would have reacted, "Not important at all. I like to paint my house." The salesperson would have then had the opportunity to cite an *appropriate* benefit.

As a rule of thumb, the first reaction question should be open-ended. This encourages further involvement by the prospect. However, if you are faced with an overload of responses, it's smart to use reaction questions that are closed-ended.

USING THE FEATURE/BENEFIT/REACTION SEQUENCE IN YOUR PERSONAL LIFE: The Feature/Benefit/Reaction sequence can also work in your personal life. Suppose that someone wanted to persuade his or her spouse to go back to Omaha for the Christmas holidays. That person might use the Feature/Benefit/Reaction sequence like this:

Feature:	*Honey, it says in the paper here that Midwest Airlines is offering reduced family fares to Omaha on Christmas Day.*
Benefit:	*We could spend Christmas with the folks in Omaha and not worry about the expense,*

since it would be so much cheaper than usual.

Reaction: *How do you think that would be, enjoying an affordable Christmas with everyone back home?*

Spouse: *Well, that would really be nice.*

The person is appealing to the spouse's Desire for Gain (reduced air fare) and Satisfaction of Emotion (affection for the family back home).

In another example, a father could use this technique to persuade his child to study harder and get better grades in school.

Feature: *Sharon, if you spend more time studying now, you'll understand your subjects and feel a sense of mastery over them. You'll also get better grades.*

Benefit: *Understanding and mastering your subjects and getting better grades will make you feel powerful and accomplished, and you won't have to worry about other kids looking down at you.*

Reaction: *How do you think you would feel if you could walk through the halls at Central High feeling proud of yourself and "on top of it" in terms of every class?*

Sharon: *I'd feel good, I guess.*

Feature: *And Sharon, if you spend more time studying while you're still a freshman, next semester, because of your better grades, the counselors will assign you to the "college track" English, history, and science classes.*

Benefit: *You'd be in the same class with some of the most popular, accomplished, interesting kids at Central. You'd probably be able to change the whole course of your future high school life by being in those classes, in terms of the girls you'd be friends with and the boys you'd be socializing with.*

Reaction: *How much more fun do you think you might have if you get to go through the rest*

*of high school with the kids in those
classes?*

Sharon: [Giggling.] *It would be more fun, I guess.*

THE HEART OF YOUR SALES PRESENTATION

You are now ready for the precise, step-by-step procedure to follow in the heart of your sales presentation.

To move smoothly from Step Four: Sell the Company to Step Five: Fill the Need, use the following transition statement:

- ♦ *"There are several important features about* [your product or service] *that I'd like to tell you about."*

Then you go right into the Feature/Benefit/Reaction sequence. In this procedure, you will stress the intangible benefits your product or service provides. You will especially stress the benefits that will appeal to your prospect's dominant Buying Motives. Here is how it works:

1. Name a feature of your product or service.
2. Paint a vivid, word picture of the benefits that feature provides.
3. Ask a reaction question tied to that benefit.

To recap, the *feature* represents important information about your product or service: the fact a product is compact or portable, or a service is extensive. The *benefit* highlights what the feature will do for the potential buyer and can appeal to one or a combination of the prospect's buying motives: Desire for Gain, Fear of Loss, Comfort and Convenience, Security and Protection, Pride of Ownership, and Satisfaction of Emotion. The *reaction* question draws out the response the prospect will base his or her buying decision on.

The Feature/Benefit/Reaction sequence serves two functions. First, it allows you to demonstrate to prospects how their needs can be met through your product or service. Second, it allows you to uncover your prospect's true attitude toward your benefit or service. Let's take a closer look at this procedure.

Suppose you are selling a telemarketing service. You might use Feature/Benefit/Reaction sequences like these:

Feature:	*We handle every detail of your telemarketing program. We hire skilled, experienced personnel, prepare scripts, and do the on-going supervision of those employees.*
Benefit:	*You'd have that whole load off your shoulders — someone else to take over that complete responsibility.*
Reaction:	*How would you feel about being relieved of those details and worries, and having more free time to relax and enjoy that new boat of yours down at the marina?*
Prospect:	*Well, it sure would be nice not to have to worry about doing it myself.*
Feature:	*We submit a daily report to you.*
Benefit:	*This means each day you'll receive a list of pre-scheduled appointments with thoroughly qualified prospects: people who have a genuine interest in, and need for, the product you sell.*
Reaction:	*How would it affect your profits if your sales staff were spending its time in front of qualified prospects with the authority and funds to buy?*
Prospect:	*Well, theoretically profits should be higher, since the salespeople would probably make more sales.*

Notice, that each reaction question is open-ended, which encourages your prospect to freely express his or her reactions to the feature and benefit presented. Thus, you will know what your prospect really thinks about your product or service at this point in the presentation. The only time you can know what your prospects are thinking is when they are talking.

Why will the Feature/Benefit/Reaction sequence be so effective for you?

- When you name an honest, accurate feature of your product or service, you are establishing credibility. Your product or service actually is, has, or does definite, concrete things.

As a professional salesperson, your goal is more than just making a sale now. You want the sale to wear well. You want the sale to help you establish an ongoing relationship that turns the prospect into a long-term client.

The prospect, on the other hand, buys emotionally, then justifies those decisions logically. When your prospect wakes up at two o'clock in the morning and mulls over this purchase, it's the tangible *features* that will make this sale wear well. Therefore, you have taken care of this step. You have named the features; you have let your prospects know the real, tangible product or service they are spending their hard-earned dollars to buy. You are giving them reasons to decide that their purchases make good, logical, business sense.

> ◆ When you paint the intangible benefits that relate directly to the prospect's Six Buying Motives, you answer the prospect's unasked question: "What will it do for me?"

Therefore, you have also taken care of this step. In the benefits portion of this sequence, you help your prospects visualize exact ways in which their current situations will improve if those purchases are made. Your statement of benefits should relate directly to your prospect's Buying Motives: Desire for Gain, Fear of Loss, Comfort and Convenience, Security and Protection, Pride of Ownership, and Satisfaction of Emotion. Your statement of benefits should help the prospect think: "Aha! If I'd had that product or service the last time I faced this problem, I could have been more effective, more successful, and had less worry and hassle," or whatever benefits may apply in your own selling situations.

> ◆ Lastly, you asked a reaction question, "How would that add to your peace of mind?" or "What impact would that have on your department's productivity?" or "What do you think might happen to the speed of the production line if you installed this system?"

The reaction question should always relate directly to your statement of benefits. The question should be open-ended to encourage your prospect to talk freely and to give you an honest, complete reaction to those benefits.

This reaction question accomplishes two exceptionally important goals for you. Recall that everyone buys for his or her own reasons. In Step Five: Fill the Need, you want to *keep your presentation focused on the things of greatest importance to this specific prospect.* Your reaction questions give you the opportunity to test the accuracy of the features and benefits you are now presenting, to find out if you really have zeroed in on this prospect's most important problems and needs, and are offering solutions that will really motivate this person to buy.

For example, suppose you are selling computer equipment and start to list the benefits:

> Salesperson: *Our equipment is "user friendly." It's so easy that even a child can use it.*

However, you are speaking with an experienced computer buff who most likely is skilled in every technical aspect of many different computers. After stating the benefit, you ask your reaction question:

> Salesperson: *How important is it to you that this equipment is simple and easy to use?*

> Prospect: *It isn't important at all. Beginners may prefer "toy" computers, but I'm ready to get right down to business. I want a computer I can program to do any operation or application required, without those silly distracting little pictures.*

You are still ahead of the game. Now you *know* what she is thinking.

On the other hand, suppose this prospect responds enthusiastically:

> Prospect: *You know, I've never worked with one of these "visual" systems before. I think I might really enjoy it for a change. I can still program it, right?*

In that case, you know you have made an accurate judgment, and you are offering this prospect something that will truly solve her problems or fill her needs precisely.

I've met many salespeople over the years who were sure they already knew their prospect's motives, and already knew what features and benefits to stress. This can be a costly mistake. The vital importance of getting feedback from your prospect was brought home for me by a story a reservation agent for

Singapore Airlines told me when I did training for them. "I nearly lost a sale by assuming I knew what my prospect wanted," the agent related. And she told this story:

She had been speaking to a tour operator in Las Vegas, who had called to check on group tour flights to Singapore. The agent was proud of a new feature that her company was offering: free cocktails on any transcontinental flight, in both first class and coach. "All the passenger has to do is put out his or her glass, and presto, it will be filled," she stated exuberantly. "This new service can save a passenger considerable expense on a long flight." She went on to enthusiastically stress this feature and benefit to the tour operator.

Finally the tour operator stopped her mid-sentence. "My group isn't interested in free cocktails," she said irritably. "We're Mormons, and we don't take kindly to hard liquor!"

What should the airline agent have done instead? If she had known about the Feature/Benefit/Reaction sequence at that time, the conversation could have gone like this:

Feature:	*Cocktails are free on all transcontinental flights.*
Benefit:	*This means that your people will have all the drinks they want, no matter what class of service they're traveling in.*
Reaction:	*How important do you think that would be to people in your group?*
Prospect:	*It wouldn't be important at all. We're Mormons; we don't drink, you know.*

The agent could then have gone on to more meaningful features and benefits for the prospect, instead of *un*-selling the tour operator by harping on a feature and benefit that was mildly insulting to this group. Had this airline agent known about and done a good job in the Approach and Qualification steps, she would have already asked what kind of group would be traveling to Singapore and what their interests might be.

There are dozens of sound, legitimate reasons why someone would buy the product or service you sell, but *only a few of these reasons are important to each individual prospect.*

Very few salespeople realize this. Most salespeople who are unaware of this important fact tend to "oversell" — to bombard their prospect with reason after reason for buying. This is not only unnecessary, it is counterproductive. Your reaction questions, on the other hand, help you keep your presentation focused precisely on each prospect's individual, genuine needs.

Your reaction questions help you achieve a second important goal, too. As a rule of thumb, your reaction questions should be open-ended to encourage your prospects to talk freely. This involves the prospects fully, and as illustrated above, when your prospects are talking, you know what they're thinking. They are thinking about your product or service, because you're keeping their attention focused on the benefits they will receive if they buy your product or service.

When you are doing the talking, on the other hand, your prospect's minds could be wandering; they could be distracted by pressing problems at work or home. When they are contemplating and describing the benefits they could receive, you know they are thinking about the ways in which their current situation could improve if they decide to buy the product or service you sell. They are mentally "trying it on for size," and that's exactly what you want them to do.

BENEFITS TO THE PROSPECT
VS. BENEFITS TO THE CONSUMER

Sometimes a salesperson will confuse the benefits to the end-consumer with the benefits to the prospect, who may be the dealer, distributor, or store manager. Suppose, for example, that a salesperson represents a pharmaceutical company and is calling on a drugstore owner to sell a generic brand of aspirin. The salesperson hasn't done her homework in the Approach and Qualification steps and doesn't know what is important to that prospect. She says:

Feature: *Laboratory tests have shown All-Clear brand aspirin acts safely and quickly to provide temporary relief from simple headaches and muscular aches and pains.*

Benefit: *This means that your customers will get quick pain relief from minor aches and pains.*

> Reaction: *How do you think your customers will feel if they know they can get this quick relief by purchasing All-Clear at your store?*
>
> Prospect: *Okay, I guess.*

What do you do if the prospect is half-hearted about generic brands? Happily, the Feature/Benefit/ Reaction sequence also works with prospects who are not strongly negative in their response, but *are* in the unsure zone. The salesperson tries again:

> Feature: *Henderson Pharmaceuticals created All-Clear as a cut-rate "generic" brand, which still provides the same quality ingredients and pain-relieving benefits of name-brand aspirins.*
>
> Benefit: *This means you can stock more bottles of All-Clear than the name-brand aspirin for the same price, therefore reducing shelf-space requirements and increasing sales per square foot.*
>
> Reaction: *How would you feel if you could increase the revenue per square foot of shelf space in the over-the-counter drugs portion of your store?*
>
> Prospect: *Now you're talking.*

In this case, of course, the benefit to the consumer is that the aspirin provides the same temporary relief from aches and pains as the more expensive brand-name aspirin, which saves money. The benefit to the store owner, on the other hand, is increased sales per square foot by not having to stock so many name brands.

Notice the two levels of benefits in this next example. A salesperson with a line of plumbing fixtures for hardware stores calls on the store manager.

> Feature: *These faucet fixtures are high quality stainless steel.*
>
> Benefit: *By offering them you would generate customer loyalty, because these fixtures work so well your customers would have minimum service calls to plumbers.*

Reaction: *If quality products like these are important
to your customers, how do you think
offering them might increase your profits?*

However, the hardware store manager would sell these same
faucets quite differently to his own customers:

Feature: *These high-quality, stainless steel Water-
Tight Fixtures are the best we offer.*

Benefit: *Because they're high-quality stainless
steel, they fit so well they are most likely to
be trouble-free.*

Reaction: *How important is it to you to save money
on plumbing costs down the road?*

The benefit to the consumer is a long-lasting, trouble-free
product; the benefit to the store owner is customer loyalty and
increased profits.

WHICH FEATURE AND BENEFITS?

How do you know which features and benefits to stress in Step
Five of your sales procedure? From the input you gathered in
Step One: Approach and Step Two: Qualification. You now
know your prospect's problems, needs, values, and the Buying
Motive most likely to prompt this person to make the purchase.
In Step Five: Fill the Need, *stress only the features and benefits
that zero in on these specific needs.*

HOW MANY FEATURE/BENEFIT/REACTION SEQUENCES?

How many Feature/Benefit/Reaction sequences should you use
in Step Five of your presentation? Our research indicates that
three or *four* are sufficient. If you have done a thorough job in
Step One: Approach and Step Two: Qualification, you have
discovered exactly what this person wants or needs to buy.
Your prospect's response to your reaction questions now tells
you how accurately you have judged his or her needs. Three
Feature/Benefit/Reaction sequences, aimed precisely at what is
important to each individual prospect, are usually enough to
persuade anyone to buy or act now. If that is not enough, you
will learn in the next chapter how to come back and supply your

prospects with even more sound reasons to buy and still exert almost no pressure at all.

Think how this approach differs from the way most salespeople conduct sales calls. If the product or service has fifteen important features and benefits, how many do they stress? Sixteen, right? That's too many. More than three or four overloads the listener and creates too much pressure, causing the prospect to retreat. The Track Selling System,™ on the other hand, helps you see things through your prospect's eyes and provide genuine, beneficial service. With the Track Selling System,™ because you accurately zero in on the prospect's dominant Buying Motives and you help the prospect "try on" those benefits beforehand, you only *need* three or four Feature/Benefit/Reaction sequences to make the sale.

IN WHAT ORDER OF IMPORTANCE?

Suppose you have chosen three Feature/Benefit/Reaction sequences that are on-target for your prospect. You know one is good, the second is even better, and the third is so ideal for that prospect it would knock his socks off. How should you present them? Our research shows that *you will be most effective if you present your Feature/Benefit/Reaction sequences in increasing order of desirability to the prospect.* That is, first present the feature and benefit that you know he will like. Next, present a feature and benefit he will *really* like. Third, present a feature and benefit he will *love.* Building in that order carries the prospect to an emotional high.

Also, as a rule of thumb, the first reaction question should be open-ended. This will, of course, induce your prospect to become fully involved in contemplating the possible benefits. It is possible that your prospect could become too involved, and you may be faced with an overload of responses. If this happens, use a closed-ended question to temporarily stop your prospect and return his or her attention to your next Feature/Benefit/Reaction sequence.

You control the participation of your prospect by the types of reaction questions you ask. If you are not getting as much reaction as you like then ask open-ended reaction questions. If you are getting more reaction than you want, your next question could be closed-ended, or in some instances your reaction might be a statement instead of a question. For example, if in the qualification step your prospect told you that quality was extremely important and the benefit you are talking about stresses quality, you wouldn't say, "How important is quality to you?" The prospect has already told you that, so your reaction might be "and you have already told me how important quality is to you."

"WHAT'S THE PRICE?"

As you ask your reaction questions, listen to what your prospect has to say. Each time you receive a lukewarm or negative reaction, that tells you not to stress that feature or benefit again in your presentation. However, the prospect's enthusiastic reactions will help you zero in on the real reasons the prospect has for buying the product or service you sell, and these are the features and benefits you will stress most in the rest of your presentation.

There are dozens of legitimate logical and emotional reasons for a person to buy the product or service you sell. This technique helps you stress only those of most importance to each individual prospect.

After completing your three Feature/Benefit/Reaction sequences, always ask:

- *"Do you have any questions?"*

If the prospect asks a question, answer it. Then again ask, "Do you have any other questions?" Keep asking until your prospect runs out of questions.

Hopefully, somewhere in that list of questions will be this one: "Yes, I have a very important question. What's the price?"

This prospect has already made positive decisions about you, your company, and your product or service. The next Buying Decision, in precise, psychological order, is the price.

It is much better, psychologically, if your prospects bring up the subject of price. Normally that question will come up very naturally during this portion of your sales presentation. If the prospect doesn't ask, you will have to bring up the subject. You might make a statement such as, "I suppose you're wondering about the price?'' Before you quote the price, make sure you summarize the features.

To quote the price, use the following statement:

- *"For your* [summary of features to be included], *the price is* [quote the price]."

Again, these two sentences should be memorized and used word for word. The three sentences you should commit to memory for Step Five: Fill the Need are:

- "[Prospect's name], *there are several important features I'd like to tell you about our* [name of your product or service]."
- *"Do you have any questions?"*
- *"For your* [summary of features to be included], *the price is* [quote the price]."

Read all three sentences over as many times as required to memorize them. When you are ready, write them from memory in the space below.

Here are some examples of how you might use the last two sentences at the end of your Fill the Need step:

Salesperson:	*Do you have any questions?*
Prospect:	*Yes, I do. What is this going to cost me?*
Salesperson:	*For the package we've outlined, including one carrier pick-up and delivery of your product, a direct distribution network across the country, computerized tracking of the transportation service, and computerized dispatch billing, your investment is* [quote the price].

Salesperson: *Do you have any questions?*

Prospect: *What's the price?*

Salesperson: *For your complete grounds maintenance service including weekly mowing, edging, clipping, pruning, weeding, and fertilizing, the price is $200 per month.*

Salesperson: *Do you have any questions?*

Prospect: *What's the cost?*

Salesperson: *For your initial order of five gross of snap fasteners, size MM, in black, the price is $2,900.*

Salesperson: *Do you have any questions?*

Prospect: *What does it cost?*

Salesperson: *For your hot air balloon ride of one hour, in the area you have identified, for four people, the price is $200.*

Salesperson: *Do you have any questions?*

Prospect: *What does this policy cost?*

Salesperson: *For your car insurance on two automobiles, including the liability, collision, and uninsured motorist coverage, the annual premium is $430.*

As I mentioned earlier, when you quote the price, I strongly suggest you don't use the word "cost." For some reason "cost" is a negative impact word. Instead, use words like "investment," "fee," "price," and "annual premium" — *anything* but the word "cost."

REVIEW OF THE TRACK SELLING SYSTEM™ TRANSITION SENTENCES

Let's review the Track Selling System™ phrases from each step you have memorized. They are:

STEP TWO: QUALIFICATION

+ "[Prospect's name], *I would like to tell you about our* [name of your product or service]*; however, in order for me to do the best job I possibly can for you, I need to ask you a couple of questions. Is that all right?*"

Optional statements:

+ "*May I ask what you like most about ...?*"
+ "*Would it be fair to ask what you like least about ...?*"
+ "*Has anything changed?*"

STEP THREE: AGREEMENT ON NEED

+ "*As I understand it, you are looking for something that will* [summary of important information you gathered in Step Two]. *Is that correct?*"

STEP FOUR: SELL THE COMPANY

+ "*May I ask how much information you have about* [your company's name]*?*"
+ "*I understand. Let me quickly cover a couple of things that I think would be important to me if I were in your position.*"

STEP FIVE: FILL THE NEED

+ "[Prospect's name], *there are several important features I'd like to tell you about our* [name of your product or service]. "

"*Do you have any questions?*"

"*For your* [summary of features to be included], *the price is* [quote the price]. "

SAMPLE DIALOGUE FOR STEP FIVE: FILL THE NEED

In the following conversation between salesperson and prospect, notice that Gerri feeds back to Dick three benefits she knows he cares about.

Salesperson: *Dick, there are several, important features I'd like to tell you about our Hawaiian tours. One of the things that sets us apart from other tour companies in Hawaii is that we'll put a tour together that will allow you to choose any of three islands. What that means to you is that you decide how you want to spend your time. That may mean that on a two-week vacation, you spend one and a half weeks on Maui, because you like the coral reefs, or because you like the tours we talk about there, or that you only spend three days on Kauai and maybe a single day and night in Honolulu. It sounds like you and your wife wouldn't mind limiting your time on that island. Wouldn't it be nice to have that personal kind of flexibility, using our planning resources, but letting you pick exactly where you would like to spend the bulk of your time?*

Prospect: *Boy, that sure would be nice. That didn't happen to us in Mexico. They told us how much time we were supposed to spend in each area, and many times our likes didn't match up with theirs. One place that they seemed to be pushing, we felt that we'd seen enough in half of a day.*

Salesperson: *Another feature that I would like to tell you about our tours is that we handle all the transfers from where you get on the plane, to your greeting at each island, to actually driving you to your hotel accommodations and back, to the starting point of each scheduled tour. What that means is that we've worked out an arrangement with the local people on all the islands in Hawaii, so that when you get off that airplane, you*

*go to a specific sign posted and easy to
find, that says, "Happiness Is Hawaii
Tours meet here." You'll be met by a local
tour guide, and a special ceremony will
take place to show you some island greeting customs. I don't want to ruin the
surprise for you, but most of our travelers
are pretty pleased by the way they're
treated. Many say they feel like royalty.
Best of all, you don't have to look at a map
and struggle to find your hotel in a new
location. You'll be delivered right to the
front door. Have you ever had the experience of trying to spend time trying to
figure out whether it's more economical to
go by cab, bus or trust your sense of
direction in a strange rental car?*

Prospect: *Boy, I guess you must have been along on
our Mexican vacation. I looked pretty
foolish to my new bride when I took the
wrong turn to our hotel.*

Salesperson: [Laughs.] *Another thing that I think would
appeal to your family is that on this tour
package, on each island, each family
member, for one price, can pick one
special activity that they can engage in for
no extra charge. What that means is that
your daughter can have a guided tour
around the island if she'd like to see that.
At the same time, your son could be out
there having a scuba-diving lesson. And
you could be having a great time trying to
catch that fish of a lifetime on a deep sea
fishing excursion, while your wife might be
shopping in a local area, with a native tour
leader telling her what some of the neighborhood bargains might be. How would
you like to be able to have each of your
family members choose their own favorite
event without any extra money out of your
pocket?*

Prospect:	*That seems almost too good to be true. I'm sure this is going to cost me a lot.*
Salesperson:	*That's almost the best part of our vacations. The pricing. Do you have any questions?*
Prospect:	*Yeah, I guess the big question. I'm pretty excited about some of the things you've told me, but I still have to keep this within our family budget. What is it going to cost me to do all this?*
Salesperson:	*Dick, for your Hawaiian winter vacation package, that would give you round-trip airfare for your son from Boston, you and your family from Los Angeles, free transfers from airports to all islands, individualized sports and tour activities, and all lodging, your investment for the whole vacation would be $3,500.*

WHEN THE NEED IS FILLED

When you Fill the Need with a Feature/Benefit/Reaction sequence, the prospect sees how your product or service meets his or her needs and is willing to buy. In the next step, Act of Commitment, you will learn to close the sale — and feel good about yourself in the bargain.

THINGS TO REMEMBER

- In Step Five, you help your prospect make positive decisions about your product or service and the price by using the Feature/Benefit/Reaction sequence.
  - Name a *feature* of your product or service.
  - Paint a vivid, word picture of the *benefits* that feature provides.
  - Ask a *reaction* question tied to that benefit.
- A feature is a fact about your product or service: it's size, shape, color, frequency, availability, what it is or does.
- A benefit is something intangible that answers the prospect's question: "What will it do for me?"
- People buy benefits, not features.
- Don't confuse the benefits to the end-user with the benefits to your prospect if they are not the same, for example a retailer. Appeal to your prospect's needs, not necessarily to the consumer's.
- Present three Feature/Benefit/Reaction sequences in increasing order of desirability to the prospect.
- *Sell*, don't tell.
- Use the Feature/Benefit/Reaction sequence to determine your prospect's dominant Buying Motives.

EXERCISES

1. Identify a tangible or intangible feature of your product or service, and the corresponding benefit(s) and Buying Motive(s) that it addresses:

   Feature:

   Benefit(s):

   Buying Motive(s):

   Reaction:

2.   a. Review the written plan you have prepared for each of the previous Track Selling System™ steps.

   b. As you prepare your Step Five plan, you will have to use your imagination. Since this is a one-sided exercise, you will not be able to hear your prospect's reactions to any questions you have asked. Therefore, arbitrarily decide which features and benefits this person is most likely to find important. Compose your Feature/Benefit/Reaction sequences for this prospect accordingly, either on a separate sheet of paper or in the space below.

WRITTEN PLAN FOR STEP FIVE: FILL THE NEED

Write out the transition sentence you memorized:

"[Prospect's name], *there are several important features I would like to tell you about our* [your product or service]."

   a. Feature:

   Benefit:

   Reaction:

   b. Feature:

   Benefit:

   Reaction:

c. Feature:

Benefit:

Reaction:

Fill in the second sentence you memorized:

"Do you have any questions?"

Fill in the third sentence you memorized, dealing with price:

"For your [summarize all features to be included], *your price is* [quote the price]. *"*

3. In the space below, practice summarizing the features of your product or service and quoting the price:

15

STEP SIX: ACT OF COMMITMENT

Now that you have helped your prospect make the first four Buying Decisions positively, your prospect's only remaining decision is when to buy. And when is it? *Now.* Now is the time to ask for the order — to "take up the collection." *Now* is the time to ask for whatever act of commitment you had as your objective for this sales call.

WHEN IS A CLOSE NOT A CLOSE?

It's not actually true that you "close" a sale. This term gives beginning salespeople the impression that once they have closed, they have finished the transaction. Veteran salespeople know that a *close* really means the *opening* — and opportunity — of a new cycle of business.

Maybe that's why the average salesperson finds it difficult to close. When you close, it's not the wind-up of a sale you're facing, but the moment of truth — evidence of how well you opened the presentation in Step One and Step Two, your understanding of the prospect's needs in Step Three, why they should buy from your company in Step Four, and how well you met those needs in Step Five.

If a salesperson would close only *one* time, I think productivity would increase by *fifty percent.* Not long ago I was out in the field with a sales force of ten, and not once did I see any of them even try to close the sale. Most "closes" go something like this:

Salesperson: This phone system has quality parts, well put together.

Prospect: That's good to hear.

Salesperson: It takes a lot of heavy use.

Prospect: Using phones is a big part of our sales and other operations.

Salesperson: What does it do for your business to know that customers won't be cut off at busy times?

Prospect: Good point.

Salesperson: We use state-of-the-art fiber-optics in our transmission lines.

Prospect: Fiber optics? We're impressed with it.

Salesperson: And you know it delivers clear sound, local or long distance. How might static-free phones help your telemarketing people?

Prospect: Quite a bit, especially with prospects.

Salesperson: The system also carries the conference-call feature and multiple line capacity.

Prospect: [Interested.] Uh-huh.

Salesperson: You can set up the conference call yourself, without having to make special arrangements with the phone company.

Prospect: That would be a big help.

Salesperson: This conference-call capacity will save you time for calls in the continental United States.

Prospect: [Very interested.] Uh-huh.

Salesperson: How would this time-saver help you in a crisis?

Prospect: I really don't know if now is the right time to lay out money for a phone system.

Salesperson: Remember, there's a two-year warranty on parts and labor.

Prospect: *I'm not too sure I ought to commit myself now. I'd like to think it over. Give me a call next week.*

Salesperson: *Well, if you feel you're not ready now.*

Prospect: *I'll call you later this week.*

Salesperson: *Sure. No problem. Thanks for your time.*

The bottom line? This salesperson is afraid of asking for the order.

Has that ever happened to you?

CAREFUL GROUNDWORK PAYS OFF IN THE CLOSE

You have come through important steps of the Track Selling System.™

In Step One: Approach, you introduced yourself to your prospect and established warm rapport.

In Step Two: Qualification, you asked the right kinds of questions to help you qualify this prospect as a real, potential buyer. You discovered this person has a need for your product or service, and has the authority and budget to buy. You discovered what is important to this person and the motives most likely to prompt him or her to buy.

In Step Three: Agreement on Need, you presented a capsule summary of the important information you gathered in Step One and Step Two, to clarify and verify the information you received. From this point forward in your presentation, you know that you and your prospect are working in complete accord, toward common goals.

In Step Four: Sell the Company, you supplied your prospect with the information required to help the person decide that your company operates competently and with integrity, and why they should buy from your company.

In Step Five: Fill the Need, you helped your prospect visualize the ways in which your product or service solves their problems or fills their needs.

You have also discovered that the steps of the Track Selling System™ parallel your prospect's Five Buying Decisions, and these decisions are made in precise, psychological order. Again, these decisions relate to the Seven Steps in the following way:

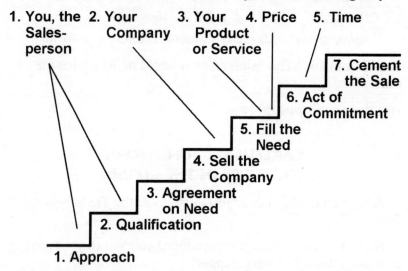

1. You, the Salesperson   2. Your Company   3. Your Product or Service   4. Price   5. Time

7. Cement the Sale

6. Act of Commitment

5. Fill the Need

4. Sell the Company

3. Agreement on Need

2. Qualification

1. Approach

You have laid careful groundwork, moving your prospect smoothly through the preceding Buying Decisions positively. Can you see how closing the sale should be the logical conclusion to your well-given presentation? You will find closing the sale to be no more difficult — and no more important — than any of the preceding Buying Decisions.

The closing technique, if done properly, does the following:

- It increases the odds that you will close in the first or second try.
- It keeps you from creating a high-pressure situation that puts your sale in trouble.
- It gives you the flexibility of trying to close several times without antagonizing the prospect.
- It establishes you as a credible sales representative, whose aim is to serve the buyer.
- It increases your productivity, in both the short and long run.

"TAKING UP THE COLLECTION"

Studies show that 62 percent of all salespeople never ask for the order. Is it any wonder then that eighty percent of those who call themselves salespeople are ineffective and unsuccessful? The people who make up this 62 percent may be timid, unsure of when to ask, or may fear rejection.

I recall a young saleswoman who worked for a Los Angeles fruit juice company, which her father owned. She told me about a salesman who had been calling on her company for over three years, but so far, the company hadn't bought anything from him. Finally she asked her father, "Dad, how come you have never bought anything from that salesman?"

"Because," her father replied, "he's never asked me to buy anything."

Many salespeople don't ask for the order because they (perhaps unconsciously) fear rejection. As long as they don't ask, they can't be rejected. This doesn't make sense, of course, because the prospect is not rejecting the *person* or making a personal attack. The prospect is just saying no. No to the proposal. Maybe even, no ... for now.

No should serve as a challenge — a reason for learning how to persuade the prospect more appropriately.

Kids understand this instinctively. When you tell them no, they know it doesn't mean you don't love them anymore; it just means no. In the following example, my teenage son "sold" me on lending him my car, regardless of my no. He didn't take it personally at all. He just calmly continued to sell me.

"Dad," he said, "I want to borrow your car tonight for graduation."

I said, "No, you're not going to borrow my car. Your own car runs perfectly well. Use that."

He understood that when I said no, it didn't mean I didn't like him or didn't love him anymore. It just meant that he couldn't use my car.

So he said, "Dad, I've got an important date tonight and using your car would really make a great impression."

Again I said, "No. You're not going to use my car. Use your own car."

He understood the generation gap, and he knew that for some reason he was failing to get me to understand his situation as he understood it. So he gave me another opportunity, and asked me a third time.

This time I was adamant. "Ron," I told him, "you have that car home by one o'clock sharp!"

Well, you get the point. If you aren't regularly asking for the order on your calls, just imagine how much more effective you'll be when you begin doing it even *once*.

And *if* you get an objection, " the Track Selling System's™ Guaranteed Close — a precise, step-by-step procedure for asking for the order five times — lets you keep coming back, without creating a tense, pressure-filled situation between you and your prospect. I am not suggesting that you close the sale five times, four times, or even three times because it has been my experience that outstanding sales performers close the sale one time and it's closed. However, by knowing the Guaranteed Close sales procedure and having developed the ability to close the sale five times you will be prepared to deal with objections you encounter. The reason the outstanding sales performers are able to close a sale one time and have it closed is because they do a one hundred percent job in each of the preceding steps. Closing the sale truly is the logical conclusion to a well given presentation. However in the real world that you and I sell in, many times we don't do a one hundred percent job in each of the other steps. Therefore being prepared to deal with objections will pay off.

THE ETHICAL WAY TO CLOSE

The negative image of salespeople comes, in part, from the old techniques of closing. These techniques include the "Impending Event" close: "Buy now, because the price goes up at the first of the month!"; the "Assumptive" close: Assume that the prospect is going to buy, and start filling out the order; or the "Alternative Choice" close: "Do you want the washer and dryer in white or in gold?" Recently I saw a very respected publication offering tips to salespeople on closing the sale and they advised the salesperson to answer a prospect's question as follows:

> Prospect: *Does this appliance come in the heavy duty model?*
>
> Salesperson: *Do you want it if it does?*

These and other old methods of closing a sale were established forty years ago. Can you imagine using those types of closes today, on today's knowledgeable buyers?

In contrast, the *World Class Selling* close serves the prospect. There's no manipulation, just skill. As Sheryl Diller, Account Executive for Volt Technical Service, said, "I have yet to find a close that is as effective and non-threatening as the one you taught me."

ASKING FOR THE ORDER

THE FIRST CLOSE

You will have the opportunity to close five times, if needed, but the first time is so simple you may be surprised.

The following statement will help you greatly. Again, I recommend that you use this precise wording to achieve maximum effectiveness and success.

- *"If we can* [summary of action to be taken], *can you think of any reason why we shouldn't* [summary of desired act of commitment]*?"*

Such simple words: "If we can ... can you think of any reason why we shouldn't ...?" And just like that, you have effectively asked for the order or act of commitment.

I don't think you'll find a softer sell or a more low-pressure close anywhere. This close will fit comfortably for you no matter what your own personality or the varied personalities of your prospects. It will fit comfortably for you no matter what product or service you sell. It will fit comfortably for you whether you are asking for the actual order or another act of commitment — any "next step" in the procedure that will lead to your successful sale somewhere down the road.

Some sample closing questions might be:

- *"If we can* guarantee delivery by the 15th, *can you think of any reason why we shouldn't* go ahead?"

- *"If we can* schedule the training of your technical people next week, *can you think of any reason why we shouldn't* order the equipment?"

- *"If we can* write your policy to be effective on Friday noon, *can you think of any reason why we shouldn't* get your fleet protection in place for you?"

These sample closing questions are short, simple, direct requests for the order. Yet at the same time, they exert almost no pressure.

SUMMARIZING FUTURE ACTION

After the words, "If we can ... ," you give a summary of the action to be taken. In the examples above, the summaries promised delivery by a specific date, personnel training at a definite time, and a specific date on which the insurance coverage would take effect.

Your summary of action to be taken might be the promise of a specific price, inclusion of specific components, a promise of definite follow-up service, and so on.

After the words, "... can you think of any reason why we shouldn't ...?" you've made your direct request for the act of commitment. You have asked the prospect to go ahead, order the equipment, get the fleet protection in place, and so on.

In short, you have asked your prospect to make a positive decision to buy or act *now*. You have "taken up the collection."

This question is not meant to imply that your product or service will take care of your prospect's needs. You have already said that in Step Five: Fill the Need. The philosophy behind the closing question is, *"If we will do business with you, will you do business with us?"*

ASKING FOR AN ACT OF COMMITMENT

This closing question is equally effective when your goal on a sales call is not to make a sale, but rather to get an act of commitment for the next step that will lead to a sale at a later date. For example:

- *"If we can* coordinate schedules, *can you think of any reason why we shouldn't* set up a demonstration on Thursday?"
- *"If we can* get together with your technical people to get the specs on this, *can you think of any reason why we shouldn't* put together a proposal?"
- *"If we can* get loan approval, *can you think of any reason why we shouldn't* meet again next week to get the papers ready for escrow?"

Naturally, you wouldn't commit to a date or time that doesn't fit with your company's ability to deliver. Whatever fits with your schedule of requirements is what you use.

What Not to Say

What makes the *exact* wording of this closing question — "If we can ... can you think of any reason why we shouldn't ... ?" — so effective?

First, be aware of words and phrases that are *not* a part of this request for the order. For example, I do *not* recommend that you use words like *now, today, this afternoon,* or *right away.* Words and phrases that urge direct action take your close out of the realm of a simple, low-key, low-pressure request for a decision, and into the realm of high pressure selling.

As a professional salesperson, you use persuasion, not pressure. Your request *implies* that immediate action will be taken, *but no actual words to that effect are used.*

Here are examples of high-pressure, low-response closes — of what *not* to do:

- " ... can you think of any reason why we shouldn't finish the paperwork now?"
- " ... can you think of any reason why we shouldn't get this service started for you immediately?"
- " ... can you think of any reason why we shouldn't get this equipment ordered right away?"

Now, notice how easy, conversational, and non-threatening —
low pressure — the same questions are without the "loaded"
words:

- " ... can you think of any reason why we shouldn't
  finish the paperwork?"
- " ... can you think of any reason why we shouldn't get
  this service started for you?"
- " ... can you think of any reason why we shouldn't get
  this equipment ordered?"

Another negative-impact word to avoid is "sign." We have all
heard the admonition, "Never sign anything," and so have your
prospects. The words "sign" has negative connotations. Therefore, whenever your sale requires your prospect's signature, say
anything *but* "Please sign here." Instead, say:

- "Will you write your name here?"
- "Will you initial this, please?"
- "Would you write your OK here?"
- "May I have your autograph here?"

The Psychology of the
Track Selling System™ Close

Now that we have discussed what the Track Selling System™
close *doesn't* say, let's explore what is *does* say. Notice the
word "we." "We" is used to reinforce the concept that you
and your prospect are working as a team. You and your prospect are not adversaries; you are working together to achieve
common goals.

Notice how odd it would sound — considering that you and
your prospect had been building rapport, working together to
define and solve his or her needs or problems — if you said:

- "If I can deliver this equipment on Monday, can you
  think of any reason why you shouldn't go ahead?"

"We" also means that both you and your company have to
deliver.

Next, the word "think" is important. It focuses the prospect on
his or her own thinking, rather than on objections.

Last is the most important aspect of this question: the fact that it is a *negative question*. The question, "If we can ... can you think of any reason why we shouldn't ...?" does not ask them to *buy*; it asks them if they can think of a reason *not* to buy. If you have done an effective job in Step One through Step Five, helping your prospect make each of those Buying Decisions positively, the answer you can expect to hear is no.

Now this is a subtle and extremely effective piece of strategy. Why? Because psychologically, it is easier for most people to say no than yes. *When they say no, it means they have just bought.*

However, there is an even subtler, more important reason why it is easier for your prospects to say no to you. Most likely, seventy-five percent of the salespeople they have encountered in the past have been incompetent and ineffective. Your prospects, therefore, are both experienced in and comfortable with saying no to salespeople. Thus, you give them a simple invitation to say what they are psychologically most comfortable saying.

When your prospects say no to you, however, you've made your sale. Making the sale is the logical conclusion of your ability to parallel or "track" your prospects' Buying Decisions step by step. Making the sale is also the result of your belief in the quality of your product or service, your belief that your prospects will be better off after making the purchase, and your conviction that your product or service is of more value to your prospect than the money you make from the sale. Throughout the sales procedure, you have conducted yourself with integrity every step of the way. At all times you have appealed to your prospects to act in their best interests and for *their* reasons.

So why have you made the sale? Because you have offered your prospects genuine, beneficial service.

THE DISCOVERY OF THE FIRST CLOSE

I would like to tell you how I discovered this closing process. One afternoon in my early days in the insurance business, I was calling on a couple in Pasadena with my mentor, Tiny Lint. At that time I closed a sale like most insurance salespeople I knew; I got the application out early and started filling it out so I wouldn't frighten the prospect later on, when it came time to ask for the order.

Tiny and I presented a health plan to the couple, and when the husband asked his wife to get the names and addresses of their doctors, I assumed we were making the sale and completed the application.

However, I was surprised to find out that when I asked the husband to sign the application, he had an objection.

"I don't want it.".

Let me tell you, that is a tough objection to overcome. I used all the best sales techniques I knew at the time, trying one thing after another, but nothing overcame the husband's repeated assertion, "I don't want it." Obviously, I didn't make the sale.

Later, as Tiny and I analyzed what went wrong, he suddenly observed, "We're making a one-shot close. We're either closing the sale, or the sale is lost for good." It was a win/lose, yes/no, one-shot deal. I agreed that once I had placed the application in front of the prospect and asked for a signature, regardless of whatever fast-talking "techniques" I used, if the prospect wasn't ready to buy I wouldn't close the sale. We needed a technique to keep the possibility of the sale open when the prospect raised an objection.

After going over and over this problem in my mind, I finally came up with this close: "If you can qualify for this plan, can you think of any reason why you shouldn't have this protection?"

Tiny approved. "Roy, word for word, it will work."

We left the coffee shop for our next appointment: an engineer from The Jet Propulsion Laboratory in Pasadena. I presented a supplemental health insurance program to the prospect. The prospect asked the amount of the premium. I quoted the premium and used the closing statement for the first time: "If you can qualify for this plan, can you think of any reason why you shouldn't have this protection?"

"No," the prospect answered. He had just bought.

It worked the first time it was used, and it has worked thousands of times since then. This closing statement, or a variation of it, sells everything imaginable — from vacations to computers, airline reservations to spark plugs, lasers to grain bins — and it will work for you.

Of course your prospect will not always say no or buy right away. However, your skill as a professional salesperson includes your balanced, low-pressure response to any objections, stalls or delaying tactics. Later on in this chapter, you will learn to handle objections respectfully and effectively, and learn how to close up to four more times, if need be.

A WORD ABOUT HIGH-PRESSURE TACTICS

Several years ago, I was consulting for a large, landscaping firm in San Diego. This company used a two-call sales cycle. In the first call, the salesperson completed the Approach, Qualification, and Agreement on Need steps, and measured the prospects property. This information was then used to design a landscaping proposal for the prospect.

One day I accompanied a 21-year-old salesperson on his second sales call, where he intended to present his company's proposal. He had been in sales for just six months. He had started as a landscape worker three years earlier, was then promoted to foreman, and later advanced to sales. "My greatest problem in selling," he told me, "is closing the sale." I assumed he meant, like most salespeople, he was afraid to ask for the order.

We entered the prospects' home, and before long it became clear that he had done an outstanding job on his first call. The prospects were a young couple, and they hit it off beautifully. After re-establishing rapport, he suggested that the couple move to the dining room table so that he could present the proposal. He again did an outstanding job. He painted effective word pictures, explaining to the wife how she could walk on the stepping stones around the side of her home onto the back patio, partially covered by a canopy. He described the barbecue area in the left-hand corner of the patio and the flower bed down by the right-hand wall. She could see herself standing there, in the middle of all that beauty.

About this time the husband asked, "How much is this?"

"About fifty-seven hundred dollars," the salesperson told him.

"That's not bad," said the husband, "if you do all the things that you say you'll do. Not bad at all. Let me think it over."

"What is there to think over?" asked the young man. "Do the front now, the back later."

"No, it's a lot of money. I want to make sure it's the right decision."

"There must be something I haven't explained," persisted the young man. "Something you don't understand. Otherwise, we could go ahead and get it started now."

"No," the husband repeated, "I made the decision a long time ago that I just don't buy anything on the first call. I want to talk it over with my wife. We'll let you know."

Clearly, the conversation was escalating into a high-pressure situation. The wife rose from the table, walked to the kitchen and looked for something to do ... to get away from the pressure and discomfort of the situation.

The young man said to her, "Do you mind coming back in here and sitting down until I finish this presentation?"

I couldn't believe it! I had thought this young fellow was *afraid* to ask people to buy. If he asked these people to buy one time, he asked them six or seven times. The situation got worse and worse. He may have "won the argument," but he certainly lost the sale.

When we left that sales call, I advised him: "You don't have any problems in closing. You just don't know *how* to close. You wait until we show you how to close the sale," I assured him, "and you'll be dynamite."

Well, today that young man *is* dynamite. Ninety days after he trained with us, he became the top producer in the company.

SAMPLE DIALOGUE FOR
STEP SIX: ACT OF COMMITMENT

Note that Gerri wastes no words and asks the act-of-commitment question based on her knowledge of exactly what Dick wants for his vacation.

Salesperson: *If we can book the flights from Los Angeles and Boston on December 18th, can you think of any reason why we shouldn't send the Jacobson family on a two week Hawaiian vacation, that could be the beginning of a tradition?*

Prospect: *No, I can't. Go ahead and make reservations. I can't wait to tell my wife and kids.*

Salesperson: *Great. Let's figure out the best way to pay for it. Which would you prefer: American Express, MasterCard, or one of our payment plans that can be deferred over three months, with a little bit of extra interest?*

Prospect: *Like I said, we have that money in our savings budget. I'd like to go ahead and put in on American Express, and then pay it in one lump sum when the bill comes in.*

HANDLING OBJECTIONS

Notice how Gerri, the salesperson, expertly takes her prospect through the Track Selling System™ ... and Dick has just bought.

In the real world, things don't always happen so logically. What if Dick had said yes, raised objections, or put off the decision? Despite your careful groundwork, when you ask: "If we can deliver the product or service to suit your needs, can you think of any reason why we shouldn't go ahead?", your prospect might actually answer *yes*.

"Yes," your prospect might say, "I can think of reasons why we shouldn't. I want to think it over ... Your price is too high ... I want to get another bid ... I'm not sure if your company really can do what you're telling me it can."

A Case of the FUDs

What is going on here? The prospect is experiencing the "FUDs": Fear, Uncertainty, and Doubt.

However, if you listen carefully and really think about what your prospect is saying, you will uncover some truly valuable information that will enable you to get an act of commitment in the long run.

> Prospect: Well ... I've been buying from Sally Jones for the past five years, and in all honesty, I'm really hesitant to make a change.

If you listen, you'll hear exactly what this person has FUDs about: *you, the salesperson.*

> Prospect: Frankly, I never heard of your company until you walked through that door. What you're telling me really sounds great, but this is an important purchase, and I'd really like to do some more investigating before I make my decision.

What does this person have FUDs about? *Your company.*

> Prospect: Hey, this machinery really does a great job, but I'm a little concerned about all those push buttons. Sure, it's convenient, but are all those mechanisms going to function well, or is this thing going to cause me headaches with repairs?

This person has FUDs about *your product.*

> Prospect: The price is too high.

These FUDs are about *the price.*

> Prospect: I want to think it over.

These FUDs are about time *to buy.*

As you can see, fears, uncertainties, and doubts can usually be traced directly back to one or more of the Five Buying Decisions. Connecting the objection with a Buying Decision tells you that the prospect did not make that Buying Decision positively. The prospects' FUDs serve as your "report card," pinpointing the areas of your presentation that were not completely effective and the Buying Decisions that have not yet been made positively.

As a professional salesperson, you need not be deterred by FUDs. Instead, use them to improve your techniques. They can alert you to areas you will need to handle more effectively on your future sales calls. FUDs show you exactly where your presentation was weak. When your prospects express FUDs, what they're really saying is: "You haven't convinced me to buy."

ACKNOWLEDGING THE OBJECTION

This awareness, in itself, doesn't help you solve your current problem — to help that prospect buy or act now — and your prospect is stalling on that decision.

I have been promising that you will learn a precise, step-by-step procedure that covers all points in the sales process and leaves nothing to chance. Overcoming objections is no exception to that promise.

You may find our philosophy totally different from any other way of handling objections. In fact, you may find it downright startling. Here is how simple it is:

No matter what objection a prospect raises, respond with one of the following statements:

- "I see."
- "I understand."
- "I can appreciate that."

You acknowledge the objection — and nothing more.

How is this different from how most salespeople handle objections? Most scenarios would go like this:

Prospect:	*I want to talk it over with Bill.*
Salesperson:	*What do you mean, you want to talk it over with Bill? I've told you everything you need to know. What's Bill going to tell you that you don't already know?*

Prospect:	*I want to shop around.*
Salesperson:	*You've got to be kidding. With as little as you know about this product or service, you'd be dangerous out there shopping around.*

In short, most salespeople don't *handle* objections. They *react* to them by arguing.

You, however, are a professional. You don't react, you *act*.

Act, Don't React

A negative response will do nothing for the success of your sale. As a professional salesperson, you've worked hard throughout the Seven Steps of the Track Selling System™ to establish genuine, warm rapport. You've demonstrated your integrity and good judgment. You've worked hard to establish yourself as a friend, with genuine concern for your prospect's problems and needs. You've asked the right kinds of questions to uncover your prospect's concerns, problems and goals. You've worked hard to offer solutions that truly solve those problems or fill those needs. You've kept yourself in complete alignment with your prospect — seeing the situation through the other person's eyes — and offered real, beneficial service.

If you now react to objections by arguing, you will destroy the groundwork you have worked so hard to establish. Arguing puts your prospect on the defensive, and probably destroys all chances for making the sale.

- "I see."
- "I understand."
- "I can appreciate that."

What will this simple acknowledgment do for you? It will complete the Communication Cycle.

Conversation is like a game of catch. One person tosses a verbal thought to someone else. The thought is absorbed, and another thought is tossed back. The lines of communication remain open. This free exchange of verbal thoughts is called the Communication Cycle.

After registering an objection, your prospect is waiting for what you will do or say next. Your prospect is listening with an open mind. That's the whole secret. You can deal with an *open* mind.

What happens if you try to meet that objection head on, by arguing? "What do you mean you've got to talk to someone else? Heck, we spent six full days talking about this thing. You know everything you need to know right now." Click! The prospect's mind turns off. There's no more communication.

"What do you mean, 'The price is too high'? We've got the best equipment in the world." Click! No more communication.

Many times, the objections your prospect will raise aren't even logical. You couldn't argue with them, if you wanted to. "I want to think it over." How logical is that? Do you suppose that if you said "Okay" and walked out, your prospect would sit in the office, dim the lights, hold the phone calls, put his chin in his hands, and sit there thinking it over? You know better. There's no way you could argue that point with your prospect, even if you wanted to.

Many times, salespeople do try to overcome objections, however illogical, by arguing with their prospects. They point out dozens of reasons why those objections aren't valid. Then the prospect goes on the defensive, giving more and more reasons to support the objection. The salesperson continues to react by giving more and more reasons why the objection is invalid. Some salespeople are pretty glib talkers, and win the argument, but lose the sale.

At this point, both salesperson and prospect are tossing verbal thoughts faster and more heatedly, but those thoughts are not being *caught*. Neither one is really listening to what the other is saying. The Communication Cycle is destroyed.

There's a better way of dealing with objections than hitting them head-on. *Act*, rather than *react*. Saying, "I see," "I understand," or "I can appreciate that" keeps the lines of communications open and demonstrates that you've caught the conversation ball. You've acknowledged that person's concern, and your response tells your prospect that you remain in complete alignment. The Communication Cycle has been completed, allowing a free exchange of ideas to continue.

WHEN AN OBJECTION ISN'T REALLY AN OBJECTION

When the prospect says yes instead of no, listen carefully — he or she may be making a statement or asking a question rather than giving you an objection.

> Prospect: *Can you deliver to me by the first of the month?*

This isn't an objection — it's a question. What do you do? Work out a delivery schedule that fits.

What if the prospect says:

> *Prospect:* $ _____ *is a lot of money!*

This, too, is not an objection. It's simply a statement.

> *Salesperson:* *I can appreciate that. Yes, it is a lot of money, but not nearly as much as you'd be losing with a machine with slower output.*

In fact, the odds are that your prospect didn't even *mean* the objection in the first place.

Did you ever voice objections you didn't really mean? Did you ever walk into a department store, fully intending to make a purchase, but when the clerk approached and said, "May I help you?" you blurt out, "No thanks, I'm just looking."?

The clerk realized what was going on and made a quick retreat, leaving you to shop in privacy. Suppose that clerk *hadn't* retreated? Suppose he or she had said, "What do you mean, you're just looking? You must have intended to buy something or you wouldn't have come in here. What do you want? A jacket? A sweater? You must want *something*!"

How would you react? In all probability, you'd exit that store in a hurry. You really *do* want to buy, but you really *don't* want to be pressured.

Well, your prospects are no different from you. After your first attempt to close the sale, if your prospect voices an objection, simply acknowledge the objection and nothing more. Act, don't react. In all probability, the prospect didn't even mean the objection.

A WINNING TEAM

When you acknowledge the objection, you again demonstrate your sensitivity to the prospect's problems or needs. You are seeing the situation through the other person's eyes. You and your prospect are not combatants. You are a team, working together to arrive at a solution that will be in your prospect's best interest.

When you do this, your prospect's face will register a whole new perception of you. "Here, finally, is a salesperson who really *is* different," your prospect will likely think. "A salesper-

son who really *is* a professional. Who really *does* understand."
People buy your product or service not so much because they
understand it as because they feel *you* understand *them*.

"What about the objection? Nothing at all has been done to
overcome it."

I understand.

When you say "I see," "I understand," or "I can appreciate
that," you *are* taking the first step toward handling objections
by acknowledging them. When your prospects voice objections,
they are not rejecting you. They may not even be rejecting the
product or service you sell. They may, in fact, be planning to
buy your product or service. All they are saying to you is:
"You haven't convinced me to buy. I still have FUDs."

So acknowledge those objections. Let your prospects know you
empathize with their concerns. Then you'll get back to the job
of selling, by giving the prospect additional reasons to decide to
buy your product or service.

And that constitutes the second close.

THE SECOND CLOSE

The second close goes like this:
1. Acknowledge the objection.
2. Re-establish your areas of agreement.
3. Add a new Feature/Benefit/Reaction sequence.
4. Ask for the order again.

1. Acknowledge the Objection:

"I can appreciate that."

Notice that your second close begins by handling the prospect's
objection: by *acknowledging* it. You don't meet the objection
head-on or try to persuade the prospect the objection is ill-
founded. You simply acknowledge the objection — nothing
more.

For example, if the prospect says: "I want to think it over,"
your response could be: "I see." If the prospect says: "Your

price is too high," your response could be: "I understand." If the prospect says: "I want to shop around," your response could be: "I can appreciate that." In over 35 years of selling, these three phrases are the only ones I have found that work.

2. RE-ESTABLISH YOUR AREAS OF AGREEMENT:

After acknowledging the objection, re-establish your areas of agreement. Give another Feature/Benefit/Reaction sequence to provide the prospect with more reasons to buy or act now — more answers to the unasked question: "What will it do for me?"

> Salesperson: *Bob, we agreed that you like the compact size of this equipment. You like the fact that it has the accurate, foamless filling feature. We also agreed you liked the saniflow filter that's going to keep the Department of Health off your back.*

3. ADD A NEW FEATURE/BENEFIT/REACTION SEQUENCE:

> Feature: *In addition, this equipment has forty percent fewer moving parts than any other equipment of it's kind on the market today.*

> Benefit: *This fact is going to increase your cash flow. You won't have to keep as many spare parts in inventory. You will have lower maintenance costs and far less downtime with this equipment.*

> Reaction: *How would you like to take that extra money you've been spending on spare parts and maintenance, and use it to refurbish and upgrade some of your other equipment?*

4. ASK FOR THE ORDER AGAIN:

People buy for their own unique reasons. In the second close, give the prospect another reason to buy or act now — another way your product or service solves the problem or fills the need. Note that you are still appealing to the prospects to buy for *their* reasons, not yours.

Ask them for the order again exactly as you did before:

- *"If we can* schedule delivery and installation of the equipment by the end of the month, *can you think of any reason why we shouldn't* go ahead?"

You might feel strange using that same wording, "If we can ... can you think of any reason why we shouldn't ...?" a second time. However, studies show that people remember 77 percent of what they see and only fourteen percent of what they hear. It's not likely that the prospect will think you're repeating yourself when there's only a fourteen percent chance the person heard you the first time.

Here's another statistic — one you've heard before: Sixty-two percent of salespeople never ask for the order *once*. At this point in *your* sales procedure you've asked for the order not once but *twice*. How much do you think this fact alone will affect your success in selling?

Salesperson:	*If we can schedule delivery of the XYZ computer by the end of the month, can you think of any reason why we shouldn't set it up?*
Prospect:	*Sounds good. I'd like to think it over. Maybe look at a couple more companies.*
Salesperson:	*I can appreciate that. As we agreed, you liked the power of the XYZ computer, its built-in hard disk and expansion connector.* [Repeat of features] *Now, in addition, XYZ has a large, easy to view black-on-white video screen.* [New feature] *Your employees can spend long hours at their PC without having to worry about eyestrain and fatigue.* [New benefit] *Do you think the large, easy-to-view XYZ computer could increase the work output in your office?* [New reaction question]
Prospect:	*It sure would add to our productivity.*
Salesperson:	*If we can schedule delivery of the XYZ computer by the end of the month, can you*

> *think of any reason why we shouldn't set it*
> *up?* [Second close]
>
> Prospect: *No, let's go ahead.*

In both your first and second closes, you name honest, accurate features of your product or service, and you paint vivid, word pictures of those honest, accurate benefits. Then you ask for the order by saying: "If we can ... can you think of any reason why we shouldn't ...?"

No matter what your personality, would this procedure make you feel uncomfortable? Would it make your prospect feel uncomfortable? We don't think you'll find a softer or more ethical closing procedure anywhere.

THE SECOND OBJECTION

What happens if the prospect objects to your second close? Many times he or she doesn't reveal the real reason for holding back. In fact, the prospect may not even recall what he or she said. Prospects tend to say the first things that come to mind: "Sounds good," "I'd like to think it over," "The price is too high," or "I want to shop around." Some buyers are trained to say no to your first offer, regardless of what it is. Your objective is to get to the *real* objection. Only then can you speak to it and, thus, serve the prospect's real needs.

Fortunately, you get another chance to do that now.

THE THIRD CLOSE

With the old way of closing, many salespeople would be three-quarters of the way out the door by this point. "What? Risk rejection a *third* time? How far can I push this prospect, anyway? You've got to be kidding!"

World Class Selling offers you not just a guaranteed procedure, but a philosophy you can count on:

* The purpose of making your sales call is to be of service to the customer.

When you believe this philosophy, and you truly believe your product or service solves this prospect's problems or fills his or her needs — your prospect will be better off after making this purchase than before — and your product or service is of more value to this prospect than the money he or she is paying.

Then continue to try to persuade your prospect to buy or act now.

The procedure for your third close is:

1. Acknowledge the objection.
2. Re-establish your areas of agreement.
3. Uncover the real objection.
4. Handle the objection.
5. Optionally, add a new Feature/Benefit/Reaction sequence.
6. Ask for the order again.

1. ACKNOWLEDGE THE OBJECTION

You have already learned the three statements you can use to acknowledge the objection, no matter what the objection might be:

- "I see."
- "I understand."
- "I can appreciate that."

2. RE-ESTABLISH YOUR AREAS OF AGREEMENT

You have also learned how to re-establish your areas of agreement. You simply say:

- "[Prospect's name], we agreed you liked this feature ... this feature ... and this feature."

3. UNCOVER THE REAL OBJECTION

In your first and second close, you simply acknowledged any objections that were raised. You knew those objections might not be real ones and there's no point in making your prospects defend objections they may not really mean in the first place.

Because your prospect is still not yet convinced to buy, now it is time to uncover what the real objection might be.

Here's how you do it. Ask the prospect:

- "[Prospect's name], there must be something you don't like. Would you mind telling me what it is?"

This question is dynamite! It has worked for successful sales-people throughout the world.

What is it like for a prospect to be asked this question? One prospect described the effect like this: "When the salesperson asked me that, it was almost as if the person had gotten up out of his chair and had come around the desk to sit beside me. The two of us worked together to arrive at a solution."

This statement offers two benefits. This first is that it allows you to demonstrate your sensitivity and understanding. It shows you are seeing the situation through your prospect's eyes, and you remain in complete alignment with the person's problems and needs. Remember, your prospects buy your product or service not so much because they understand *it* but because they feel *you* understand *them*.

The second benefit is: It will uncover your prospect's real objection to buying or acting now.

Now that you've got the real objection out in the open, you're going to have to *deal* with it.

4. HANDLE THE OBJECTION

In your first close, your prospect's objection might have been: "Your price is too high." In your second close, the prospect might have voiced the same objection. By the third close, the prospect's response might be: "Hey, I've told you twice already: The price is too high!"

Remember: People don't buy price; they buy *value*.

The *third* objection should be an indication that your prospect is interested, but that he or she does not see the *value* of your product or service. He or she has FUDs about your price.

The objection you uncover in this third attempt to close the sale may be exactly the same as before. Or it may be totally different — a concern you were completely unaware of. Whatever the objection, you'll know it is probably genuine.

This third close is dynamite!

Your first close was so soft your prospects might not have even realized that you asked them to buy. When you came back and asked for the order the second time, do you suppose they *knew* you were asking for that order?

You'd better believe it.

It may have come as a surprise to them. For perhaps the first time ever, here they were face to face with a salesperson who actually asked for the order.

Yet, because of their past experiences and their own expectations, they may feel a little pressure at being asked to buy. That's why the third close is dynamite. It takes them totally off the defensive. In the third close, you might say:

- "Tom, we've talked about a lot of things you liked about this equipment. You liked the compactness, the accuracy of the filter, the fact that is has 40 percent less moving parts ... a lot of things you really liked. *There must be something you don't like. Would you mind telling me what it is?*"

Again, this sentence is so important that you should memorize it and write it below:

Notice, you're not arguing. You're not putting the prospect on the defensive. If anything, you're giving the prospect the opportunity to tell you exactly what's on his or her mind. Then you can deal with it, to the best of your ability, and turn the situation around.

WHEN YOU CAN'T OVERCOME THE OBJECTION: Now, this doesn't mean you're going to be successful one hundred percent of the time. There's a real world out there, and in the real world you're going to run into some objections you *can't* overcome.

Suppose that you ask for the order the first time, and the prospect says:

> *Prospect:*   *It's company policy that I get three bids*
> *before making a purchase of this size.*

Okay. Maybe that's the real objection ... and maybe it's not. So
you test it with your second close. And the prospect says:

> *Prospect:*   *I really like your product or service, but I*
> *do have to get two more bids. It's company*
> *policy.*

You've heard that same objection twice, so you're pretty sure
it's the real one.

Give it one more test — the *third* close:

> *Salesperson:*   *We agreed that you liked the fact that this*
> *equipment is going to cut your testing*
> *costs, give you more accurate results and*
> *free your employees for more creative*
> *tasks. There must be something you don't*
> *like. Would you mind telling me what it is?*

What does your prospect say?

> *Prospect:*   *There's nothing at all that I don't like*
> *about the equipment, but it's company*
> *policy that I get three bids, and I can't*
> *change that.*

You know that is probably the *real* objection. How are you
going to handle it? In all honesty, there's nothing you *can* do.
It's company policy, and you are not going to change that.

What you *can* change is your objective for that sales call. It's
going to be impossible for you to make the sale now, so go
after the act of commitment. You might say:

> *Salesperson:*   *I understand. Ms. Prospect, when are you*
> *going to get the other bids?*
>
> *Prospect:*   *This Wednesday.*
>
> *Salesperson:*   *I see. If we can schedule a meeting on*
> *Thursday, after you've gotten the other*
> *bids, can you think of any reason why we*
> *shouldn't get together to talk about it*
> *then?*

You've gotten the act of commitment.

What if your prospect says to you: "Hey, I've told you three times already. I don't want your product or service! There's the door. If you're not out of here in two minutes, I'm going to call security!" I strongly suggest you get through the door in less than two minutes.

Don't shut that door of opportunity behind you, though. You might say: "Doug, I'm really sorry I couldn't help you. We really do have a solution for your problem. I'd like to leave my card, and if you have any questions or if anything changes, please give me a call. I'm sorry I couldn't be of service to you." And leave.

That kind of situation isn't very likely to happen, because you've taken the time to establish warm rapport. If it does, keep in mind why you've made the sales call: to be of service. It's not going to change *your* life if the prospect doesn't buy your product or service, but it might change his or hers. If you sincerely believe that, you're going to hang in there and do everything possible to help your prospects make their buying decision positively.

Most of the time when you get an objection, you'll find you *can* do something to turn the situation around. Let's suppose that you've asked for the order three times. And every time, the prospect has said, "Your price is too high." That's the kind of situation you *can* turn around ... by getting in there and doing a good job of selling. People don't buy price; they buy value. So show your prospect more ways in which your product or service represents good value, and turn the sale around.

In this chapter, you'll learn to keep on selling ... to ask for the order a total of five times, if necessary.

That doesn't mean I expect you to close five times on every sales call. I'm firmly convinced that if you close only twice, you'll be amazed at your increase in productivity. If you then use the third close, discover the real objection and deal with it, your productivity will zoom.

You won't offend the prospect by asking for the order three times. Not when you ask:

- "If we can ... can you think of any reason why we shouldn't ...?"

Who could take offense with that? Or with the question:

◆ "There must be something you *don't* like. Would you mind telling me what it is?"

5. ADD AN OPTIONAL FEATURE/BENEFIT/REACTION SEQUENCE

As part of handling the prospect's genuine objection, you can add a new Feature/Benefit/Reaction sequence to move the prospect in a positive direction. You do this to emphasize the value of your product or service — to answer your prospect's unasked question: "What will it do for me?"

Because you know the prospect's real objections, you will find it easy to focus the benefits in the precise area where your prospect's real objections lie.

Salesperson:	*There must be something you don't like. Would you mind telling me what it is?*
Prospect:	*Well, to be honest, I needed a freight quote once and I called your company. I was told to talk to a Mr. Griddle, but he never called me back. Nothing! I don't want to deal with that kind of person.*
Salesperson:	*I understand. He is no longer with us. We agree entirely with you, but the new man in this area has been in the business for fifteen years and is a true professional. The problem simply no longer exists. Our company protects you from all the daily risks you face in your business.* [New feature] *You need never again experience unexpected losses.* [New benefit] *How would it feel to know that that whole area of responsibility is something you don't have to think about again?* [New reaction]

6. ASK FOR THE ORDER AGAIN

You've pointed out to your prospect new ways in which your product or service solves the problem or fills the need. You've supplied your prospect with new reasons to buy or act now.

Now it is time to ask for the order the third time.

This time, however, make the request short and to the point. For example:

- "Let's set it up."
- "Let's get started."
- "How about letting me set this up for you?"

THE FOURTH CLOSE

For the fourth close, this is the procedure:

1. Acknowledge the objection.
2. Cite the penalty for not buying or acting now.
3. Optionally, add a new Feature/Benefit/Reaction sequence.
4. Ask for the order again.

1. ACKNOWLEDGE THE OBJECTION

By now, you're getting to be an old hand at acknowledging those objections:

- "I see."
- "I understand."
- "I can appreciate that."

2. CITE THE PENALTY FOR NOT BUYING OR ACTING NOW

This is the new step. To do it, paint a vivid, accurate, word picture of the negative results that may occur if this prospect does not make a positive buying decision now.

This doesn't mean being the bearer of bad news. Since you know your prospects will be better off after making the purchase, let them know you're just as seriously concerned about their success as they are. You're still appealing to your prospects to buy for *their* reasons and in their own best interests.

For example, you might say:

- "Mr. Prospect, as I understand it, it's a matter of examining the information for a few days. So the only

> thing that will happen between now and the time you commit is that it will cost you in efficiency, quality and service. That doesn't make sense, does it? Let's set it up."

Or you might say:

> ♦ "Ms. Smith, your company is manufacturing a superb product, but you've mentioned the serious problems you're having moving your product off the shelf. Ms. Smith, we've worked together to design a marketing program that will boost your sales by at least ten percent, and every day you delay the decision to put this program into action you're taking valuable profits from your company's bottom line."

Or you might say:

> ♦ "Jack, your competitor, LMN Company, changed to this system six months ago, and they've cut their operating costs by eight percent. Can you continue to remain competitive when they can produce these goods at a lower cost than you?"

These are not scare tactics. These are your honest appraisals of the damage that can occur if the prospect does not take advantage of the benefits your product or service provides.

3. ADD A NEW FEATURE/BENEFIT/REACTION SEQUENCE, IF DESIRED

Optionally, you may now present a new Feature/Benefit/Reaction sequence, giving your prospect another good, sound reason to buy or act now.

If that's not comfortable for you or not appropriate in this particular situation with this particular prospect, simple move directly into your fourth request for the order.

4. ASK FOR THE ORDER

This fourth request for the order should be short and to the point:

> ♦ "Let's set it up."
> ♦ "How about it?"

+ "Let's do it."

Do you think your prospect will be upset by your persistence? Will this person feel that you are aggressive or offensive?

Not in the least. Every step of the way, you have shown sensitivity and understanding of this prospect's problems and needs. You and your prospect have been functioning as a team, each striving to achieve the same goals. You have exerted almost no pressure at all. How could anyone take offense with that?

THE FIFTH CLOSE

In the fifth close, acknowledge the prospect's objection, and try something creatively different. Use your imagination — the key to making it happen.

THE COMPROMISE

You might offer a compromise:

+ "How about trying this product or service in just one of your stores? See for yourself how well this works for you, and then make your decision."

THE DISCOUNT

You might offer a reduced price:

+ "Bob, I just can't bring myself to walk out of here without getting your problem solved. How would you feel about placing your first order at a 20 percent discounted price?"

THE FREE TRIAL

You might suggest a free trial period:

+ "Jean, how would you feel about trying this product or service free for a week, and then making your decision?"

THE ZANY CLOSE

We would hope, however, that you'll come up with something far more creative, unexpected, unique, and downright zany. Perhaps something like this:

- "Why do you think I carry this violin case around?"

Here's how one seasoned salesperson did the fifth close:

Tom was selling for a clothing manufacturer. He made his annual visit to Harry, his buyer in New York, who represented a major department store that had been carrying Tom's line for years.

Tom gave the buyer the royal treatment. He and his wife took Harry and his wife out to dinner, to the theater, then to the 21 Club after the show. They laughed, ate, talked, and had a great time.

The next day, Tom went back to pick up the order.

Harry said, "Sorry, Tom, but we're not picking up your line this year."

Tom thought fast and said, "Harry, may I use your phone." Tom called his wife and said within earshot of Harry, "Honey, remember how much fun we had last night with Harry and Ruth? Remember how great that play was? The delicious Shrimp Scampi? And remember how I promised you a fur coat from the commission I was going to make on the sale?

"Well," he continued, "I'm not going to be able to buy you that coat. And Harry, here, will tell you why."

And he handed the phone to Harry.

Tom's wife got her coat.

ASKING FOR THE ORDER

Your own personality, the personality of your customer, and the situation itself will be your guideline. Ask for the order the final time. Keep this request short, direct, and to the point, such as:

- "Let's do it."

THE SEQUENCE IS FLEXIBLE

Occasionally, you might want to use your fourth or fifth close as your second or third close. In actual selling situations, you'll have enough rapport with your prospects that you can tell which close to use when, or try again if you guessed wrong.

A FINAL RUN-THROUGH

Let's return to our old friends, Gerri and Dick. As you observe Gerri going through the closes, notice first, how expertly she serves her customer, and second, how much more of the procedure you're aware of than you were earlier in this book.

THE SECOND CLOSE

Salesperson: *If we can book the flights from Los Angeles and Boston on December 18th, can you think of any reason why we shouldn't send the Jacobson family on the two-week Hawaiian vacation that could be the beginning of a tradition?*

Prospect: *[Flatly.] Thirty-five hundred dollars. I'm kind of surprised that it's under my budget, but this is really the first time that I've investigated Hawaii, and I haven't checked out any of the competition. If you're able to put together that kind of package in the islands, I might want to call ABC Travel or one of the other well-known travel companies before I commit. Why don't you call me next week after I get those other prices, and then maybe we can do business, if the comparisons look good.*

Salesperson: *I can appreciate that. [Acknowledgment] Dick, we agreed you liked the fact that you'd have the ability to pick the amount of time you'd spend on the three islands, and the fact that you're going to be picked up and taken to your hotel without any additional problems or planning on your part. You also liked the fact that Happiness*

*is Hawaii Tours builds in activities that
can be individualized to you and your
family for one price.* [Agreement on
features] *In addition, we've put together a
variety of dining choices for different age
groups that are on our tours.* [New fea-
ture] *What that means* [Benefit] *is that
your teenage daughters, at no additional
charge to you, can go off and dine with
other teenagers who are on the tour group,
with food that wouldn't necessarily appeal
to a gourmet and contemporary music,
while you and your wife are having a very
special candlelight dinner somewhere else.
All of these dinners are chaperoned, if the
children are under eighteen. And, of
course, you and your wife aren't going to
need any chaperones.* [Laughs.] *Wouldn't
it be nice to give your seventeen-year-old a
chance to meet other young people without
your having to sit through noise that you
would never call "dinner music?"* [Reac-
tion]

Prospect: *I can sure remember the times we went to
my daughter's favorite restaurant, with
dinner ruined because the music was so
loud we couldn't talk. I'd sure like to not
hassle with that issue on vacation.*

Salesperson: *Well, Dick, if we can book the flights from
Los Angeles and Boston on December 18th,
can you think of any reason why we
shouldn't send your family on a two-week
Hawaii vacation that could become a
tradition?*

Prospect: *I'm getting closer and closer to really
committing to this, but I feel like I should
probably call my son, talk it over with my
wife, and get back to you next week, Gerri.*

THE THIRD CLOSE

Salesperson: *I understand.* [Acknowledgment]*We talked about a lot of things you liked: the special-ized tours, all of the transfers being handled, the fact that you can have a special dining experience, depending on the age group — a lot of things you liked.* [Agreement on features]*There must be something you don't like. Would you mind telling me what it is?* [Asking for the objection]

Prospect: *Well, you've spent a lot of time with me, and I feel like you've really listened to what I want on a vacation. However, I had a friend at the office who went on one of these tours. They told him it would be individualized, but they felt like cattle. What I mean is, they woke them up at a certain time and marched them out, and made them participate. They felt like the local people were watching them at a distance because they were such a large group. They never felt relaxed or welcome. I don't want that for my family vacation.*

Salesperson: *I see.* [Acknowledgment] *That wouldn't be the kind of vacation you described you wanted to offer your family. Rest assured that Happiness is Hawaii Tours wouldn't have grown as large as we have, and developed such a good reputation, if we didn't live up to our bargain of individual-ized, personalized choices, using local people as guides, so you'll feel a part of the culture, not apart from the culture.* [Meeting the objection]

Prospect: *You're sounding awfully convincing. You just about answered all of my objections. I would like to talk it over with the family and give my son a call. You can call me at the end of the week. No, I just remembered I'm going to be out of town on business the*

*last three days of the week, so you can call
me the following week.*

THE FOURTH CLOSE

Salesperson: *I understand.* [Acknowledgment] *Dick, it
sounds like you're a busy man. You've got
your business trip coming up, some holiday
shopping and planning to do, and it pretty
much sounds like Hawaii is the place
you're going to take your* family. *The only
thing that is going to happen between now
and then is that you're going to spend a lot
of time trying to figure out comparative
activities and prices. While you're doing
that, you'll be spending a lot of your
valuable time, the prices can go up, and
it's even possible that you could lose
availability on some of the flights we
checked for you. I'd hate to see that happen.* [Citing penalties] *We've pretty much
talked about everything you wanted to
accomplish on this trip. I'd like to be a
part of making that happen for you, and
giving your kids and your wife the kind of
vacation you've wanted to plan for a long
time.* [Feature/Benefit/Reaction] *Let's go
ahead and set it up.* [Asking for the order]

Prospect: *Gerri, I think you must know me better
than I imagined, but I feel like I'm not
supposed to buy from the first person who
calls me.*

THE FIFTH CLOSE

Salesperson: *Dick, as you know we've spent a lot of time
together!*

Prospect: [Laughs] *Well, you may be right! You
know, you've done an awfully good job of
painting a pretty nice picture of this
upcoming Hawaiian vacation. I would like
to get that choice made so we can spend*

> *our time anticipating and packing for it,
> instead of spending all of our time plan-
> ning for it.*

Salesperson: *Okay, great. Let's figure out the best way
to pay for it. Which would you prefer:
American Express, MasterCard or one of
our payment plans that can be deferred
over three months, with a little bit of extra
interest?*

Prospect: *Like I said, we have money in our savings
budget. I'd like to go ahead and put it on
American Express, and then pay it in one
lump sum when the bill comes.*

Salesperson: *Great, Dick. I assure you that you've
really made a great choice about coming
with us on a Happiness Is Hawaii Tour.*

CONCLUSION

You were promised that the techniques and procedures you
learn in this book would be comfortable for you. They'll work
in any selling situation. They'll fit right in, no matter what your
own personality is. Can you think of any reason why The
Guaranteed Close procedure wouldn't be comfortable for you?

If you sincerely believe that these procedures will not only be
comfortable for you but also effective, can you think of any
reason why you shouldn't go out and put them to work for you
on your next sales calls?

The Act of Commitment can lead to the opening and opportunity of a new cycle of business. The next step, Step Seven:
Cement the Sale, gives you this opportunity.

ACT OF COMMITMENT

- Closing the sale is the logical conclusion to your well-given presentation.
- When asking for the order, use the negative question technique, partly because people find it easier to say "no" than "yes."
- Use the closing statement *exactly* as it is worded.
- Don't use words or phrases like: "now," "today," "this afternoon," "right away," or "immediately," because they put pressure on your prospect.
- For the same reason, use any word but "sign."

THE SECOND CLOSE

- Acknowledge the objection with: "I see," "I understand," or "I can appreciate that."
- Re-establish your areas of agreement.
- Add a new Feature/Benefit/Reaction sequence.
- Ask for the order again.

THE THIRD CLOSE

- Acknowledge the objection with: "I see," "I understand," or "I can appreciate that."
- Re-establish your areas of agreement: "We agreed that you liked this, this, and this."
- Uncover the real objection: "There must be something you don't like. Would you mind telling me what it is?"
- Handle the objection.
- Optionally, add a new Feature/Benefit/Reaction sequence.
- Ask for the order. (Keep it short.)

THE FOURTH CLOSE

- Acknowledge the objection with: "I see," "I understand," or "I can appreciate that."
- Cite the penalty for not buying or acting now. Paint a vivid, accurate, word picture of the negative results that may occur if this prospect does not make a positive buying decision now.
- Optionally, add a new Feature/Benefit/Reaction sequence.
- Ask for the order again.

THE FIFTH CLOSE

- Come up with an imaginative, even zany, final close.
- Then say: "Let's do it," "Let's get started," etc.

EXERCISES

ACT OF COMMITMENT

1. How have you handled your fear of closing in the past?

2. What do you fear most about asking the prospect to buy?

3. Develop a closing strategy that you can use to ask a prospect to buy or get an act of commitment.

    a. Summarize the features, quote the price, and close:
       For your [product or service], which includes:

       your investment is:

    b. If we can:

       can you think of any reason why we shouldn't:

    c. Possible objections:

4. Think about actual selling situations in which your goal is to get an act of commitment rather than to make an actual sale. On a separate sheet of paper, or in the following space, create three closing questions that would be appropriate to use to ask for an act of commitment in your own selling situations:

    *   *"If we can* [summary of action to be taken], *can you think of any reason why we shouldn't* [summary of desired act of commitment]*?"*

a.

b.

c.

WRITTEN PLAN FOR THE ACT OF COMMITMENT

Please review the written plan you have prepared for the previous Track Selling System™ steps. After reviewing it, on a separate paper or in the space provided, write out what you plan to say to this specific prospect when you "take up the collection" or close the sale.

If we can:

[summary of action to be taken], can you think of any reason why we shouldn't:

THE FIRST CLOSE: ASKING FOR THE ORDER

Think about the specific product or service you sell and the kinds of situations you face when it is time to ask for the order. On a separate piece of paper or in the space provided, create three closing questions that would be appropriate to ask for the order in your own selling situations. Remember, the closing question is:

- *"If we can* [summary of action to be taken], *can you think of any reason why we shouldn't* [summary of desired act of commitment]?*"

1.

2.

3.

HANDLING OBJECTIONS

1. In your sales experience, what are some typical FUDs that you have encountered from prospects?

2. How would you handle the FUDs now?

3. Fill in the Buying Decision that applies to each of the following situations. The Five Buying Decisions are:
   1. Salesperson
      a. Integrity
      b. Judgment
   2. Company
   3. Product or Service
   4. Price
   5. Time

   a. *"I'll discuss it with my staff and get back to you in a week."*
   Buying Decision:

   b. *"I can get the same thing cheaper from someone else."*
   Buying Decision:

   c. *"In all honesty, I'm not convinced you can meet our delivery schedules. I'd like to shop around before I decide."*
   Buying Decision:

   d. *I plan to talk with a couple other salespeople, and then I'll give you a call."*
   Buying Decision:

   e. *"I don't think that equipment is exactly what I had in mind."*
   Buying Decision.

3.   See for yourself how appropriate it is to acknowledge any
      objection that a prospect might raise by responding with:
      "I see," "I understand," or "I can appreciate that." Use
      each of these responses, in any order you choose, in reply
      to the objections listed below.

      a. *"I want to think it over."*

         What You Might Have Said Before:

         Your Response Now:

      b. *"Our company policy requires me to get at least two
         more bids before a purchasing decision is made."*

         What You Might Have Said Before:

         Your Response Now:

      c. *"ABC company sells that very same coverage for less
         money."*

         What You Might Have Said Before:

         Your Response Now:

      d. *"If I open my account with your competitive bank,
         they'll give me a free safe-deposit box."*

         What You Might Have Said Before:

         Your Response Now:

      e. *"I want to shop around."*

         What You Might Have Said Before:

         Your Response Now:

4. Describe a statement that you have or could have received from a prospect that was not an objection — merely a comment or request for more information.

THE SECOND CLOSE

Review the areas of agreement you established with your prospect in the sales plan you are preparing. Also, review the Feature/Benefit/Reaction sequences you have already presented to your prospect. With that in mind, prepare a written plan for your second close on that same sales call.

WRITTEN PLAN FOR THE SECOND CLOSE

1. Acknowledge the objection:

2. Re-establish your areas of agreement:
    [Prospect's name], *we agreed that you liked:*
    [Feature]:
    [Feature]:
    and [Feature]:

3. *In addition* ... [new Feature/Benefit/Reaction sequence]:
    [Feature]:
    [Benefit]:
    [Reaction]:

4. *If we can* [summary of action to be taken]:

    Can you think of any reason why we shouldn't [summary of act of commitment]?

5.   Prospect's possible objection:

THE THIRD CLOSE

1.   Write a short statement or question that you'd feel comfortable using when you ask for the order the third time.

2.   Check each statement below that you would *not* use when you are closing your sale.
   a. "Let's get this service started for you right now."
   b. "If we can guarantee the quality you need, can you think of any reason why we shouldn't place the order today?"
   c. "Would you mind initialing this for me, please?"
   d. "If you sign the order today, I can have your service started by nine o'clock tomorrow morning."
   e. "Will you sign this purchase order, please?"
   f. "I'll need your okay on this order form."
   g. "If we can schedule our work crew to begin on Thursday, can you think of any reason why we shouldn't get this project underway?"
   h. "Let's get this contract signed now."
   i. "Shall we set it up?"
   j. "If we can add the Broad Form Endorsement, can you think of any reason why we shouldn't get this coverage in place for you right away?"

   (See answers at end of chapter.)

3.   Imagine, if you will, what objection your prospect might raise at this point in your presentation. It might be the one voiced previously, or it could be a totally new one. Write that imagined objection in the space provided.

Objection:

What *new* Feature/Benefit/Reaction sequence could you now present, aimed at the specific objection?
Feature:

Benefit:

Reaction:

THE FOURTH CLOSE

Think about the specific product or service you sell.

1. What penalty might your prospect suffer if he or she does not decide to buy or act now?

2. Write an optional Feature/Benefit/Reaction sequence you could use on your own sales call.

3. Write a short statement that you could use in this fourth request for the order.

Acknowledge the objection:

Cite the penalty for delaying action:

Feature:

Benefit:

Reaction:

Ask for the order:

THE FIFTH CLOSE

What are three ways in which you might close for the fifth time?
Consider workable compromises and humor. Use your imagination.

1.

2.

3.

ANSWERS TO THE THIRD CLOSE, EXERCISE TWO:

You would not use statements A, B, D, E, H or J.

16

STEP SEVEN: CEMENT THE SALE

In Step Six: Act of Commitment, you asked your prospects if they could think of any reason why they shouldn't buy or act now. If the prospect responded no, you made your sale.

But *your* commitment to your customer hasn't ended. It is only the untrained salesperson, like the guy in the cheap, blue suit, who thinks that once you have made your sale, your involvement is over. As a professional salesperson, you have the ability to help the prospect buy now and wear well, or get an act of commitment and wear well. Step Seven: Cement the Sale shows you how to keep your buyer satisfied after the sale.

DON'T SELL 'EM AND FORGET 'EM

To "sell 'em and forget 'em" is negative and self-defeating. This attitude produces dissatisfied customers and a drop in sales. It is negative to ignore customers just because they have plunked down their money. They respond by canceling orders and spreading word about your dismal follow-up after purchase.

It is much more positive — for your customer and for you — to follow up after the customer has placed an order. Make it known that your company provides support before *and after* the order is taken — for example, technical assistance, training,

installation and effective communication. Here is what you want
to convey to the customer:

> Salesperson: *My success is dependent on your success
> and your happiness with our product or
> service. Rest assured that I'm going to do
> everything on my end to make sure that
> happens.*
>
> Prospect: [Smiling] *I guess this is a long-term rela-
> tionship.*

HELPING YOUR CUSTOMER
AVOID BUYER'S REMORSE

A strange thing happens to all of us after a purchasing decision
has been made. Suppose that you have just decided to buy a
new, luxury car. You are in the showroom right now, bursting
with pride. Your new car is the most beautiful car you've ever
seen. You can hardly wait to get it home to show your family
and friends. You can hardly wait to take the car for a drive and
enjoy the luxury appointments and smooth, quiet ride.

But what happens as you drive that car off the showroom floor?
You begin thinking: "Maybe the color is too bright. Maybe if
I'd haggled a little longer, the dealer would have dropped the
price. Maybe I should have waited a couple months to see next
year's models. Maybe I should have shopped at a few more
places before I bought this car."

What you're suffering from is a universal syndrome called
buyer's remorse.

Your prospects are no different from you. When they wake up
at two o'clock in the morning and realize that they have committed hard-earned dollars to making this purchase, they, too,
need to be reassured that their purchasing decisions were wise
and their purchase makes good, logical, business sense.

Remember: Your prospects buy emotionally, then justify their
decisions logically. So in Step Seven, you want to make sure
that your sales wear well by reminding your prospects of the
logical reasons that made their purchases wise. You will assure
them that their buying decisions make good, logical sense.

REASSURING THE CUSTOMER

How can you give this reassurance?

* Review the *logical* reasons for the purchase or act of commitment. Remember: It is the logical reasons that make a sale wear well.

* Express your thanks for the order or act of commitment.

* Promise to provide any required follow-up action.

These three parts do not need to be presented in any special order. For example, if you were selling storage systems, you might say:

* *Thank you for your order, Jack.* [Expressing thanks] *You'll find this system is completely compatible with your present equipment, takes up minimum space in your computer room, and will handle all of your storage requirements not only today but also four or five years down the road.* [Reviewing logical reasons for purchase] *Your system will be delivered on the fifteenth, and I've put it on my calendar to call you on the sixteenth to see if there's any way I can help you get the system into operation smoothly.* [Promise of follow-up action]

If you were selling automobile insurance, you might say:

* *Mr. Thomas, you've made a wise choice. You've filled in the gaps in your previous coverage and set realistic liability limits. You also know that you've received the most competitive rates available.* [Reviewing logical reasons for purchase] *I assure you that I'm always available to answer your questions. I will be calling you in three months to see if there are any changes needed in your insurance coverage, but feel free to call me any time.* [Promise of follow-up action] *Thank you, Mr. Thomas.* [Expressing thanks]

If you were selling personnel training manuals, you might say:

* *It has been a pleasure working with you, Mrs. Weatherby. You'll find these manuals not only cut training costs dramatically, but also give your employees the exact skills required in your company's operations.* [Reviewing logical reasons for purchase] *Thank you for your order, Mrs. Weatherby.* [Expressing

thanks] *I will be here Monday morning at nine o'clock to begin working with your staff on the most effective ways to use these manuals.* [Promise of follow-up action]

To return to our old friends, Gerri and Dick:

Salesperson: *Dick, I assure you that you've really made a great choice about coming with us on a Happiness is Hawaii Tour. In fact, I'll find out the name of the tour guide who will meet you at your first stop in Hawaii and call you back with that, so you'll know who is in charge of the first leg of your trip.* [Promise of follow-up action]

I appreciate your taking the time to really talk with me and let me know what you wanted in a vacation, so that we can have you as one of our satisfied customers who returns year after year. [Giving thanks]

As you said, you were looking for a vacation that would become a family tradition, and I'm confident that you will want to go back year after year after year. Because of the history that Hawaii brings to us and the individual planning that gives you freedom as your children's interests change, many families never have to shop the other choices. They call Happiness is Hawaii first. I know you made a great choice. [Review of logical reasons for purchase]

Now, your flight arrangements and travel documents will be in the mail next week, to arrive at your home within two weeks. Also, a week before your scheduled departure — probably before the second week in December — you'll receive an itemized itinerary for each family member. It will list the places where the guides will meet you, dinner choices, and how soon you need to pick your preferences. You should have an enjoyable evening at home just

> *customizing everyone's vacation.* [Promise of follow-up action]
>
> *If there are any questions that come up between now and then, feel free to call me. I'm usually in the office until about eight o'clock each night, and I'll be happy to answer any questions you, your wife, or any of your children may have about how this vacation may be the best for all of you. I'm looking forward to hearing from you when you get back from your vacation. Give me a call and tell me how it went. And if you're anywhere near our office in Century City, please come in. I would like to meet you in person. Dick, thanks for the time and have a great vacation.* [Expressing thanks]

Prospect: *Thanks so much, Gerri. I'll let you know how it goes, and I do hope to meet you.*

Why is it so important to communicate to a customer that you care about the person after the close? Cementing the sale means *keeping* the customer who is still a prospect for more products or services. A customer who is a prospect is more valuable than a prospect who remains a prospect.

RETURN PHONE CALLS

Return phone calls. Managers and employees who support sales count on you to continue with Step Seven. Returning calls promptly is part of your customer responsibility, and it's good business. *Not* returning calls gnaws at the connection between customer and supplier.

Customer: [Sounding disgruntled] *All I wanted was a little information. Not even the decency of a return call! What happens if I'm really in a jam?*

Sometimes you might communicate to a customer:

- "I'll get that information to you by next week."

If you find you won't have the data by that date after all, call as soon as you know, and report:

◆ "I don't have that information yet, but I'm working on it, and I will get it for you as soon as possible."

People stay with you as customers not because they feel they understand your product or service, but because they feel *you* understand *them*. If salespeople *initiate* calling a customer to make sure there is satisfaction, it puts them in a much different position than if they *receive* a call from a customer and have to react to it.

Cementing the Sale is a *continual* process. It involves everyone employed by your firm. Coworkers either sell or *un*sell your organization all the time. How a person answers phones or greets clients in person can make or break customer loyalty.

LET THE BUYER BE AWARE: REVIEWING THE BENEFITS

Customers buy for *emotional* reasons, but when they wake the next morning, they stay sold for *logical* reasons. In this final step of the Track Selling System,™ you review the details of the purchase. You assure your customers they made the best choice by buying your product or service. You communicate your company's product or service has been refined through X years of successful usage. You let the buyers know who to phone for their questions. You make it clear this is the beginning of a long association — that you won't take their investment and ignore them.

CULTIVATING THE CUSTOMER CONNECTION

"Thank you."

These two simple words can make the difference between a disgruntled customer and a loyal, long-term customer. Expressing thanks can be just as simple — and productive.

Even a simple thank-you card can cement a sale and sustain a good customer relationship. Several years ago at a meeting of the Sales and Marketing Executives Association of Nevada, held at a Las Vegas restaurant, I sat down to breakfast and noticed that on the corner of each table was a card with a cowboy motif and the words, "Thank you, pardner."

What was the story behind the card? It had been put there by the woman who was to speak that morning. Her printing firm sold coin-wrapping paper to casinos. It had started only three years before, yet by now they had fifty percent of the coin paper business in Las Vegas and eighty percent in Reno.

What was behind her success?

"I sent a thank-you card to my first customer," she explained. "Three years later, the card is still sitting on his desk. It's the same one you have before you now."

She sent *one* card to *one* customer. The *one* buyer gave her *four* additional accounts, which amounted to a substantial portion of her business.

So don't stint on saying thank you. It's good for morale and good for business. Send your customers a thank-you card expressing appreciation for their business. Add a personal touch that shows how you know what interests them, when possible. For example, if your customer is a photography buff, you might clip out a magazine article on photography, attach your business card, and mail it with the note, "This might be of interest to you." Make a phone call to make sure the sale is wearing well. Let them know what your follow-up will be, and when you will call on them. It all adds up to nurturing the customer connection.

KEEPING THE CEMENT FRESH

Cementing the Sale well firms up your success in personal plans and business. It opens up future opportunities. It establishes long-term relationships and creates a resource for prospects, which is what successful companies are all about. The salesperson who continues to serve, deserves. *Service after sale is nothing more than caring in work clothes.*

THINGS TO REMEMBER

* Review the *logical* reasons for the purchase or act of commitment.
* Express your thanks for the order or act of commitment.
* Promise to provide any required follow-up action, and follow that up.

EXERCISES

1. Develop a summary statement that you can use with your customer to review the logical reasons for his or her emotional purchase.

2. What have been your experiences in generating loyalty from your clients?

3. How do you communicate to a customer that you care about him or her after the close?

4. In what new ways might you Cement the Sale with your customers?

17

MASTERING THE SEVEN STEPS
OF THE TRACK SELLING SYSTEM™

Now that you know the Seven Steps of the Track Selling System,™ it is time to become so comfortable with them they feel like second nature.

Your keys to success are *motivation* and *practice*. If you truly believe that the Track Selling System™ will make you more professional, more effective and more successful, you'll be willing to spend the time required to achieve these skills.

Remember when you learned to drive a car? Remember how frustrated you were, trying to keep in mind the mechanical details of shifting, braking, steering, and so on? At the same time you were trying to keep in mind the rules of the road, plus exercise good judgment as you met unexpected conditions in which you'd had no previous experience.

Now when you get into your car, you don't give the details a second thought. You perform the functions automatically and can give your full attention to the road.

That's just how it is with the Track Selling System.™ At first you will feel clumsy and awkward. You will find yourself on Step Five and realize you've skipped Step Three and Step Four completely.

Don't let that discourage you. Each time you move through the seven-step procedure, you'll find it becoming more comfortable and natural. You *will* achieve success, but it *does* take practice.

PERFECT PRACTICE MAKES PERFECT

The most effective method of learning the Track Selling System™ is role play. I've heard seasoned salespeople say role play is not the real world. That's correct. It is not the real world. However, a salesperson will not do much better in the real world than he or she does in a role play situation. I'm not talking about your situation now because you are just learning the Track Selling System.™ However once you have the Track Selling System™ mastered (You'll do that through role play.), you won't do much better in a real world selling situation than you do in your role play scenario. I've made many sales calls with salespeople and have them destroy any possibility of making the sale. Then after the call was over they would say to me it only happened because I was with them and made them nervous. It is pretty easy to imagine what a great job we did on a sales call when in reality, if the call had been secretly video-taped, I wonder how many times we would have been proud to have it shown to our peers.

It is pretty easy to sit on the side of the dance floor and mentally do Saturday Night Fever. However when we get on the floor and do the dance, many times it does not turn out nearly as well as it did in our imagination. Many times it is easy for us to imagine what a great job we did on a sales call, when in reality it could have been greatly improved.

It is great if you have a fellow salesperson, a friend, a spouse, or someone else you can role play with, however that's not too important in the beginning when you're just learning the Track Selling System.™ If you don't have someone to role play with, use a tape recorder and play both the salesperson and the prospect. Refer to the role play exercise form in the forms section of this book.

Throughout this book you have been developing the sales presentation plan and the same format should be used for your role playing exercises. In the beginning, don't be concerned about being smooth or glib. Be more concerned with following your outline, especially utilizing the transition statements. Each time you go through role play, you'll become more confident. Just as you did when learning to drive a car, you will find yourself forgetting the mechanics and able to concentrate more completely on what your prospect is saying and doing.

Many years ago a great salesperson said the thing that moved him from the minor leagues of selling into the major leagues is when he went to his boss and asked him if he could role play how a sales call should be made in front of all his peers. Once he was able to do that, never again did he have a problem dealing with a prospect.

Can you imagine how successful you would be if you could get on stage in front of all your peers and role play how a sales call should really be made?

Every hour invested in role play will pay off for you many times over in the real world of selling.

GOING ALL THE WAY
THROUGH THE SEVEN STEPS

Here is a dialogue between a salesperson and a prospect that goes all the way from Step One: Approach to Step Seven: Cementing the Sale. In this situation, a major bank has hired a business-development salesperson to call on corporate prospects and attempt to sell their new computerized cash-management system. The bank has bought a list of local business owners and investors who move a large volume of money in various money-market instruments on a daily basis.

On this call, the prospect is not a current customer of the bank the salesperson represents.

> *Salesperson :* *Good morning, Mr. Harrison. I'm Bob Jamison from Downtown National Bank. How's your day going?*
>
> *Prospect:* *Pretty busy, thank you. Have a seat.*
>
> *Salesperson :* *Busy, huh? How do you go about getting all of this business?*
>
> *Prospect:* *Well, I guess I really shouldn't complain. I've been very fortunate in my major investments, and after a couple of lean*

*years things are really beginning to pay off
for me.*

Salesperson :   *Mr. Harrison, I know you specialize in
handling tax shelters and investing tax
shelter funds. Fill me in on how you go
about deciding which tax shelters you will
represent.*

Prospect: *Well, I used to be a tax attorney and got to
research and do all of the investigation in
investing for my clients. After a while, I
realized I was making more money for
them than I was for me. It was a tough
decision to stop practicing law, but I don't
think I've ever been happier than I am
right now — or more financially secure.*

Salesperson :   *That takes a lot of courage, to break away
from a profession like law that you've
spent so many years studying. What gave
you the incentive to do that?*

Prospect: *I think I got tired of not being able to
schedule my time. I did a lot of work in
international tax shelters, so many times I
would receive phone calls from my foreign
clients during their daytime, which was my
nighttime. I think my wife and I finally had
our sleep interrupted one too many times,
and I took a long, hard look at what I
could do to change that.*

Salesperson :   *So now you handle various tax shelters,
both domestically and internationally, for
yourself, and other specific clients?*

Prospect: *I function as a broker — mainly make the
choices where we will invest the money
available, whether that would be a pool of
client money or my own liquid assets. I
choose among various tax-shelter offer-
ings, and I'm constantly moving funds to
the money market.*

Salesperson :   *What's your pet project, currently?*

Prospect: I've invested a lot of money in the investigation and testing of wind-generated power equipment.

Salesperson : You mean those windmill farms we see on top of the hills near the freeway leaving town? My children have always thought they were pretty funny-looking.

Prospect: Those "funny-looking" machines your kids laugh at may look pretty silly, but they're making me a lot of money!

Salesperson : How are you currently deciding how and when to move the money you are responsible for when it's available for reinvesting?

Prospect: Currently, I've been working with my banker, who I call when I want to check on current market rates, stock options, and other items in my portfolio. That's his specialty, so he's usually able to get me the information I need in a short period of time. When the time is right, I move the funds I've invested in the market into a tax-shelter offering of my choice.

Salesperson : How many times in a typical day might you call your banker for that information, Mr. Harrison?

Prospect: By the way, Bob, call me James. I'd say some days I only call him once, but many days I call him as often as six or seven times, depending on other investors who might call me to check current changes they have heard are available.

Salesperson : What do you like best about working with the bank that currently handles this part of your business?

Prospect: Well, I've been with them now for about ten years and they handle all of my family accounts, my legal accounts, and now, my cash-management requirements.

Salesperson : James, if you could change one thing about the way your cash-management *transactions are done, what would that be?*

Prospect: *Well, Bob, I'd say that because I'm used to investing with some international clients, many times I want to check on rates for them after our normal business hours, and I'm unable to do that. I have access to that information from 8 a.m. to 6 p.m. with my bank, so I have to tell my overseas clients to call back the next day.*

Salesperson :   *I see. How are you currently billed for the cash-management services you receive on a monthly basis?*

Prospect: *It varies by the number of calls that I make into the bank and the length of time I tie up the bank's computer. It can vary from $300 to $800 a month. That's based on the $200 monthly flat fee and the $10 per phone call charge, plus the overseas billing when it's necessary to check on those transactions.*

Salesperson :   *James, what kinds of reports do you get to show you the status of your various accounts? Also, how often are those reports generated and received by you?*

Prospect: *I only get a report in hard copy every two weeks. I can call up and get a verbal status report at any time, although it costs me $10 each time I ask for a computer check.*

Salesperson :   *How do you use those reports in managing your various tax shelters and accounts?*

Prospect: *I use them regularly in tracking how my investments are paying off, and also in reporting to my investors and investment groups, who call in periodically as they see a new offering come up.*

Salesperson :   *So would I be correct in understanding that having those a little more often might help you answer some of the investors' questions?*

Prospect: *Yes, it sure would! Many times they can't wait, and I end up making a lot more expensive, inquiry calls into the bank computer.*

Salesperson :   *I know we haven't met before, but when I called you about coming out and discussing some of the services of Downtown Bank, you seemed fairly interested in hearing about our cash-management program specifically. What attracted you to our particular method of cash management?*

Prospect: *Well, you've certainly been spending a lot of money advertising in the right places. I've seen you in Business Week, the Wall Street Journal, and some of the people I exercise with mentioned being pretty happy with some of the new things you're doing. I just wanted to have the opportunity to see what's going on in the marketplace.*

Salesperson :   *Exercise? Where do you go to exercise?*

Prospect: *Across the street, at the Maintown Athletic Club. I used to try to get up early and jog before I came to work, but that didn't work out as a steady routine, and this is handy enough that I think it has become a habit.*

Salesperson :   *You must be doing something right. You look pretty trim to me.*

Prospect: *[Laughs.] Thanks. It doesn't come as easy as you get a little older.*

Salesperson :   *James, as I understand it, you're looking for a cash-management system which would allow you to get current market information, preferably on a 24-hour basis, wouldn't be costly to check status several times daily, and could generate reports more often than twice a month. Is that correct?*

Prospect: *That would be quite nice — very nice, as a matter of fact. Do you have something that could do that, Bob?*

Salesperson :   *We've got a lot of solutions at Downtown National Bank. In fact, let me ask you:*

How much information do you have about
Downtown National Bank?

Prospect: Well, I like to think I'm keeping up to date
on most of the major banking forces in our
town, but I really don't know very much
about you, other than what I've read. And
what the guys at my exercise club say.

Salesperson: I understand. Let me quickly cover a
couple of things that I think would be
important to me if I were in your position.
Downtown National is the twelfth-largest
bank in the United States. We have over
$31 billion in assets and almost 20,000
employees. We started out as primarily a
consumer bank, then expanded into commercial, and are now heavily developing in
the areas of trust and portfolio management. We also have a number of subsidiar-
ies — fourteen, to be exact — in the
United States and seven overseas in Lon-
don, Hong Kong, Australia, and a number
of other places in the Far East. We feel
we've positioned ourselves well for both
interstate and international banking, as the
regulations have loosened over the past
two years.

James, there are several important features
I would like to tell you about our cash-
management program. One is that we have
a flat fee per month. What that means to
you is that you can either call up once a
day, once a week, or ten times a day to
check for yourself and your investors. It
won't cost you any extra money. How
would it help to know that you could
budget a certain dollar amount every
month for those services, instead of waiting
for the bill to come and have it be a surprise?

Prospect: Well, I think that would be very nice.
Sometimes, when it gets up to the high end,
it plays havoc with my budgeting. Also, I

*bill my investors based on how often they
use my services, and many times having to
count which one made more calls can be a
time-consuming project for my bookkeeper.*

Salesperson : *We also have the most up-to-date computerized equipment at Downtown National,
which we've dedicated to our cash-management project. What that means to you is
that we have a faster turnaround time on
print documents, which would show the
daily activities on all of the funds you're
working with. That means you wouldn't
have to wait the two weeks you mentioned
between reports. In fact, for one fee you
could receive up to twelve printouts per
month. How might that help you inform
your investors and keep them from calling
your office so often?*

Prospect: *Well, I think it would be marvelous. I could
let my secretary and my staff handle many
of their questions instead of having to
make a personal call to get the information
from my banker. You see, because the
information is so confidential, I'm the only
one who's authorized to call. If the reports
were more frequent, I'm confident they
would answer most of the questions. I've
got one older man who will probably still
call me daily, but it should satisfy most of
the investors.*

Salesperson : *The next feature I'm really excited to tell
you about is an option we have in our
cash-management program that's not
offered by anyone else at this time. That is,
for an additional flat fee of $250 per
month we can put a computer on your desk
with an attached printer. What that would
mean was that you could have information
24 hours a day, just by pressing the access
codes on a machine near your desk.
Wouldn't that kind of flexibility put you
ahead in the market and attract other*

*investors to work with you, knowing that
you had the most modern equipment and
constant access to rates?*

Prospect: *I'll say it would! You mean, I could actually have a computer sitting right here on
my desk? That would be pretty impressive
to some of my more aggressive clients, who
feel I'm a little older and therefore, you
know, not as well informed as some of my
younger competitors.*

Salesperson : *Do you have any questions?*

Prospect: *Bob, you quoted a few prices, depending
on options, but I'm curious as to how much
this whole package might cost me.*

Salesperson : *Glad you asked. James, for your cash-
management system that would give you
one flat fee, regardless of the number of
inquiries, up to twelve printed readouts per
month and your own desktop computer,
your investment would be $550 per month.
If we could get our programmer out here
next week to start putting your numbers
into the system, can you think of any
reason why you shouldn't be the first in the
building to have a 24-hour cash-management system?*

Prospect: *You know, it sure sounds exciting to me,
but I'm really not in a position to move all
of that money yet. I just wanted to listen to
what Downtown National was doing in this
area.*

Salesperson : *I can appreciate that. We agreed you liked
the flat fee. You liked the fact that you
could have up to twelve hard copies a
month. You really liked the fact that you
could have a computer on your desk to
give you unlimited, around-the-clock
access to all your financial information. In
addition, we programmed this with the
most simple language that's available in
the marketplace. What that means is that*

not only could your secretary or one of the clerks get information when a client called, but with very little effort, you could easily master the computer. How would that be? And show all of those investors that you're really not an old-fashioned lawyer but a modern money-manager.

Prospect: *Hmm, that would certainly open a few eyes! It would absolutely surprise my son, who thought I wouldn't come anywhere near a computer.*

Salesperson : *Great, James. Then, if we can get our programmer out here next week to start putting your numbers into the system, can you think of any reason why you shouldn't start having a 24 hour-a-day cash-management service available to you and your clients?*

Prospect: *Well, Bob, it's just that I think this is a big decision. Like I said, I've been with my bank for over ten years now, and it means changing a lot of things in addition to my cash-management system. I'd like to talk it over with my banker before I make a final decision.*

Salesperson : *I understand. We've talked about a lot of things you liked. You liked the fact that you could count on a flat fee, the 24-hour access available, and a lot of other things you liked. There must be something you don't like. Would you mind telling me what it is?*

Prospect: *Well, to be honest with you, I feel that my banker has become a personal friend. As I got excited about your system — and I really did — I kept seeing the face of my old banker-friend, and I felt badly about how tempted I am to go with you. I just really don't know the proper way to let him know I'm thinking of changing bankers.*

Salesperson :   *I can sure appreciate that kind of loyalty, and I would certainly look forward to earning that from you someday. Staying up to date in the market means taking risks and leaving old things behind. Including some old friendships. That never comes very easy. Since Downtown National is the only bank that's offering this, you may have to make this decision. Sure would like to have you as one of our customers, and watch you manage your own money on your own time, and not have those sleepless nights you talked about earlier. I bet your wife wouldn't believe it if you told her you could get all your calls at the office, now, because you're clients only want the latest information straight from your computer.*

Prospect: *You know, Bob, that does make sense. Let's get started. When can the programming people put the numbers on my new system?*

Salesperson :   *They can be out next Tuesday, James. I assure you that you have made an excellent choice in converting to our new cash-management system. In fact, many of our customers don't call it our cash-management system, they call it their cash-management system. That's because they have access in their office any time they want it. I'm confident this is just the beginning of a much more simplified way for you to handle all of that international and domestic business. It's also a great way for you to get your hands on today's computer, painlessly. You'll have to let me know what your son says about his modern, "high-tech" father.*

I'll call you next Tuesday to set up a specific time for the programmers to come out to work with your secretary and the records from the existing bank, so we can

*get all the numbers up to date. You'll be
proficient on that computer before the end
of the month. I sure do appreciate you
taking the time to see me today, and I look
forward to a long relationship with you.
James, there's a user's group that meets
monthly over lunch to discuss various
applications of your new system. I'll make
sure your name gets added to the invitation
list, in case that could be of extra value to
you. I'll talk with you next week.*

Prospect: *Good-bye, Bob, and thanks very much.*

THINGS TO REMEMBER

- Perfect practice makes perfect.
- Practicing the Seven Steps helps you become comfortable and successful with them.
- Role-play with a partner, using a written script to take you through the Seven Steps.

EXERCISES

Fill in the following steps of the complete Track Selling System™ for a sales call you have coming up. Prepare yourself for the sales call by using this as a script to role-play with a partner.

Prospect's name:

Prospect's title:

Prospect's company:

Kind of business:

Date and time of appointment:

Your specific objectives on this sales call:

STEP ONE: APPROACH

Introduction (exactly what you will say when you first greet this prospect):

Rapport building (five open-ended questions to encourage this person to talk freely about personal interests):

    1.

    2.

    3.

    4.

    5.

STEP TWO: QUALIFICATION

[Prospect's name], *I would like to tell you about our* [product or service]:

However, in order for me to do the best job I possibly can for you, I need to ask you a couple of questions. Is that all right? [Write five open-ended questions to qualify this prospect and uncover problems or needs.]

1.

2.

3.

4.

5.

Ask all the questions necessary to give you the information you need.

STEP THREE: AGREEMENT ON NEED

As I understand it, you are looking for:

Is that correct?

STEP FOUR: SELL THE COMPANY

May I ask how much information you have about [your company's name]:

I understand. Let me quickly cover a couple of things that I think would be important to me if I were in your position.

STEP FIVE: FILL THE NEED

[Prospect's name], *there are several important features I would like to tell you about our* [name of product or service]:

Feature:

Benefit:

Reaction:

Feature:

Benefit:

Reaction:

Feature:

Benefit:

Reaction:

Do you have any questions? For your [summary of features]:

The price is:

STEP SIX: ACT OF COMMITMENT

If we can [summary of action to be taken]:

Can you think of any reason why we shouldn't [summary of act of commitment]:

STEP SEVEN: CEMENT THE SALE

[Prospect's name], *I assure you* [reasons why this buying decision makes good, logical business sense]:

Thanks very much. I'll [summary of follow-up action you will take.]:

PART 3

WORLD CLASS SELLING IN THE REAL WORLD

Now that you know the philosophy and the procedures of the Track Selling System,™ how do you take it out into the real world? The next seven chapters will help you do just that. You'll find out how to:

- Deal with unexpected sales situations, like prospects who want to buy what you don't think they need.

- Maintain a professional appearance (unlike the guy in the baggy, blue suit).

- View yourself as being in the people business, not the product business.

- Manage your time effectively.

- Set goals designed for your success.

- Build a successful career in sales.

- Use *World Class Selling* in your personal and work life — with your employer, your significant other, your family, and friends. Because the Track Selling System™ is about service, use it is an act of caring — of giving, not taking.

As you read this last part, think of yourself as a sales professional. You've had the training now to justify that title. So go on. Polish your skills, reach for your star, and be proud to sell the *World Class Selling* way. You can do it!

18

WHAT IF . . . ?

The Track Selling System™ will take you successfully through real-world sales situations. Occasionally, though, you may encounter unusual situations — situations not specifically covered in the Track Selling System™ or the Guaranteed Close.

You have been learning both the procedures *and* the philosophy. The *procedures* you have learned will carry you step-by-step through your complete sales call, leaving nothing to chance. When an unusual situation arises, you can rely on the *philosophy* to help you respond to the situation, acting within the ethical guidelines you've learned.

Now let's take a look at how the procedures and philosophies of *World Class Selling* apply to some "What if ... ?" situations.

- You walk into your sales call and the prospect says, "I'm busy, I don't have time to talk with you. Leave your brochures and price lists and I'll get back to you." What do you do?

This is strictly a matter of *procedure*. You've already learned exactly what to do. Open your Step Two: Qualification presentation with the words:

+ *"Mr.* [Prospect's name], *I would like to tell you about our* [product or service]. *However, in order for me to do the best job I possibly can for you, I need to ask you a couple of questions. Is that all right?"*

If your prospect gives you approval, begin by asking good qualification questions as you learned to do in Step Two of your sales procedure. For example, you might ask:

+ "How are you presently handling your problems with such-and-such?"

+ "How is that working out for you?"

+ "How do you feel about ... ?"

+ "What is your opinion about ... ?"

+ "What is your biggest worry about ... ?"

+ "May I ask what you like most about ... ?"

People prefer talking to listening. No matter how busy your prospects are, you will usually find they have plenty of time to talk about what *they* want to talk about with a salesperson who sincerely listens.

Remember the first two steps, Approach and Qualification, are the only two steps in the Track Selling System™ that are interchangeable. In this situation it is apparent you need to address the business reasons for your call. However, there are no shortcuts in the selling process, therefore it is necessary to move back into rapport building as quickly as possible. In this situation, these two steps can go back and forth between qualifying your prospect and establishing rapport.

It is possible that the prospect really is too busy to talk. You have to respect that, but again don't just hand the person your brochure and price list. Your goal is to be of service to the person. In order to do that you have to have certain information. At this point it would seem the objective would be to get an appointment to come back at a time more convenient to the prospect when he or she has the time to discuss how you might be of service.

+ You are on Step Three: Agreement on Need, and your prospect begins asking you about the price of your product or service? In the sales procedure, you recall, price is not handled until Step Five: Fill the Need. What do you do?

Act, don't *react*. Maintain control. You must keep the steps of the sales procedure in precise order to carry the prospect smoothly through the Five Buying Decisions, in the precise order.

How do most sales people *react* to that question? They answer it. They tell the prospect the price, and what they've done is jump from Step Three: Agreement on Need all the way to the end of Step Five: Fill the Need where the subject of price is handled.

Then the prospect asks you about your company. If you *react* by answering the question, you've jumped back to Step Four: Sell the Company, and before you know it you're all over the place and have lost control.

Act, don't *react*. When the prospect asks you a question about the price, say, "Joe, I'm glad you asked me that. That's an important question. *In order for me to determine the best price I can give you, I need to ask you a couple of questions. Is that all right?*"

You must always respond to your prospect or you lose communication. You stay on track by following your response with a question: "In order for me to determine the best price I can give you I need to ask you a couple of questions. Is that all right?" Then ask questions related to price such as quality, delivery, service, and all other factors in your business that relate to price.

- Your prospect wants to buy your product or service, but you personally feel it doesn't meet the person's or company's needs. What do you do?

First, keep in mind that people buy for their reasons, not your reasons or their company's reasons. In the prospect's mind, the purchase may make complete sense. The person may feel the purchase will help him or her gain something, avoid losing something, provide comfort and convenience, security and protection, pride of ownership, or satisfaction of emotion. The purchase may not make sense to you, but it may make perfect sense to the prospect.

For example, I went on a sales call once with a woman representing a computer time-share company. She was calling on a bank manager, and the two of them were asking questions back and forth. The manager said, "As I understand it, I'll have a computer on my desk and all I have to do is put in the information and I'll get the answers right here on the screen, right?"

The salesperson said, "No! You don't *need* a computer on your desk. All *you* will need is a hard copy."

The conversation went on. And a little later, the bank manager said, "How long is it going to take me to learn to operate the computer?"

The salesperson said, "I already told you: You don't *need* a computer. All *you* will need is a hard copy."

When we left, I asked that salesperson, "Couldn't he have a computer?"

"He doesn't *need* one," she said.

"Well, he *wants* one," I said.

Wouldn't it be a lot easier to sell him something he wants, something the prospect feels will help him or her gain something or avoid losing something, or any of the other Six Buying Motives that prompt people to buy? If the computer sitting on the bank manager's desk wasn't going to work with the system, or if it was going to foul up the computer operations in any way, that's a different story. Would you refuse to sell someone a yacht, with your reason being the person doesn't *need* a yacht?

Suppose your prospect wanted to buy a $150,000 Rolls Royce so long it had to have hinges to get around the corner. Would you tell that person, "No, you can't buy that Rolls Royce, because you don't *need* it!"

People buy for *their* reasons, not *your* reasons. It is a good point to keep in mind.

   • Your prospect wants to buy your product or service, but
     you know making the purchase will be damaging to the
     person or the company. For example, it simply won't
     work well under these particular circumstances. Or
     paying for the product or service will put the company
     in a precarious financial condition, etc. What do you do?

This situation is a whole new ball game. For example, if the computer the bank manager wanted wasn't compatible with the rest of the equipment, or its use would destroy the capabilities of the time-share program itself, that's another thing entirely. You have no right to sell people things they don't want, can't use, or can't afford.

Here is an example of how one insurance salesperson handled a situation of this very same kind. After he'd read the prospect's policy, he said, "I think what you've got right here is perfect for your needs. I would hurt you if I changed your policy." And he walked away from a $50,000 sale.

The prospect, needless to say, was stunned. He said, "I can't believe what I've just heard! I've had five other salespeople in here looking at this policy. Every one of them said it was terrible. Every one of them suggested I buy something else. I'm really glad to hear you confirm what I've thought all along: my present coverage is exactly what I need."

A couple of weeks later, the salesperson's phone rang. It was a friend of the prospect whose coverage wasn't changed. The man on the other end of the line said, "My friend told me that if I ever wanted to meet an honest salesperson, I should call you."

The salesperson met with the referral and sold him a $500,000 policy!

The salesperson said, "I'd hurt you if I changed your policy." He walked away from a $50,000 sale and made a $500,000 sale instead.

That's not always going to happen to you. You may walk away from a sale and never hear from the prospect again. You may get no referrals. That's reality, but you've acted with integrity, and in the long run, it's going to pay off.

- The prospect wants to buy your product or service. He or she has genuine need, but no budget available to make this purchase. What do you do?

If there's no budget available and you know no budget ever *will* be available, you have little choice but to thank the prospect for talking to you and be on your way.

Before you take that step, ask some good qualifying questions to find out as much as possible about the company's budget. Could you make it easier for the prospect to buy if you offered installment payments? Will the purchase of your product or service help the company cut current costs, and could the saved money be used to make the payments? Could the money come from another department or another budget? Could the money be borrowed? Is it possible money for the purchase will become available in the future?

If so, go for an act of commitment. Make arrangements now to meet with the person at a later date, when the funds *will* be available and the purchase *can* be made.

   ◆ The prospect says he or she has no earthly use for the product or service you sell, but you know a genuine need really does exist. What do you do?

Many times, you will find prospects are truly unaware that problems or needs exist. They are perfectly happy with things the way they are. It's your responsibility, as a professional salesperson, to ask the right questions to uncover the real problems or needs that exist. It's possible your product or service is quite new, the prospect isn't aware it exists, or isn't aware of the ways in which it could improve his or her present situation. It becomes your responsibility to assume the role of educator, painting vivid, word pictures, and helping the person understand the benefits your product or service provides.

It is possible you will meet with prospects who are so engrossed in the daily running of their business they simply haven't kept up with current trends. Again, they're unaware of the benefits your product or service provides. You might use third-party influence, again painting vivid, word pictures of the ways businesses like theirs have used your product or service and gained beneficial results.

In short, it's up to you to help the person become aware that problems or needs really do exist, and of the ways your product or service solves the problems or fills the needs.

TRUSTING YOURSELF, THE PROCEDURE AND THE PHILOSOPHY

The Seven Step procedure is designed to work on every sales call you make, no matter what personality you or your prospects have and no matter what product or service you sell.

When unusual situations arise, think back to the procedure itself, and you will usually find a way to adapt it to the situation. If you don't find the answer in the *procedure*, let the ethical *philosophy* guide your actions.

Your goal is to help the customer buy or act now, because the decision is in your prospect's best interests. You are a professional. Your goal is to serve.

THINGS TO REMEMBER

* *World Class Selling* procedures and philosophy will carry you through unexpected selling situations.

* Always respond. Never react.

* If the prospect says he or she is too busy to talk with you, say: "[Prospect's name], *I would like to tell you about our* [product or service]. *However, in order for me to do the best job I possibly can, I'd like to ask you a couple of questions. Is that all right?*"

* If your prospect asks you about price prematurely, maintain control by saying: *"That's an important question. However, in order for me to determine the best price I can give you I need to ask you a couple of questions. Is that all right?"*

* Your prospects buy for *their* needs, not yours. They may want your product or service even if you think they don't need it.

* If you are convinced your product or service is not right for the prospect, walk away from the sale.

EXERCISES

With both the procedure and philosophies of *World Class Selling* in mind, write the action you would take if faced with the following situations.

1.   *What if...* you walk into your sales call and the prospect says, "I'm busy, I don't have time to talk with you. Leave your brochures and price lists, and I'll get back to you."?

2.   *What if...* you are on Step Three: Agreement on Need, and your prospect begins asking you about the price of your product or service? In the sales procedure, you'll recall, price is not handled until Step Five: Fill the Need.

3.   *What if...* your prospect wants to buy your product or service, but you personally feel the customer doesn't need it?

4. *What if*... your prospect wants to buy your product or service, but you know without a doubt making the purchase will be damaging to the person or company? For example, it simply won't work well under these particular circumstances? Or paying for the product or service will put the person or company in a precarious financial condition, etc.?

5. *What if*... The prospect wants to buy your product or service? The person has genuine need, but no budget available to make this purchase.

6. *What if*... the prospect says he or she has no earthly use for the product or service, but you know a genuine need really does exist?

19

THE IMPACT OF YOUR APPEARANCE

How you look has a strong impact on how your prospects perceive you as a professional. Your physical appearance can help you convey the positive visual message: "Here, *finally*, is a competent, successful, *professional* salesperson."

Because most prospects have had negative experiences with ineffective salespeople, they have negative expectations of you at first. It is your caring and skill in *World Class Selling* that will put you in the top twenty percent, but it's your *appearance* that will make the first impression.

When you dress like a professional, people treat you like one. This translates into greater sales for you and your company.

EFFECTIVE DRESSING

Clothing is a matter of personal taste, current style, your budget limitations, and even the area in which you live.

What goes on in your prospects' minds when you walk into your sales call wearing the proverbial, baggy, blue suit? Do you look as though you have been successful in your sales career? Do you look like the kind of person who could help your prospects achieve success?

You should dress as well as the most successful person in your profession. People like to associate with winners, and your attention to the way you dress is one way you show yourself to be in the winner's circle.

GOOD GROOMING

Your professional image starts with basics: good grooming. Keep yourself clean and organized. There is no second chance to make a first impression. The first assessment lasts.

I travel a lot, and I'm not overjoyed about taking long trips in a suit and tie, but I do it. Why? Because people see me as a professional, and they treat me differently because of that.

Keep your clothing clean and well pressed. Make sure your shoes are well polished, and replace the heels when they begin to wear down. If you are a man, carry an extra tie in the glove compartment of your car. Then, if you spill something on the one you are wearing, you've got a handy spare. If you are a woman, carry an extra pair of stockings. If the ones you're wearing develop a run, you can change. Your attention to details — little things — make a big difference.

THE BEST WITHIN YOUR BUDGET

Everyone works within practical budget limitations when selecting a wardrobe. Purchase the best-quality clothing you can afford. This doesn't mean you mortgage your house, but it does mean you take time to plan how you dress — in addition to being neat and clean, your clothing fits with your sales environment.

This may restrict you in your selection of clothes, but everything you wear will reflect your dedication to quality and success. Your appearance has a strong impact on your prospects' perceptions of you as a professional and a strong impact on your success.

WHAT TO WEAR

As a rule of thumb, dress one notch better than your prospect. This is not a matter of "one-upsmanship" at all. You are simply creating a visual image of professionalism and success.

What do I mean by "dressing one notch better?" Suppose you and your prospect are both men. Your prospect usually wears slacks , a dress shirt, and a tie. You should wear slacks, a dress shirt, a tie ... *plus a jacket.*

Suppose you and your prospect are both women. Your prospect usually wears a skirt, blouse, and blazer. Dressing one notch better means you would wear a matching suit or a dress.

When you and your prospect are of opposite sexes, the same guidelines apply. Wear what would be appropriately considered one notch above what your prospect wears.

Here is a true story that happened to one salesperson selling farm equipment. This salesperson was making a call on a farmer. He knew that the farmer always wore Levi's and a plaid shirt, so he was wearing exactly the same thing: Levi's and a plaid shirt. He figured this would help put the farmer at ease.

On this particular sales call, the salesperson was accompanied by one of the managers of the farm-equipment company. The manager was wearing a suit. What happened? The salesperson couldn't get the farmer to talk with him. The farmer insisted on directing his questions to the manager — the man in the suit.

If you have ever priced farm machinery, you know it can cost hundreds of thousands of dollars. The buying decision the farmer faced was an extremely serious one. By wearing a suit, the manager of the farm-equipment company gave the visual impact of being more knowledgeable and professional, and that's the person the farmer wanted to talk with.

What do you suppose the salesperson learned from this experience? How do you suppose he dressed for his future sales calls?

Little things — attention to details — make a big difference.

YOUR AUTOMOBILE MAKES
AN IMPRESSION, TOO

Your automobile can also help you create an image of professionalism and success, and this has nothing to do with the year, make, or model of your car.

How does the exterior of your car look now? Is it clean?

How does the interior of your car look now? Is it tidy, or is it piled high with sample cases, maps, papers, or other things that could give your prospects the impression you are disorganized or disorderly?

You never know when your prospect might be glancing out the window as you drive up. A dirty car or one that is bulging with stacks of papers and samples in disarray can destroy the professional image you are working so hard to create.

Are the materials you need for each sales call neatly organized, all in one spot, ready to pick up as you leave the car to make your call? How will it look to your prospect if you drive up, then spend five minutes digging through stacks of rubble to find the materials you need?

If necessary, stop a block away from your prospect's office. Sort out the materials you will need on the sales call. With your materials conveniently at hand, you'll be able to step from your car with dignity and confidence.

NO SMOKING, PLEASE

If you smoke, don't smoke on a sales call. Ever. If your prospect doesn't smoke, your smoking will be offensive. Even if your prospect does smoke, your own smoking is simply not businesslike. It creates a distraction for you, taking your mind off the business at hand.

Suppose you're on Step Three of the sales procedure, Agreement on Need. You are giving your prospect a capsule summary of the important information you gathered in Step One and Step Two. You stop to light a cigarette. And what happens? You lose track of your train of thought and lose your composure. It isn't worth the risk.

Can you imagine the effect it would have on your sale if you carelessly dropped ashes on the prospect's rug or accidentally burned a hole in the prospect's desk?

A salesperson was making a presentation to a prospect's company's board of directors. The group was seated around the company's newly-purchased, expensive, teak conference table. This salesperson's service had a long sales cycle. He had worked for a long time uncovering this company's problems and needs and designing a program to fit those needs. Finally, it was time to ask for the order.

The salesperson lit a cigarette and put it in the ashtray. He got so engrossed in the conversation, he didn't notice when the cigarette dropped out of the ashtray onto the table and was burning the company's new conference table.

The amazing thing about this story is: The salesperson got the order. However, the president of the company called the salesperson's company the next morning and asked that this particular salesperson never set foot in their building again.

So put your cigarettes away when you are making sales calls. It isn't worth the risk.

NO COFFEE, THANKS

I advise that you don't drink coffee or accept any other refreshments while on a sales call. Again, this can distract both you and your prospect from your established goals. Suppose you're on a sales call, chatting with your prospect, asking good, open-ended questions and establishing warm rapport. You are drinking a cup of coffee the prospect was kind enough to give you. You reach for a pen, knock over the cup of coffee, and it spills on the important papers the prospect has laid out!

What effect will this have on the warm rapport you were working so hard to establish? What effect will it have on your ability to make a successful sale?

It isn't worth the risk. Say "No, thank you," when your prospect offers you a cup of coffee or other refreshment. Express your appreciation for the thoughtfulness of this gesture, but politely decline. You aren't going to offend anyone.

LITTLE THINGS MEAN A LOT

An executive once said to me, "You know what really bugs me about salespeople? They drive the wrong way on the arrows."

If there was ever a perfect opening for a reflective question, this was it. So I said: "On the arrows?"

He said: "Yes. My office overlooks the company parking lot, and from my desk I can watch salespeople when they drive up. There are huge arrows painted on the concrete telling you the direction to drive when you come into the parking lot, in each one of the parking aisles, and when you leave. I just hate salespeople who are so dumb they drive the wrong way on the arrows."

Now what is this executive going to say to the salesperson for not buying? Is this Stanford Ph.D. going to say to the salesperson: "The reason I am not buying your product or service is because you drove the wrong way on the arrows."? Of course not. He is going to say: "Your price is too high, I want to shop around, I need to get three more bids," etc. Think about this example when you question whether people buy emotionally or logically.

You just never know. Little things — your attention to detail — make a big difference. You give yourself every possible opportunity to succeed by avoiding conduct that presents any potential for destroying your own success.

THINGS TO REMEMBER

- You have only one chance to make a first impression.
- Keep your clothing neat and clean.
- Buy the best clothing you can afford.
- Dress one notch better than your prospect.
- Keep your car neat and clean.
- Don't smoke or drink coffee or other refreshments while making a presentation.
- It's the little things that make the big difference.

EXERCISES

1. Below is a description of men's and women's attire. Check each one that would help send a visual message that the wearer is a true professional.

    a. Freshly polished shoes

    b. Stockings with runs

    c. Crisply creased trousers

    d. Shoes with worn heels

    e. A blouse with a plunging neckline

    f. A jacket and trousers with clashing fabric patterns

    g. A tasteful business suit

    h. A tie with food stains

    i. Ostentatious or gaudy jewelry

    j. A slip that shows

    k. A freshly cleaned and pressed dress

    l. A shirt with frayed cuffs

    m. An overflowing purse

    n. Pockets bulging with keys and other objects

    o. A tie the wrong width for today's fashion

    p. A skirt the wrong length for today's fashion

    q. Lapels the wrong width for today's fashion

    r. A well-coordinated jacket, skirt, and blouse

    s. A slinky, sequined dress

    t. A neatly pressed blazer

20

YOU'RE IN THE PEOPLE BUSINESS

The greatest weakness of today's salespeople is that they are product-centered, not people-oriented, and are sadly unaware of this shortcoming. Be aware: It is your *people* skills that will make your product knowledge pay off.

On most sales calls today, how do most salespeople spend the majority of their time? Telling their prospects every physical detail about the product or service they sell.

People buy not because they understand your product or service, but because they feel *you* understand *them*. People buy emotionally.

YOU AREN'T IN THE PRODUCT BUSINESS

As a professional salesperson, you need to be more people-oriented than product-oriented.

If you sell insurance, don't think of yourself as being in the business of selling insurance. You're in the people business.

If you sell computers, you are not in the business of selling computers. You're in the people business.

You are not in the business of selling cars, banking services, temporary help, commercial aircraft, imported tea, or any other products or services. As a professional salesperson, you're in the *people* business. It is your people skills that make your product knowledge pay off.

A novice salesman who was an avid gardener took our training to learn to organize the Los Angeles International Flower and Garden Show. "I enjoy people," he said, "but I have often felt uncomfortable 'schmoozing' with them. Since learning the Track Selling System,™ my entire attitude and perception of sales has changed. I simply need to sincerely ask rapport-building, fact-finding and feeling-finding questions that are open-ended. I have also learned the value of listening.

"Now, pulling this show together will certainly be a challenge — an exciting adventure. *We're in the people business*, and having the opportunity to work with the down-to-the-earth kind of people in the horticulture industry is going to be very rewarding. I can't wait to see the thousands of people pour through the doors!"

SEVEN WAYS TO IMPROVE YOUR PEOPLE SKILLS

In Chapter Six, you learned one of the easiest ways imaginable to help your prospects decide that they like you: let them do the talking. The more your prospects talk, the more they will like you. No magic, no personality overhaul, no manipulation. Let your prospects do the talking. This technique is just as effective with your friends and family members as it is with your prospects.

Here are seven quick and easy techniques to improve your people skills. These techniques don't require magic, personality changes, or manipulation of any kind.

- Smile. It's the number one sign of friendship in any language. The Chinese have a proverb: "A man who cannot smile should not open a store." Think about it. Give a smile and you will get a smile in return.

- Develop a genuine interest in others. When you have sincere interest, it shows. Look directly at people when they are talking. Let your facial expression register your interest. Ask good, open-ended questions to let people know you really care. The secret is to be intersted, not to attempt to be interesting.

- Talk in terms of the other person's interests. You will never meet anyone who doesn't have time to talk about what *they* want to talk about. Your time is better spent encouraging your prospect to discuss his or her interests, needs, and priorities rather than launching into a discussion about yourself, your experience, your product or service, or how great your company is.

- Use the other person's name. Using a name builds personal rapport and shows you are listening with respect. Be careful, however, not to overuse the person's name, which is even worse than not using it.

- Give compliments. Everyone loves a compliment when it is genuine. Sincerely praise prospects on their business success, helpful employees, the location of their facility, decor of the office, and so on. Make a concentrated effort to give at least three sincere, honest compliments every single day of your life. You will be amazed at what it will do for your relationships.

- Listen. It is the greatest compliment you can pay. Your prospects like salespeople who listen more than they like salespeople who talk too much. When you assume the role of listener, it relaxes the sales climate. As you listen, you are demonstrating that you truly care about the other person and are genuinely interested in what he or she has to say. Everything your prospect is telling you is valuable information you can store and use to solve that person's problems or fill his or her needs. Listening establishes you as a warm, likable person — the kind of person your prospect would enjoy having as a friend

- Make the other person feel important. Every person *is* important. Let people know you realize this. Show your prospects the respect of being willing to serve their needs. When you are sincerely impressed by something other people are, own or have achieved, let them know it. Make the other person feel important.

You can tell a lot about the character of other individuals by the way they treat the people around them who can do nothing *for* them or nothing *to* them.

Successful selling and successful living should be pretty much the same. The same skills that can help you become more successful as a professional salesperson can also help you become more successful as a human being.

FOUR FACTORS THAT DETERMINE YOUR SUCCESS

As a professional salesperson, there are four factors that will determine your success with people.

- ◆ Your impact. First impressions may not be fair, but they are a fact of life. Your prospect's initial impression will have a strong influence on the success of your sale.

  Find a full-length mirror and stand in front of it, dressed exactly as you dress for your sales calls. Carry the materials you carry when you make your calls.

  This is exactly what your prospects are seeing. What visual impact are you creating when you first walk into your sales calls? How will your prospects size you up? Remember: You only get one chance to make a first impression.

- ◆ Your sensitivity. This means how sensitive you are to your prospects — their personalities, their moods, their business, the things they are trying to accomplish.

  How well do you read between the lines — sense the same feelings your prospect is feeling? How well do you respond, letting your prospect know that you really *do* understand?

- ◆ Your perception. How do you perceive your prospects' problems and needs? How do you perceive their marketplace? Are you conveying to your prospects that you are viewing the situation through *their* eyes? Is your thinking meshed with theirs? Are you seeing the same realities they face?

- ◆ Your judgment. How effective are the solutions you offer to solve your prospects' problems or fill their needs? Have you listened, evaluated the situation accurately, and offered something that is both practical and on-target?

EMPATHY

These four factors help you develop empathy. Empathy is your ability to put yourself in your prospects' shoes — to see things through their eyes.

It is your knowledge and understanding of people that will make your technical skills and your product knowledge pay off. You are in the people business. People buy because they like you.

I don't mean to downgrade the importance of technical skills. It is important you are well informed about the physical aspects of your product or service — what the product or service actually consists of, how it functions, and what it is capable of doing. The facts help you to establish credibility. It is important that you have the ability to convey this information to your prospects with clarity.

When it is time to "take up the collection" — time to ask for the order — you will find your people skills have made your product knowledge pay off.

BODY LANGUAGE

You may be surprised to find that the way you sit, gesture, hold your hands or your head, and so on can be giving signals to your prospects that you don't mean to send.

Your knowledge of body language can help you communicate more deliberately. It can also make you more perceptive about your prospects' moods and more capable of responding with sensitivity.

Generally speaking, upward gestures are considered positive, such as holding your head up, gesturing upward, and leaning forward in your chair. These actions signal to your prospects that you have confidence, interest, and enthusiasm.

By contrast, downward gestures are considered negative, such as holding your head down, gesturing downward, and slouching back in your chair. These actions are signals of defeat and lack of interest.

I can't begin to cover all the intricacies of body language.
However, many fine books have been written on the subject. I
urge you to learn about non-verbal communication.

WHAT IS SELLING?

In capsule form, selling is simply:

- Uncovering a problem or discovering a need.
- Offering a way to solve the problem or fill the need.
- Persuading the prospect to buy or act now.

Your technical skills are important. These skills add credibility
to your presentation. Your product knowledge is important.
This knowledge allows you to use good judgment in the solutions you offer.

When you get right down to the basic selling procedure, you're
in the people business. Your people skills make your product
knowledge pay off.

THINGS TO REMEMBER

- Try these seven ways to improve your people skills:
  - Smile.
  - Develop a genuine interest in others.
  - Talk in terms of the other person's interests.
  - Use the other person's name.
  - Give compliments.
  - Listen.
  - Make the other person feel important.
- Know the four factors that determine your success
  in selling:
  - Impact
  - Sensitivity
  - Perception
  - Judgment

21

SETTING GOALS

Now that you have these selling skills, what are you going to do with them?

Researchers from a major university followed a graduating class over a 20-year period. Do you know what they found? Only three percent of the class set goals, put those goals in writing and adjusted them over the 20-year period. They also found the three percent who set goals accomplished more, materially, than the other 97 percent combined.

Most people don't set goals, and most people don't make it in this world. Could there be some correlation?

A GOAL IS NOT A WISH

If you were to stand on a street corner and interview people passing by, how many of those people do you suppose set goals? If you asked: "Can you tell me what kind of job you'll have five years from now?" or "Can you tell me what kind of home you'll be living in ten years from now?" or "How much money are you going to have in the bank when you retire?" most of those people couldn't tell you.

Nevertheless, every one of these people would probably say:
"Oh, I'm going to have a *better* job. I'm going to have a *nicer*
home. I'm going to retire financially independent."

This is wishful thinking.

People who think goal-setting is motivational hype might take a
cue from the most successful people of all time. They all practice the principle of setting goals.

"When I graduated from college," says Curtis L. Carlson,
owner and founder of the Carlson Companies headquartered in
Minneapolis, Minnesota, "I set myself a goal of earning $100 a
week as a salesman. I've been setting goals ever since." How
well has it worked for him? The Carlson Companies is one of
the world's largest, privately-owned, holding companies with
annual sales in excess of ten billion dollars.

The goals you set should be *your* goals — things that are
important to *you*. I'm not suggesting your goals should be
related to money, jobs, homes, or anything else in particular.
When you set a goal, make sure it is something you want. If
not, you won't do the things necessary to get you there.

FACTORS IN SETTING GOALS

When setting your goals, consider these four important factors:

* Goals should be big.

Goals *have* to be big in order to get you excited. If not, you
won't do what is needed to reach them. It's pretty tough to get
excited about paying this month's car payment.

So shoot for a star. Do you want to double your income? Do
you want to be the top salesperson in your company? Do you
want to own a big, beautiful home? Do you want to take your
family on a month-long vacation in the Greek Isles?

You may think big goals are unrealistic, but is it realistic that
men have walked on the moon? That goal was set ... and it was
accomplished.

Put aside a few hours and think about what you would like to
accomplish in life. Set some goals. It will be one of the most
meaningful time investments of your life. Not only does it work,
it works so well it will become a way of life.

* Goals should be long-term.

A long-term goal is five years or longer. You need time to meet a big goal.

Big goals give you long-term direction. If you have a five-year goal, you can have a bad week and make it up. You can have a bad month and make it up. You can even have a bad year and make it up.

As you are traveling down the narrow path to success, you're going to find a giant standing right in the middle of the path. He carries a big club and when you get to that place in the path, he is going to knock you down with his club.

The club may be a large sale you are sure you are going to make — so sure, in fact, you've already spent the commission. Then the sale falls through.

The club may be when your company is re-engineering and you lose your job. It may be when the bank pulls your line of credit.

The club may be the unexpected death of someone important to you. It may be a severe illness or other personal tragedy. It may be many things.

On the path to success you're going to get knocked down again and again. When that happens, you've got to get yourself up, dust yourself off, and go at the giant with the club again ... and again ... and again. Finally, one day, you get around him, and you're home free.

There has to be some way of separating the 97 percent who don't make it from those who do. Perhaps it is the giant with the club who does the separating. There is an old saying that has withstood the test of time: "Winners never quit, and quitters never win."

Or, as the late boxer, Rocky Marciano, said, "It doesn't matter how many times you get knocked down. It's how many times you get up that counts."

When you have long-term goals, the giant's club can knock you down, but your goals remain intact. You have a temporary setback, but you go at it again, continuing to work to achieve the things important to you. Your long-term goals give you long-term direction.

◆ Goals should be short-term.

Break your long-term goal into a series of comfortable steps. If your goal is a one-month trip to the Greek Isles, set a date for the trip. Decide how you will travel, where you will stay, what you will do. Determine the amount of money you will need for the trip.

You now know how much money you will need and the length of time you have available to save. How much will you need to save each week or month to turn your dream into a reality?

Save that amount each week or month, as you have planned. When your departure date nears, make your reservations, pack your bag, and you're ready to go. Your series of short, consistent actions will make your dream come true.

If your goal is to double your income, set a specific date when you want to reach your goal. How much more annual income, in actual dollars will you need to add? Break the total into the added sales you will need to make each day, week, or month to achieve your goal. Work day by day, week by week, month by month to add the sales you need. When your targeted date arrives, you will have added all the sales you need to double your income. Your series of short, consistent actions will make your dream come true.

Remember when you were in school? On the first day of each semester you received course outlines, due dates for term papers, and dates of exams. What was going on in your head? "*This* time I'm going to do a little reading every day and a little research for my term paper every day, so I don't have to stay up all night to meet the deadlines."

Then what happened? The same old thing. At the last minute you stocked up on No Doze and stayed up all night to cram for exams and finish reports.

How much better would you have done if you had worked on a *daily* basis to achieve the goals?

A successful career doesn't just happen. It is made up of successful hours, days, and weeks. The successful days and weeks add up to successful months and years. It is the consistent actions you take on a *daily* basis that transform your dreams for a successful career into reality. Do something about it today, or you won't be there five years from now.

♦ Put your goals in writing.

Something magical happens when you put your goals in writing. The simple fact you have written your goals down takes them out of the realm of wishful thinking and transforms them into a personal commitment.

Writing your goals down helps you keep them firmly in mind. The faintest of ink is better than the strongest memory.

Writing your goals allows you to review them on a regular basis. Each time you review your goals, make a renewed commitment to working toward achieving what you have set out to do on a daily basis.

Adjust your goals as needed. Scratch off the ones you have achieved, and add new ones. Scratch off any that are no longer important to you, and again, add new ones.

Set your goals high. Don't be afraid to shoot for a star. You can make it happen. One of the greatest examples of what a human being can accomplish is the four minute mile.

In 1954, the mile was run for the first time in less than four minutes. In fact, before the twentieth century, it was an accepted "fact" that it simply could not be done. The medical profession said the body couldn't withstand the pressure — the heart would probably explode.

Then along came a young Englishman named Roger Bannister, who didn't know it couldn't be done. He ran the mile in three minutes and 59.4 seconds.

In 1979, another Englishman, Sebastian Coe, set a new world record by running the mile in 3 minutes and 49 seconds. The amazing thing is that in that same race, there was another individual who ran the mile in 3 minutes and 55 seconds and his time was only good enough for tenth place. Can you imagine ten people in the same race ran the mile in less than four minutes and yet for ninety years it couldn't be done. The record for the mile has changed hands several times in the past few years and as of the writing of this book, Steve Cram holds the record for the mile at 3 minutes and 46.3 seconds.

Set your goals high, and as a well-known commercial says: "Just Do It."

THINGS TO REMEMBER

- Goals should be:
  - Big
  - Long-term
  - Short-term
  - In writing

EXERCISES

1. What is your definition of a goal?

2. What experiences have you had in setting goals? Were you successful in achieving your goals? Why or why not?

3. What career goals have you set for yourself?

4. What goals have you set for your personal life?

22

MANAGING TIME EFFECTIVELY

In the following chapter we talk about building a success-ful, professional sales career. A successful career is made up of successful years, successful months, successful weeks, successful days, and even successful hours.

As professional salespeople, you and I have many activities we have to be involved with on a daily basis — activities that contribute to our success and activities that don't. The old cliché of plan your work and work your plan is given more lip service on managing time effectively than all other ideas combined. When most salespeople say they plan their work, what they are really saying is they plan on showing up for work.

As a professional you have to know not only what to do and how to do it, but also how to organize your activities, set your priorities, and plan effective use of your time. This is the only way to harvest important objectives.

It is important to allow yourself time to consistently work toward your goals, on a daily basis, not only in your professional life, but your personal life as well.

There is only one thing you can do with time: spend it. How you spend your time will directly affect your success. Time is given to us without prejudice. Each person on earth is granted the same 24 hours each day. Have you ever noticed how some people get more accomplished than others in the identical 24-hour period?

Why is it that some people can zip through 57 assorted tasks in any given day while others only accomplish two or three tasks and then complain they were "too busy" or "didn't have enough time" to finish the rest?

Are those high achievers wizards? Do they have a magical formula? Are they hyperactive? Do they simply have more stamina — more adrenaline flowing?

You will find the people who accomplish more than average don't have any more stamina than the rest of us. If you question these people you will probably find a common denominator: They prepare a written plan of all the tasks they hope to accomplish each day, and then plot along task after task until every job on the list has been checked off.

To keep your own career and personal life in good balance and to keep your personal objectives in mind, picture your allotment of time in terms of a Wheel of Activity. At the hub of your Wheel of Activity is planning. It is the most vital aspect of every professional salesperson's day.

By planning, I mean planning every aspect of your day — how you use each valuable hour.

For example, plan the order in which you will make your sales calls with no retracing of steps — the most efficient routes — so you will spend less time traveling between calls.

Prepare written plans for every sales call you make. Do you know exactly what your objectives are on each call. Use the sales plan form as outlined on page 380 of this book. Plan to allow yourself time for all essential activities for your professional and personal success.

Here is a lesson in planning that one steel company executive paid $25,000 to receive. I pass it on to you for free.

This executive hired an efficiency expert. "I'm going to show you how to manage and run this business," the expert said.

"I already know how to manage and run this business," replied the executive. "I just don't know how to get it done. If you can show me how to get it done, I'll pay you anything within reason.''

"I can increase your effectiveness by fifty percent immediately," said the expert, "if you'll just do this:"

- Write down the six most important things you have to do to make your business grow. Write these six things in your own order of priority.

- Tomorrow, pull out that list and go to work on number one. Don't even look at the rest. When you've finished number one, go on to number two. Don't worry if you don't finish all six. Just work on one job at a time, in order of priority. This way you'll know you are spending your time on the most important thing you should be doing to build your company.

- Try it for awhile. Share it with your staff. Then let me know how it's working.

Several months later, the efficiency expert received a letter from the executive saying this was the most important lesson he had learned for the success of his business. Enclosed with this letter was a check for $25,000.

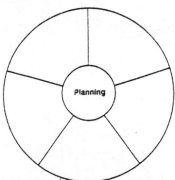

ONE: PROSPECTING

On your wheel of activity there are five spokes. The first spoke is prospecting. I've had salespeople say to me: "I can sell. I just don't like the prospecting part of it." If you can't prospect, you can't sell. For many salespeople prospecting is not the most enjoyable activity. However, you know it is vitally important to your success. If you don't have ample prospects, you are not going to have many customers.

I recall when I first started selling life insurance I set myself an objective of making forty cold telephone calls a day. I can recall sitting down at the telephone and my hands would shake as I dialed the numbers. The sweetest sound in the world was a busy signal. I used to call home every four or five calls just to talk to someone friendly — or at least occasionally friendly. I never enjoyed doing it even though I could tell you how much money I earned every time I dialed the telephone. One of the secrets I have found with successful salespeople is they will do the things necessary even though they may be things they dislike doing.

During prospecting, good salespeople let the prospect know they want to be of service — they appreciate the need to establish rapport with the prospect. Through discussion, they find out what the prospect needs by communicating at the *prospect's* level of understanding and applying this information to the *prospect's* requirements.

Set aside time daily for prospecting as an ongoing activity — a part of every day, every week. Prospecting is the salesperson's gold mine.

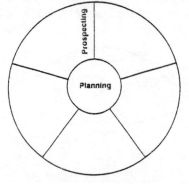

TWO: SELLING

It doesn't do you much good to have a lot of prospects if you don't follow up. That's what selling is about: finding people to sell and selling the people you find.

How does this relate to your planned use of time? You have to allow yourself plenty of time for direct contact with your prospects in order to get your product or service sold. You will have to plan time available for selling when your prospects also have available time.

Be aware of the "golden hours" in your workday when you are most successful at contacting and meeting with prospects.

Don't waste this valuable selling time doing less productive tasks, such as paperwork.

For example, if you are selling life insurance, you may find your most productive selling hours are in the evening, when you can talk with husbands and wives together. This means you will use your daytime hours for your paperwork and planning, so your evenings can be devoted to direct contact with your prospects.

If you are selling real estate, your most productive selling hours may be evenings and weekends. If you are selling business-to-business, your prospects will usually only be available during business hours.

Plan ahead so you can schedule your non-selling activities at times when it is not possible to meet with prospects. Then, during the hours when your prospects are available to see you, you are also available to see them.

Keep in mind that selling also means finding what a prospect needs and serving those needs. You will continue to prosper if you effectively answer the prospect's unasked question, ''What will it do for me?''

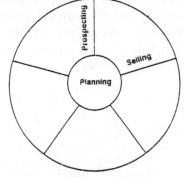

THREE: SERVICE

Good service means: If you don't forget your customers, they won't forget you. If you take care of this end, it will make your job a lot easier. Customers who are happy with your service will keep you busy.

Plan time to give service not only right after the sale, but as an ongoing activity. Your sale is not a one-shot deal. It is an opportunity for you to turn a prospect into a long-term client.

Even if you only spend ten minutes a day on service, you will see surprising and satisfying results. How long does it take to pick up the phone and check back with a customer to make sure a sale is wearing well, find out if any conditions have changed, or ask if there are any additional services you could provide?

Most salespeople "neglect" to take the short minutes required to make these phone calls. How can you prevent yourself from forgetting these important phone or face-to-face calls? Schedule them on your calendar. After you have made a successful sale, jot down on your calendar the exact dates, at appropriate intervals, that you will make service calls.

Think what this one simple act of planning can do for you. At regular intervals, you will have repeat contacts with this customer. You will be maintaining rapport. You will find out new problems and needs the customer is facing and new ways the person can use the products or services you sell. Or, if your company develops a new product or service, you will know exactly which of your customers could benefit from its use. Think what this information could do for your ongoing sales.

When you provide continuous service, you have happy, satisfied customers. These happy customers are the greatest advertisement you can possibly have. Word spreads fast. The happy, satisfied customers provide you with referrals, and your prospecting job becomes easier for you.

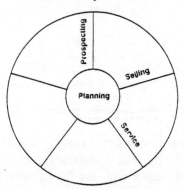

FOUR: PERSONAL

The personal spoke puts fun and relaxation in your life. Time off from work charges your batteries. If you plan your time off, you will find more fun in your life, and you will have much more energy to make it in sales.

How do you feel when you take time for family and friends, hobbies and relaxation, exercise and personal interests on a spur-of-the-moment basis? You probably feel guilty because you are "playing" when there is so much work to be done. You don't really enjoy the personal interests. When personal activities play second fiddle to business pursuits for a long time, the result can be burnout, fatigue, or even illness.

Think of the actual meaning of the word "recreation." It means re-creation — creating anew our vitality, enthusiasm, and interest in life. It is essential for personal growth.

When your work activities are scheduled and under control, and your personal activities are planned in advance, you will find you can truly enjoy the things you do for relaxation and recreation. You will emerge refreshed and a more effective human being.

FIVE: STUDY

School's never out for the professional. We're living in a rapidly changing world, so keep up to date with the trends and facts that affect your business. Continue your education, get advanced degrees, read trade journals and specialized books. Take courses to improve your professional skills. Keep up with current events so you are well-informed and can converse intelligently with your prospects.

Study every day. By setting aside fifteen minutes each day for reading, the average person can complete eighteen books per year. Think of the impact the new information, insights, and philosophies could have on your professional and personal growth.

How do you get study time, even a short fifteen minutes a day? By planning the time in advance. By deciding what time of the day you are least likely to be interrupted by phone calls or other distractions, and jotting down that time on your daily schedule. When the time comes, use it exactly as you have planned it — for study.

Study also means preparing yourself each day to improve your sales presentations, instead of trying to cram information into your head a few moments before your appointment.

Whatever activities you choose, this time, well-spent, is invaluable.

DEALING WITH PROCRASTINATION

This all happens with discipline: planning your work and working your plan on a regular basis, and doing what it takes to complete both the interesting and boring parts of your work. Consistency in performance makes it work for you.

But then there's ... procrastination.

We all have the tendency to procrastinate. It is important for each of us to remember disciplined use of time pays off. Wasting time is worse than wasting money. Wasted money can be re-earned, but wasted time is gone forever.

Those who don't enjoy prospecting find it easier to avoid prospecting. It is something they will get around to "later," but not right now. Yet without prospecting, there are no prospects to sell, and your opportunities for success are diminished.

We procrastinate about staying in front of the prospect, servicing our clients, planning our own personal time, and allowing time for study. Whatever aspects of our professional or personal lives we enjoy the least, we put off until "someday." Often, someday never comes.

Each of the five activities on your wheel is vital to your success. Avoiding the activities you dislike diminishes your opportunity for success.

Professional salespeople form the habit of doing *all* the things necessary for success, even though they may be things they dislike.

FORMING HABITS OF SUCCESS

How do you form the habit of doing the things necessary for your success? By doing them ... and doing them ... and doing them ... until these activities are second nature. Even the things you dislike. Even the things you downright detest. Make time for each of these important activities each day. Write them into your plans for the day, and *do* them.

- Recognize how completing the tasks you dislike helps you accomplish your goals.
- Prioritize the tasks.
- Set aside a specific time to perform the tasks.
- Reward yourself when you have accomplished your goals.

Disciplined use of time pays off. You will be much more effective. Each day will add to your success as a professional salesperson and as a human being.

Would this technique help *you* achieve the goals that are important to you?

HORSESHOES OR MAINSPRINGS?

There is only one thing you can do with your time: spend it. When it's gone, it's gone, never to be recaptured. *How* you spend your time will directly affect your success in selling.

You can compare your use of time with how you might use a bar of steel. You can use the bar of steel to make horseshoes. They would be worth about $250.

Or you can use the bar of steel to make blades for penknives. They would be worth about $2,500.

Or you can use the bar of steel to make mainsprings for fine watches. They would be worth about $25,000.

You can spend your time only once. Will you spend it making horseshoes, blades for penknives, or mainsprings for fine watches?

THINGS TO REMEMBER

- The only thing you can do with your time is spend it.
- Prepare a written plan of your daily goals, and keep to it.
- Balance your Wheel of Activity by attending to all activities:
  - Planning
  - Prospecting
  - Selling
  - Service
  - Personal
  - Study
- Stop procrastinating by doing what's necessary for success, even things you don't like.
- Form habits of success.
- Spend your time making "mainsprings" instead of "horseshoes."

EXERCISES

1. In the space provided, write an explanation of why some people consistently accomplish more than others.

2. What have been your problems in managing your time and territory?

3. What is your allocation of your time in your personal Wheel of Activity?
   a. Planning:
   What type of planning do you currently do?

   b. Prospecting:
   List the prospecting activities you currently perform:

   List the prospecting activities that would help you to be more successful:

c. Selling:

How much of your workday is spent selling?

When are your most productive hours to sell each day?

What changes can you make in your daily activities that will allow you to spend more time each day selling?

d. Service:

List the types of service activities you currently perform:

What types of additional service activities would you like to perform?

e. Personal:

List the recreational activities you enjoy with your family and friends:

What types of additional recreational activities would you like to engage in?

f. Study:

What types of study activities do you currently perform on a regular basis?

What types of additional study would you like to engage in?

4. How can you improve your planning efforts to ensure balance in these various activities?

5. Write six things you need to do to accomplish your own personal and/or professional success. Write the items in your own order of priority.

Copy this list onto a paper to carry with you. Work on your first objective until it is completely accomplished. Then move on to number two. Don't worry if you don't accomplish every item on your list. Work on one job at a time, in your own order of priority. Judge for yourself the results you achieve.

1.

2.

3.

4.

5.

6.

23

BUILDING A SUCCESSFUL CAREER IN SALES

You most certainly can build a successful career in sales, but did you know most people don't build successful careers?

If that surprises you, look at the people around you. Most people would rather take the easy road to failure than the proven road to success.

To belong in the top ten percent of sales professionals, you don't have to be a one hundred percent better prospector, presenter, or closer. If you become just *twenty percent* better in each of the Seven Steps in the Track Selling System,™ your career will take quantum leaps.

A small difference can be the margin between a winner and second place. At 200, a baseball hitter is marginal, but at 300, the same hitter is a star. All it takes to move from mediocrity to stardom is one more hit out of every ten times at the plate.

Selling may have a poor public image, but that doesn't mean it doesn't have great potential. Business leaders tell us selling leads to excellent opportunities, whatever your sex, age, race, experience, or education. According to recent research by Herbert and Jeanne Greenberg in the *Harvard Business Review*, ''The person without sales experience — with proper training and supervision — is as likely to succeed as the experienced salesperson.'' Yet despite solid opportunities, most people don't expend the effort to build successful sales careers.

If you're seeking success, you've got to stretch your skills, steer a different course in your thinking and planning, and improve your abilities. You have to build your career by designing a blueprint that moves you forward.

That blueprint is based on the Pyramid of Success.

THE PYRAMID OF SUCCESS

The pyramid exemplifies permanency — steady, durable, and lasting for centuries. The same is true in building your sales career. If it is built solid, like the pyramids, it will last a lifetime.

There are five essential ingredients needed to build a successful sales career. These ingredients are available to anyone with a desire to succeed.

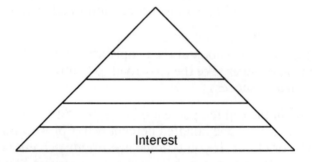

ONE: INTEREST

Interest: *the decision you make to develop, practice, and apply the information available that will cause you to become as successful as you're capable of becoming.*

Genuine interest is the solid, stable foundation of a successful sales career.

I'm sure it has crossed your mind that minimum interest by a professional can leave customers in a bad way. Suppose you are in the hospital for a serious operation — a procedure that could mean life or death. As the nurses wheel you to the operating room, you hear them chatting about your doctor: ''I hear he hasn't had any surgical training since he graduated from medical school thirty years ago!'' How much confidence would you have in this doctor?

How do your customers feel about you? Are you up-to-date on your industry, your customers' industries, and on the latest trends and developments in your business world?

What are the traits of people who show a great deal of interest in their career? They are enthusiastic, hard-working, organized, disciplined, and willing to try something new. Wherever you meet this person, these traits shine through. You sense an involvement, which is the basis of getting to the top. An interested person tends to be *successful* in the career of his or her choice.

When *you* are interested, you are excited about your career, so you continue to learn. You read books (like this one) and trade journals. You fraternize with the most successful people in your own industry. Walter Chrysler once said, ''Give me a salesperson who gets excited.'' When salespeople get excited, customers get excited. When customers get excited, they buy.

Are salespeople enthusiastic because they're successful, or are they successful because they're enthusiastic?

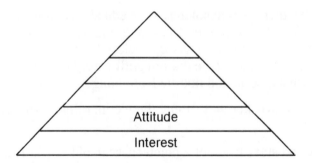

TWO: ATTITUDE

Attitude: *the idea that positive thoughts produce positive results; negative thoughts produce negative results.*

Attitude communicates your opinion of people, business, and life in general.

You may be thinking, ''Here's another one of those positive thinkers!'' There's more to it than that. William James observed that the greatest discovery of his generation was that people can change their lives by changing their attitudes.

There are only two kinds of people in the world: Those who think they can and those who think they can't. They're both right.

The negative thinker's career has a downward spiral. You find negative behavior feeding on negative thoughts. There is a story told about a man on a high bridge, getting ready to make the fatal plunge. Another man ran up to him, intending to talk him out of the suicidal leap. The two men got to talking, and ten minutes later, they *both* jumped.

The following two stories illustrate the importance of attitude:

A Russian railway worker accidentally locked himself in a refrigerated boxcar. Unable to get the attention of his fellow workers, he resigned himself to dying and started recording his thoughts on the inside of the boxcar walls: "It's getting very cold in here," he wrote. "It's very hard to breathe. I know I'm going to die. These will probably be my last words."

Sure enough, those were his last words. Just as he predicted, he died.

However, there was absolutely no medical reason for the man's death. The refrigeration mechanism in the boxcar was broken. The actual temperature never got below 56 degrees. The boxcar was well ventilated, so he did not suffocate. He was found the next morning, so he did not die from hunger or thirst.

The railway worker was simply the victim of his own negative thoughts.

The second story is about a nineteen-year-old boy in Romania, who made medical history by living for eleven days without food or water. He was buried under a ten-story apartment building during an earthquake.

When he was discovered, people asked him how he had managed to survive. "I slept much of the time," he told them. "But when I was awake, I never doubted for an instant that I would be rescued. Every waking minute of those eleven long days, I was positive I would come out alive."

Positive thoughts produce positive results. So:

- Regularly feed your mind positive thoughts.
- Look for the positive in any negative situation.
- Take action to improve a negative situation.
- Network with successful people.

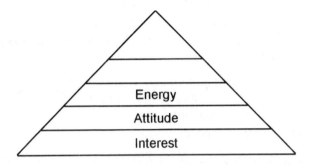

THREE: ENERGY

Energy: *developing your capacity by getting a little better every day.*

Tomorrow you could do your job a little better than yesterday ... a little better the following day ... and the next day ... and the next. Can you imagine the impact this would have on your career in one short year?

Energy is more than something physical. It is fuel for your daily challenges. It grows from interest and a positive attitude. Without it, you are like a car that remains in neutral, but when you are excited about your day's activities, you have the energy to carry you through.

Think about a time when you were facing an exceptionally exciting day. Maybe you were getting ready to go on a pleasurable vacation. The night before, you set your alarm for an hour earlier to get an early start.

What happened? The next morning, you woke up five minutes before the alarm. Your feet hit the deck and you were off and running.

Where did you get all that unusual energy? Your own enthusiasm and positive attitude gave you the energy to carry you through.

The successful, professional salesperson isn't one hundred percent better than the mediocre masses. Maybe he or she is only twenty percent better in Qualification, twenty percent better in Filling the Need, twenty percent better in Cementing the Sale, and so on throughout the Seven-Step procedure. These little differences add up to big differences. At 211 degrees, water is hot water and nothing more. But just one more degree — 212 — and the water can become steam, with the power to move a locomotive.

Several years ago at an annual dog sled race in Alaska, the race covered over 1000 miles, and lasted a grueling fifteen days and nights. The winner won by just *one second*. That *little* difference made *all* the difference.

The same is true in selling. Little differences can add up to make all the difference in the world. That's energy — developing your capacity.

FIVE: SUCCESS

Success: *the self-satisfaction in the accomplishment of something that is important to you.*

We're going to skip to the top of the pyramid in building your successful sales career. As you might expect, the top of the pyramid is *success.*

Most people don't recognize a successful person until after that person has "arrived." Then they say: "Boy, he sure was in the right place at the right time," or "She really had all the connections," or "What a stroke of luck" — as if that's all there is to becoming successful.

That's nonsense. Success isn't handed out on a silver platter. The professional salesperson has *worked* for his or her accomplishments.

Success is relative, and it means different things to different people.

To you, success may mean money — achieving a certain level of income. It may mean achieving a certain job title or owning things with status value. It may mean having time to spend with your family, establishing strong relationships, and being a positive influence on the growth and development of your children. It may mean having friends, being able to pursue your hobbies, travel, or many other things.

You need more than luck to enter the winner's circle. The professional salesperson goes for *achievement*. What makes a professional stand out? Developing the habit of doing all the things necessary to reach the top, even when they're boring or unpleasant.

When you create mental techniques, you are more motivated to handle unpleasant activities. You prepare yourself mentally by reminding yourself of the gain to you after you are done. Remembering rewards picks you up. When you set aside a specific time each day or week to finish unpleasant duties, the routine becomes automatic.

Success is achieving what *you* feel is important and the self-satisfaction that comes with that achievement. Only when *you* make clear what success means can you pursue it effectively.

FOUR: METHOD

Method: *the precise, step-by-step procedure that covers all the points in the selling process and leaves nothing to chance*

I have skipped the fourth essential ingredient in building your successful career in selling on purpose.

This is the one ingredient missing from most sales training programs and books. Yet, without it, your sales skills are like a million-dollar computer with no software. The fourth essential ingredient is method.

The *World Class Selling* method includes the Seven Steps of the Track Selling System,™ and the Guaranteed Close.

Method is a game plan for selling your product or service to your customer. Combine method with interest, attitude, and energy, and you're on top of the Pyramid of Success.

Method makes you a sales professional. It makes your mind go to details. It separates the victor from second place.

Vince Scully, one of the premier sportscasters in the country, is disciplined and operates with a method. Despite his years of experience, before he broadcasts a sports event, he arrives several days early in the city of the contest to brief himself systematically on the opposing teams and players.

It's like the actor, Sir Laurence Olivier, said: "You have to have the humility to prepare and the self-confidence to bring it off." Dedication to details, discipline, and method mark Vince Scully a professional.

The same professional traits and work habits describe a professional salesperson. A sales pro is also dedicated to details, discipline, and method for accomplishing goals. Just as Vince Scully briefs himself about the players, the good salesperson learns about the prospect and the prospect's needs. Scully prepares himself with details to make the game interesting and appetizing to receivers of his information. Similarly, the salesperson gathers and organizes details to make the presentation attractive to the prospect.

When selling becomes a procedure, it ceases to be a problem. Until it becomes a procedure, it will always be a problem. When you have *method* and you combine it with your high degree of *interest* in building your career, along with the positive *attitude* and *energy* it creates, you will become a *success*. You will witness the birth of a true sales professional.

RATING YOUR OWN SUCCESS

The Pyramid of Success is a formula for achieving success not only in selling, but also in rating your own performance and that of your salespeople during regular performance reviews, before hiring, and when considering an employee for promotion.

The pyramid helps you visualize the ingredients that propel you to success. Mark your calendar to review your progress in terms of knowledge, skill, and attitude in sixty days and in one year. In sixty days, ask yourself: "How do I measure up in these areas? What have I done to improve?" At the end of a year, review your progress with the same queries to see your improvement.

You have to master each level of the pyramid before you can move up to the next, and these levels also work synergetically. It's the interaction among the levels that is the key to attaining your goal of success.

Successful selling and successful living are pretty much the same. The same skills that can make you more successful in selling can also make you more successful as a human being.

THINGS TO REMEMBER

+ The Pyramid of Success is a proven road to success. Most people take the easy road to failure instead of the proven road to success.
+ The components of success are:
  1. Interest: Be excited and enthusiastic about your work.
  2. Attitude: Stay positive.
  3. Energy: Improve a little every day. You only need to be a little better in each area to be in the top ten percent of peak performers.
  4. Method: The Track Selling System™ is your path to success.
  5. Success: Your success is the self-satisfaction in the accomplishment of something that's important to you.

EXERCISES

1. How would you define success in *your* career?

2. Evaluate yourself in each category from one to ten, with ten as the highest:
    a. Interest:
    b. Attitude:
    c. Energy:
    d. Method:
    e. Success:

3. Based on your evaluation above, develop a plan to improve in these areas in sixty days and in one year.

MY PERSONAL CAREER PYRAMID

a. Interest:

Date in 60 days:

Objective for improvement:

Action plan:

Date in 1 year:

Objective for improvement:

Action plan:

b. Attitude:

Date in 60 days:

Objective for improvement:

Action plan:

Date in 1 year:

Objective for improvement:

Action plan:

c. Energy:
Date in 60 days:
Objective for improvement:

Action plan:

Date in 1 year:
Objective for improvement:

Action plan:

d. Method:
Date in 60 days:
Objective for improvement:

Action plan:

Date in 1 year:
Objective for improvement:

Action plan:

e. Success:
Date in 60 days:
Objective for improvement:

Action plan:

Date in 1 year:
Objective for improvement:

Action plan:

24

APPLYING WORLD CLASS SELLING
TO YOUR WORK AND PERSONAL LIFE

Sometimes you are ''selling'' even when no money is
exchanged for a product or service: Selling is simply
effective communication and we all communicate. Selling also
applies to ideas, concepts, desires, and attitudes. You might be
selling your boss on the idea of promoting you, your spouse on
the idea of making a major purchase, or your kids on the idea of
improving their grades.

Just about everything you have learned in *World Class Selling*
to help you sell your product or service will also work in *non*-
sales situations. Whether you are a professional salesperson
who wants to ''sell'' your spouse on the idea of a vacation, a
teacher who wants to ''sell'' a student on the joys of learning,
or an employee who wants to ''sell'' an idea to a supervisor,
you can use the techniques of *World Class Selling* to accomplish your communication objectives.

Think about this: A person who can't sell an idea is not much
better off than a person who doesn't have an idea.

THE JOB TRACK

Several years ago, a client of mine was making a job change. He
was interviewing for a management position of a new division

of a company. During the interview process, he gave me a call. He was being asked questions that seemed unrelated to the job he was applying for and was confused.

We developed a series of qualification questions so he could get a more clear understanding of the interview. He used the qualification questions and realized he was being considered for one of two positions.

"I thought I was applying for a job to develop a new division," he recalled. "I was actually being considered for this job *and* a position to take over an existing division. The qualification questions also uncovered that the president of the company had some concerns about my abilities. It was with this new awareness that I was able to address the issues in a very professional manner. I remembered Roy's advice: *Act, don't react.*"

By using qualification questions, my friend cleared up his confusion, kept the interview on track, and in the end, he got the job.

THE ROMANCE TRACK

One day in January, several years back, a good friend of mine greeted me with a big smile. "Chitwood," he beamed, "you'll never know what you've done for me ... how you've changed my life!"

"Changed your life?" I reflected.

"A few months ago," he explained, "I met a young lady. I took her out to dinner in December, and then I took her out again last Friday, January 6th. As we were having a drink after dinner, I said to her, 'We've known each other for two years.'"

"She said, 'What do you mean, two years? We've only dated twice.'"

" 'Yes,' I replied, 'but that's two years: '88 and '89.' And then I said: 'You're an attractive, single lady and I'm a divorced man. We seem to hit it off pretty well. Can you think of any reason why we shouldn't spend the night together?' "

"And she answered, 'No.' "

"And that," the salesman chortled, "was the beginning of a new romance."

I'm sure you recognize this story as an Act of Commitment.

THE FRIENDSHIP TRACK

Here's another way the Track Selling System™ was used in a personal setting:

I was doing a sales training program for one of our clients, Mighty Distributing System of America, in Niagara Falls, New York. The program was scheduled to start at 9:00 a.m. At 6:30 a.m., I received a call from the Chief Operating Officer, Jerry Beck, a personal friend. "Would you like to join me for a walk to the Falls?" he asked, knowing that I walked for exercise. I tried to back out. "Thanks, but I need to review my notes for the program at nine."

He persisted. "Did you ever see the Falls? It's a natural wonder."

"No," I said, "I haven't seen it."

"Roy, they're really beautiful, a sight to behold. It would be a shame to miss them while you're here."

"Maybe later," I stalled. "I want to prepare for the meeting."

"It's only a short walk," he went on. "Just fifteen or twenty minutes. I would really enjoy the pleasure of your company this morning."

"Fine, I'll be right down."

Jerry closed me three times that morning — twice on the beauty of the Falls, and once on the pleasure of my company. He closed me for *my* reasons, not his. He knew I would enjoy the sight.

He was right. What a delightful experience the Falls were. What a great way to start the day. It mentally prepared me for my upcoming meeting more than anything else could have done.

THE FAMILY TRACK

One day, a father of two teenage daughters (one bound for college the next year) approached his wife to sell her on the idea of making a major purchase. Notice how smoothly he takes his prospect — his wife — through the Seven-Step process.

APPROACH

Husband:	*Hi. Any big plans today?*
Wife:	*Oh, nothing much. I was just trying to get the sewing machine out to finish those curtains I started last summer. Great works of art take time, you know. So, what are you up to?*
Husband:	*Oh, I wanted to talk to you*
Wife:	*Okay. Sounds serious.*
Husband:	*No, nothing bad. I just have an idea I'd like you to listen to.*
Wife:	*Sure.*

QUALIFICATION

Husband:	*Before I explain that idea, I need to ask you a couple of questions.*
Wife:	*Do I need to have a lawyer present?*
Husband:	*[Laughs] Not incriminating questions. Just questions. First of all, would you like to take a vacation?*
Wife:	*That's easy. Of course I would!*
Husband:	*What would be your idea of an ideal vacation?*
Wife:	*I guess somewhere where I can relax — no phones, no responsibilities.*
Husband:	*Anything else?*
Wife:	*See interesting places. Travel.*
Husband:	*How would you feel about including the girls?*
Wife:	*That would be great. I've been thinking a lot lately. With Karen going away to school next year, we're not going to have very much time to do things together as a whole family.*

AGREEMENT ON NEED

Husband: *So as I understand it, you'd like to be able to get away from it all, visit places you've never been before, and you'd like us to spend more time together as a family. Is that right?*

Wife: Sure.

Husband: [Laying out some brochures] *Look at this. I've been looking into motor homes and recreational vehicles.*

Wife: *You mean, like Winnebagos. Aren't they expensive?*

Husband: *Some are, some aren't. There are a lot of different kinds.*

Wife: [Pointing to brochure] *And this is the one you want.*

Husband: *After looking around and talking to some of my friends who already own RVs, I think this model is best suited for our needs and budget. Since you're an equal partner in this decision, I'm sure there's some specific information you want to know.*

SELLING THE COMPANY

Husband: *This motor home is made by one of the largest RV manufacturers. The company's been in business over thirty years, and has an excellent reputation. I asked Tony Hanson about it. He has a different model, but it's very similar. He had nothing but great things to say about the company and its service.*

Wife: *You've really been doing a lot of research.*

Husband: *I've looked around ... asked questions ... compared models and manufacturers. It's been quite an education.*

FEATURE/BENEFIT/REACTION SEQUENCE

Husband:	*Let me tell you about some of the features of this model. It's got 27 feet of living space, with two separate sleeping areas.* [Feature] *So there's plenty of room to move around. The girls have their own private area, and we have our own.* [Benefit] *Remember what it was like when we went camping two years ago?* [Reaction]
Wife:	*I honestly thought we'd never speak to each other again.*
Husband:	*On the other hand, this model isn't too big.* [Feature] *It's easy to drive. Why, on our trips we could trade off driving.* [Benefit] *If we had the time, where are some of the places you'd like to go?* [Reaction]
Wife:	*You know, there are so many beautiful places right here in our own country that I've never seen.*
Husband:	*This model has a lot of luxury features, too. There's even a private compartment where we could install a shower.* [Feature] *So we wouldn't have to trade comfort for mobility.* [Benefit] *How do you feel about a shower?* [Reaction]
Wife:	*There's no question, my dear, it has to have a shower! There are still some things that are sacred.*

ACT OF COMMITMENT

Husband:	*For this model, with all the luxury amenities — providing us with the ability to explore places we've always wanted to visit, and giving us a great way to spend time together as a family — our investment would be $36,800. If we can find time later this week to visit the dealership, can you think of any reason why we shouldn't go ahead?*
Wife:	*$36,800 is a lot of money.*

Husband: *Yes, it is a lot of money, but it's a long-term investment. We agreed that you liked the size, you liked the fact that we'd be able to explore new places; and that even if we went camping in remote wilderness areas, you wouldn't have to give up the luxury of having a shower. This model has a lot of storage space.* [New feature] *There's plenty of room for our bicycles or a barbecue. There's even room for a folding picnic table.* [New benefit] *What do you think of the design?* [Reaction]

Wife: *Looks great on paper, but I'd like to see it in person.*

Husband: *If we can find time later this week to visit the dealership, can you think of any reason why we shouldn't go ahead?*

Wife: *I don't know. Maybe we shouldn't rush into this.*

Husband: *I understand. You liked the fact that we'd be able to spend more time with the girls. You liked the vehicle itself. You liked that it's easy to drive, that there's plenty of storage space, and that we have the option of installing an onboard shower. There must be something you don't like. Would you tell me what it is?*

Wife: *Once Karen starts school next fall, we're going to have tuition to think of. And then it's not going to be long before we're going to have to think about tuition for Michelle.*

Husband: *We've been very good about saving for college for the girls. This wouldn't come out of that fund. We'll be enjoying this for a long time. After we retire, we'll be able to travel and do all the things we've wanted to do together, just you and me. Let's do it.*

Wife: *Okay.*

CEMENT THE SALE

Husband: *I know you're going to like this. We all are. I know we'll have to very careful with money for the next few years, but in the long run we'll be glad we made this decision.*

THE IN-HOUSE TRACK

A former participant in my Track Selling System™ workshop told me how she had used Track Selling System™ within her company. Mary Parson was a general manager for an electronic parts company, and she was curious about applying the Seven Steps in a variety of business communications. "I'm going to work out a track to persuade my boss, Jack Cooper, to hire a new person," she said.

Jack has been away on a week's skiing trip, and has returned to his office on Monday morning. The first thing Mary does on Monday morning is to call Jack Cooper's secretary. This is what happens.

Manager: *What kind of mood is the boss in today?*

As you can see, Mary does a little pre-call investigation to find out what kind of mood the president is in before asking for an appointment.

Secretary: *Pretty good. He just saw last year's reports and he's about two feet off the ground.*

Manager: *I know how busy he is, just getting back from vacation, but I really need to see him today. Can you set that up for me?*

Secretary: *Hmm. How important is it?*

Manager: *Well, as I said, it's most important.*

Secretary: *Okay. I'll see what I can do and let you know.*

Undoubtedly, if the president had *not* been in a good mood, the manager would have delayed her request for an appointment. Timing is important. However, the secretary is able to set up an appointment, and soon Mary enters the president's office.

Just by looking at Jack's office, you can tell that he's a great ski enthusiast. There are photos of Jack skiing, a painting of a snow-capped mountain, and even a pair of skis in the corner.

Manager:	*How was your ski trip?*
President:	*Fantastic! The greatest skiing I've ever had! This was the first time I skied Sun Valley. I skied all week. I tell you, it was just fantastic.*

Mary establishes personal rapport.

Manager:	*I understand you just got last year's reports. How did they look?*
President:	*Tremendous! The greatest year we've ever had. A 69 percent improvement in bottom-line profits over the previous year. It was a great year. A lot of credit goes to you and your people for the fine job you have done.*

And that completes Step 1: Approach.

Manager:	*Jack, how important is it that we give our customers good turnaround time on service?*
President:	*Most important! This is the unique benefit we offer our customers, which they can't get anywhere else. When they have a problem, they can call us, and we can respond within an hour, two hours at the most.*

And that completes Step 2: Qualification.

Manager:	*Is this something you feel we should continue to do?*
President:	*Absolutely. This is how we build our company. It's greatly responsible for our growth, and this is how I want the company to be run.*

Mary has completed Step Three: Agreement on Need.

Manager:	*Jack, even though we've had this tremendous workload for the past year, our people have given us their very best. They've put in a lot of extra hours and*

> *energy. I've never heard a single gripe or complaint. They've really given us their very best.*

This is an example of Step 4: Sell the Company.

President: *Yes, I know that. As I said earlier, I feel they've made a major contribution to the success we've enjoyed.*

Manager: *Jack, by adding one more employee to our staff, we'll be able to get out the newsletter we've been talking about for the last couple of years. Do you know what that will do for us? One, it will improve our relations with our customers, and two, it will probably bring us additional business. How do you feel about the newsletter?*

The manager has just presented a *feature*, the newsletter; a *benefit*, improved customer relations and bringing in new prospects; and a *reaction* question: How does Jack feel about the newsletter?

President: *Well, we've been talking about a newsletter for a couple of years. I'd sure like to see it become a reality.*

Manager: *The new employee could also assist me with my workload, and I'd be able to get some of those special jobs done that you've been after me to do, but I really haven't had the time to do. That wouldn't make you unhappy, would it?*

President: *[Laughing] Oh no, absolutely not.*

Once again, a Feature/Benefit/Reaction sequence.

Manager: *Also, Jack, this new employee could give our Customer Service Department the assistance they need to handle our Customer Service workload. And you know what? We slipped on that in the past couple of months. Because of our workload, we've really not been giving them the service we used to. You've already told me how important that is to you.*

Observe that the *feature* just covered was the additional person to assist with customer service; the *benefit*, gives the customers the kind of service the employee wants them to have; and the *reaction* question, in this case, is a statement, because Jack has already told Mary how important customer service is.

Manager: *Do you have any questions, Jack?*

Here, Mary questions to release the prospect's FUDs.

President: *Only one: How much will we have to pay for this new employee?*

Manager: *We can get a qualified person who can help us get out the newsletter, help me with my workload, and give the Customer Service Department the assistance they need at our regular entry-level starting salary.*

This completes Step 5: Fill the Need.

Manager: *Jack, if we can get an ad in the paper for this weekend, can you think of any reason why we shouldn't set it up?*

President: *No, I really can't. It makes a lot of sense.*

And Jack Cooper has bought. Notice how Mary uses the closing statement, "*If we can get an ad in the paper for this weekend, can you think of any reason why we shouldn't* set it up?" This completes Step 6: Act of Commitment.

Manager: *Jack, I want you to know that I gave it a lot of thought before asking you to add another employee. I know no one likes to increase their overhead. However, we really do need this additional person. Not only do we need this employee, but by adding this person it will show the other employees that you really have been concerned about their workload and have done something to reduce it. That has to improve morale, and I know how you feel about employee morale. It's also an investment in better customer service, which has to pay off in increased profits. Also, I can tell by that stack of papers on your desk that you've got more important things to*

do today than spend all day with me. I
appreciate you fitting me into your busy
schedule. I'll get back with you later on in
the afternoon to confirm that we'll be
interviewing next week.

Notice, the completion of Step Seven: Cement the Sale. That's
it. All it took the manager was about four minutes to run
through the Seven Steps of the Track Selling System.™

THE DEVELOPMENT TRACK

Al Kauder, our Midwest manager, was a client of our company
before joining Max Sacks International. He had been hired by
his previous employer as Vice President of Sales to create a
new division, create a new brand name and product, and develop a sales staff for the new division. The company was an
industry leader and kept the new division a secret. Al used the
Track Selling System™ to build the new division.

"One day I received a call from a manufacturer's rep for a
company that would be a major competitor of ours. This competitor, who had some of the best rep groups in the country,
decided to replace all of their rep groups with a direct sales
staff.

"What a break for us! By having access to these reps we could
have complete coverage of the country. The challenge was to
convince these reps to meet with us at an industry trade show
ten days later at seven o'clock in the morning. This was a very
busy show for the reps and their meetings had all been scheduled far in advance.

"The first thing I did was to put my telephone conversation 'on
track.' I was able to convince the principles of every rep company to attend the meeting.

"We then put the meeting 'on track.' Since we had not yet
developed specific product designs, we mocked up several
designs to present. We developed a series of qualification
questions with the objective of having this elite group focus on
what a quality company is about and the value of a partnership
relationships.

"All but one company agreed to represent our line. The last company agreed after and additional meeting two weeks later.

"As a division with no products, no track record, and no existing customers, we were able to make 'the sale' with the help of the Track Selling System.™ It gave us focus, the ability to strategize each meeting, how to address 'What will it do for me?' for the reps, and the specific tactical steps each of us had to perform. It was fun, too!"

TRACKING YOURSELF

You can use a version of the Qualification and Agreement on Need steps in your personal life to assess what you need, what you want, what you have now, and the "price" you are willing to pay. Once you do the process with yourself, you are in a good position to set your goals and reach them.

I have done this throughout my sales career and in my personal life whenever I felt I wanted to make a major change. If my circumstances began to seem out of alignment with what I wanted, or out of alignment with what I *believed* I wanted or *used* to want, I would write out the steps to help assess my situation and clarify my goals. Here's how it works:

1. I would write out my larger, lifetime goals and objectives. Then I wrote down each smaller, shorter-cycle goal as it came to me. Did I still want those goals? Were they still on target? This, of course, corresponds to asking open-ended questions in Step Two: Qualification, to find out your prospect's particular needs and problems. I had to ask myself: "What do I like best about ... ?"; "What do I like least about ... "; and the all-important question: "Has anything changed?"

2. I would write out a capsule summary of this current, updated version of what I wanted and needed: "As I understand it now, I'm looking for ... "; and complete the description of what I wanted. This corresponds to the capsule summary of the Agreement on Need step.

3. I would write out what I had in my life right at that time, which corresponds to the salesperson's product or service. Did the "product" of the circumstances in my life *still fit* my specific needs and goals?

4. I would write out the challenges and difficulties I might
   be facing in relation to my goals and current circumstances, the things I had to put up with, and the things I
   had to go without. This, of course, corresponds to the
   "price." If my goals and objectives had changed, I
   wrote and rewrote the Agreement on Need statement
   until I "agreed" with myself and was clear about my
   new goals and objectives. If the "product" of my life
   didn't fit my specific goals and objectives, or if the
   "price" I was paying was too high, I knew I would
   have to make adjustments where necessary.

For example, I used this technique to decide whether I wanted
to stay on at Westland Life when that company came under the
control of Reserve Life. I decided I did want to stay.

But circumstances change. As I learned more about Reserve
Life's policies I did the Qualification and Agreement on Need
process again, and saw I *didn't* want to stay there after all, but
did want to work with compatible colleagues as an independent
insurance marketing firm and build an excellent sales force in
the techniques of the Track Selling System.™ And so two
colleagues and I formed Century 3 Insurance Marketing Corporation.

I did this process again when the Max Sacks sales training
company came on the market. I uncovered that what I was
really seeking was the opportunity to train many more salespeople, in all fields, in the valuable Track Selling System™
techniques. Using my personal, written-out version of the
Qualification and Agreement on Need steps helped me to make
a life-changing decision — to leave the insurance field after
sixteen years, buy Max Sacks and enter my new career as a full-
time, professional sales trainer.

This technique for assessing and clarifying the contents of your
mind and heart, and making them more conscious by writing
them down is not the only one you can use. However, it has
been particularly valuable in my life, and I suggest you consider
trying it not only in your sales calls but whenever you come to a
major crossroads in your life.

After all, the Qualification and Agreement on Need technique
underscores the ancient adage, "Know thyself." How can you
even begin to better yourself without this knowledge? This

technique allows you to center yourself — to establish a sound springboard for achieving your goals. It helps you get a higher, broader perspective to see the price you must pay to reach your goals.

In my own case, the capsule summary of the Agreement on Need statement provided me with an understanding of why I became a sales professional; validated that I wanted to be of service to others in the business world; confirmed that I want to enjoy the finer things of life; and helped me see that I have the need to be the best I can be, as a person and as a professional. What might you learn about yourself if you apply this Qualification and Agreement on Need technique to yourself?

YOUR OWN SPECIAL TRACK

As you can see, the Track Selling System™ is the most flexible communication process imaginable. It can be applied to every walk of life. It is a valuable people-skill, whenever you're persuading others in or out of business.

You've got to know the skill to apply it.

The Track Selling System™ allows you to be yourself. In essence, you take the Seven Steps and make them your *own* Seven Steps, using your words — your personality — so you're comfortable with them. As Dorothy Ficocello of Le Dimar, Inc. relates, "As far as personal success is concerned, I find this way of communicating to be of help in every facet of my life. Whether I'm addressing church organizations or simply trying to understand my teenage daughter, it has been of great assistance."

COACHING THE TRACK

One of the great benefits of the Track Selling System™ is that it gives management a tool to help their salespeople grow and become more effective. Having people learn and follow a selling process enables the manager to apply the principles of total quality management to the sales process. Refer to the coaching form in the forms section of this book and use this tool to critique your salespeople when accompanying them on sales calls. By providing continuous improvement to the selling process, you will develop a world class sales organization.

YOU HAVE WHAT YOU NEED

You have now read all the way through *World Class Selling*. You have done the exercises and applied the Track Selling System™ to your own product or service. You have looked for — and, I trust, found — the answer to the invisible question: "What will it do for me?"

You have the know-how. You have the knack. You have everything it takes to serve clients, earn more money, and have more fun in selling. Now you know what it will do for you.

Because you have persisted so well in closing the sale, another door just opened.

Welcome to the ranks of the top ten percent of professional salespeople — the proud top producers who know:

Selling is the greatest profession in the world.

THINGS TO REMEMBER

- *World Class Selling* can be applied to all areas of your life.
- You can use the Track Selling System™ in romantic relationships, friendships, with your family, at work, and in other situations.
- You can use Step Two and Step Three to clarify your own goals ... and reach them.

EXERCISES

1. Describe previous experiences in your personal life where you could have used the Seven-Step Track Selling System.™

2. How might you use the Track Selling System™ in your own life in the future?

a. At work:

b. With your family:

c. With your friends:

d. Other situations:

FORMS

FOR WORLD CLASS SELLING

In this section, you will find all the forms, steps, transitional statements, and questions that appear throughout the book. I have placed them here so you can find them at a moment's notice...and make use of them.

The more familiar you become with these forms, the more the Track Selling System™ will become second nature. It is also a good idea to photocopy the forms you'll need and fill them out before meeting with each and every prospect. This will ensure a professional presentation. You will see the difference that being prepared makes — in your confidence level, ability to close and financial success — and you will move closer and closer to joining the top performers who make their goals by serving their customers.

THE FIVE BUYING DECISIONS

1. The Salesperson
   a. Integrity
   b. Judgment

2. Company

3. Product or Service

4. Price

5. Time

THE SIX BUYING MOTIVES

1. Desire for Gain — $
2. Fear of Loss — $
3. Comfort and Convenience
4. Security and Protection
5. Pride of Ownership
6. Satisfaction of Emotion

SELLING TO THE BUYING MOTIVES

1. Desire for Gain — $
   Feature:
   Benefit:
   Reaction Question:

2. Fear of Loss — $
   Feature:
   Benefit:
   Reaction Question:

3. Comfort and Convenience
   Feature:
   Benefit:
   Reaction Question:

4. Security and Protection
   Feature:
   Benefit:
   Reaction Question:

5. Pride of Ownership
   Feature:
   Benefit:
   Reaction Question:

6. Satisfaction of Emotion
   Feature:
   Benefit:
   Reaction Question:

ASKING QUESTIONS

FACT-FINDING QUESTIONS

These questions uncover general and specific facts relevant to your prospects' needs.

General: "What are your budget considerations?"

Specific: "Who has the final sign-off on your budget?"

1.

2.

3.

4.

5.

6.

FEELING-FINDING QUESTIONS

These questions uncover general and specific motives, likes, dislikes and opinions — how your prospect feels.

General: "What do you hope to accomplish with your computer system?"

Specific: "How important is desktop publishing to you?"

1.

2.

3.

4.

5.

6.

OPEN-ENDED QUESTIONS

These questions permit prospects to express facts and feelings in as many words as they choose. For example: "How do you think inflation will affect your marketing strategy?"

Develop at least five open-ended questions for establishing rapport and at least five open-ended, qualifying questions, which determine your prospect's need, authority to make the purchasing decisions, and budget, in the following spaces.

RAPPORT-BUILDING QUESTIONS

1.
2.
3.
4.
5.
6.

QUALIFYING QUESTIONS

1.
2.
3.
4.
5.
6.

REFLECTIVE QUESTIONS

These questions encourage prospects to open up by "keying in" on what has been said.

> *Prospect:*   *"I'm concerned about your product's quality."*
>
> *Salesperson:*   *"Quality?"*

DIRECTIVE QUETIONS

These questions guide prospects toward a desired, specific piece of information. For example: "Would a three-month warranty be of use to your company?"

YOUR SALES PLAN

Salesperson: Company:

(Note: Your sales call should be to a new customer or, if an old one, present a new product, service, idea, etc.)

Name of Account:

Kind of Business:

Individual's Name: Title:

What is my objective on this call?

The most important things you need to know to determine need:

Product/Service you are going to sell:

How will the customer use your Product/Service?

Three most important facts about my company:
>   1.
>   2.
>   3.

What sales aids are you going to use?

What "Features/Benefits" are you going to present?
>   1. Feature:
>   Benefit:

>   2. Feature:
>   Benefit:

>   3. Feature:
>   Benefit:

TRACK PRESENTATION
STEP ONE: APPPROACH

WRITTEN OBJECTIVES FOR THE SALES CALL

Prospect's name:

Prospect's title:

Prospect's company:

Kind of business:

Specific objectives for this sales call:

WRITTEN PLAN FOR STEP ONE: APPROACH

1. Introduction

2. Rapport-Building (three open-ended questions):
   a.

   b.

   c.

3. Seven Ways to Improve Your People Skills:
   a. Smile.
   b. Develop a genuine interest in others.
   c. Talk in terms of the other person's interest.
   d. Use the other person's name.
   e. Give compliments.
   f. Listen.
   g. Make the other person feel important.

TRACK PRESENTATION
STEP TWO: QUALIFICATION

Transition statement to Step Two:

> "[Prospect's name], *I would like to tell you about our* [name of your product or service]. *However, in order for me to do the best job I possibly can for you, I need to ask you a couple of questions. Is that all right?"*

Ask several open-ended, qualification questions:

1.
2.
3.
4.
5.
6.
7.

OPTIONAL QUESTIONS

* "May I ask what you like most about ... ?"
* "Would it be fair to ask what you like least about ... ?"
* "Has anything changed?"

PROFILE OF A QUALIFIED PROSPECT

* Has a need
* Has the authority to buy
* Has the money to buy

I suggest you develop a list of standard qualification questions to use on every call. As you plan your presentation think of additional questions you may want to ask each particular prospect.

SAMPLE QUALIFICATION FORM

Mr./Mrs./Ms.   our company is different from most companies in the way we serve our customers. Most companies would just come out and sell you a furnace. We determine your needs, what you want to accomplish with your air quality system, and recommend the products that will meet your needs. In order for me to do the best job I possibly can for you, I need to ask you a couple of questions. Is that all right?

1.   Why are you considering converting to natural gas?

2.   What type of energy are you using for heating now?
      a. Water heating?

3.   What do you know about natural gas heating?

4.   What other gas appliances are you considering?

5.   How long have you owned your home?

6.   How long have you been considering converting?

7.   What type of work do you do?

8.   That's interesting. How did you get started doing that?

9.   How long have you lived here?

10.   May I ask what you like most about your current heating system?

11.   Would it be fair to ask what you like least about your existing system?

12.   Is there anyone else who you would want to include in our discussion about your heating and air quality system?

13.   What type of budget have you set up for the system?

14.   How are you planning on handling the investment?

15.

16.

Home Owner: Phone number:

                               Date of Appointment:

Address:

City: State: Zip code:

TRACK PRESENTATION
STEP THREE: AGREEMENT ON NEED

"As I understand it, you are looking for something that will [summarize the important information you gathered in Step One: Approach and Step Two: Qualification]. *Is that correct?"*

WRITTEN PLAN FOR
STEP THREE: AGREEMENT ON NEED

As I understand it, you are looking for:

Is that correct?

Is there agreement on need?

If No:
- Clear up misunderstandings.
- Use a revised Agreement on Need statement.
- Re-verify Agreement on Need.

If Yes:
- Proceed to Step Four: Sell the Company.

TRACK PRESENTATION
STEP FOUR: SELL THE COMPANY

Transition statement to Step Four:

"[Prospect's name], I'm sure that if I were in your position, there would be some specific information I would like to know about [your company's name]. *May I ask how much information you have about* [your company's name]?*"*

Then, in response to whatever the prospect answers:

"I understand. Let me quickly cover a couple of things that I think would be important to me if I were in your position."

Comment Statement:

Your prospect may have the following concerns (unspoken):

- I don't know who you are.
- I don't know your company's products.
- I don't know what your company stands for.
- I don't know your company's customers.
- I don't know your company's record.
- I don't know your company's reputation.

TRACK PRESENTATION
STEP FIVE: FILL THE NEED

Transition statement to Step Five.

"*[Prospect's name], there are several important features I'd like to tell you about our* [name of your product or service]."

FEATURE / BENEFIT / REACTION SEQUENCE

Feature: Key point or fact about your product or service

Benefit: Answers the prospect's unvoiced question: "What will it do for me?"

Reaction   Draws out the prospect's reaction to the features
Question: and benefits.

Prospect's Primary Buying Motives:

Most Appropriate Features/Benefits:

    1. Feature:

      Benefit:

      Reaction Question:

    2. Feature:

      Benefit:

      Reaction Question:

    3. Feature:

      Benefit:

      Reaction Question:

"*Do you have any questions?*" Uncovering any Fears ,Uncertainties, and Doubts (FUDs).

"*For your* [summary of features to be included], *the price is* [quote the price]."

TRACK PRESENTATION
STEP SIX: ACT OF COMMITMENT

"If we:

Can you think of any reason why we shouldn't:

If the prospect answers no, he or she has just bought. Now you proceed with the paperwork. All agreements, contracts, payment arrangements, etc. are handled at this time. In some selling situations it isnecessary to have the legal departments of each company handle the contracts. If the prospect answers yes, proceed to Guaranteed Close.

TRACK PRESENTATION
STEP SEVEN: CEMENT THE SALE

Develop a summary statement that you can use with your customer to review the logical reasons for his or her emotional purchase. Cite the features of the product or service, and cite the resulting benefits.

Thank your customers for their time and business.

Future follow-up: your next contact with the customer.

TRACK PRESENTATION
THE GUARANTEED CLOSE

FIRST CLOSE

If the prospect says yes and gives you an objection, acknowledge the objection with:

- ◆ "I see."
- ◆ "I understand."
- ◆ "I can appreciate that."

SECOND CLOSE

Re-establish areas of agreement, add a new Feature/Benefit/Reaction sequence, and close again.

"We agreed you like

1.

2.

3.

Now, in addition:

Feature:

Benefit:

Reaction Question:

Close: *"If we:*

can you think of any reason why we shouldn't:

THIRD CLOSE

Discover the real objection, answer it, and close again.

"We talked about a lot of things you liked, including:

1.

2.

3.

There must be something you don't like. Would you mind telling me what it is?"

Answer the objection to the best of your ability and close again. You can also add another Feature/Benefit/Reaction sequence (optional):

Feature:

Benefit:

Reaction Question:

Close: *"Let's set it up"* (or a similar close).

FOURTH CLOSE

Cite the penalty of delaying action (a face-saving way out). Identify what the prospect loses by postponing a decision.

For example, you might say something like: *"From what you've told me, it sounds like you have already made the decision to change suppliers. The only thing that can happen between now and the time you decide to change is that it will cost you. It will cost you in:*

That doesn't make sense, does it?"

Close: *"Let's get started"* (or a similar close).

FIFTH CLOSE

Do something different. Imagination is the key to success.

SALES EXERCISE INSTRUCTIONS

Complete this form for each prospect and give it to a partner for role play exercise.

Your Name:

Name of your company:

The specific product or serviceyou are going to sell:

Kind of customer you are going to sell (Business, Executive, Manufacturer, Purchasing Agent, Wholesaler, Retailer, Consumer, etc.):

Name and title of the person you are going to sell to:

How will the customer use your product or service?

How did the call originate? How long have you been involved with this person?

What is the *greatest benefit* to the customer?

Any special circumstances?

What is the Agreement on Need Statement?

"Buzz Words" or appropriate answers that would help your partner do a better job in role-playing the customer:

ROLE PLAY EVALUATION

Salesperson:

Product/Service Sold:

Date:

Grade each step and briefly explain:
(E) Excellent (G) Good (N) Needs Improvement

1. Approach: ( )
2. Qualification: ( )
3. Agreement On Need: ( )
4. Sell The Company: ( )
5. Fill The Need: ( )
6. Act Of Commitment:
    a. Closing Statement: ( )
    b. Handling Objections: ( )
7. Cement The Sale: ( )

CHARACTERISTICS OF THE PROFESSIONAL SALESPERSON

Please check appropriate space.

	Excellent	Very Good	Good	Needs Improvement
Personality:				
Sincerity:				
Empathy:				
Competence:				
Enthusiasm:				

Suggestions:

THE PYRAMID OF SUCCESS

THE WHEEL OF ACTIVITY

SETTING GOALS

Goals should be:

- ◆ Big
- ◆ Long-term
- ◆ Short-term
- ◆ In writing

TRACK COACHING

Observe the call, discover strengths and weaknesses in coaching and critiquing, refrain from a joint call!

Grade each stepand briefly explain:

(E) Excellent (G) Good (N) Needs Improvement

ONE: BASICS

1. Image: ( )
2. Auto Clean and Organized: ( )
3. On Time: ( )
4. Account Info Adequate: ( )
5. Product/Service Knowledge: ( )
6. Enthusiastic/Excited: ( )
7. Listening Skill: ( )
8. Mutual Understanding: ( )
9. Note Taking Skill: ( )
10. Use of Time: ( )

TWO: SALES CALL

1. Approach: ( )
2. Qualification: ( )
3. Agreement on Need: ( )
4. Sell the Company: ( )
5. Fill the Need: ( )
6. Act of Commitment: ( )
7. Cement the Sale: ( )
8. Were multiple needs developed to obtain additional sales? ( )
9. Seeds planted: ( )
10. Referrals: ( )
11. Other: ( )

THREE: POST-CALL REVIEW

1.   Rep Self Analysis:

2.   Your Discussion and Feedback (Strengths):

3.   Skills in Need of Improvement:

4.   Compared to a previous session, what has changed?

FOUR: SALESPERSON'S ACTION PLAN

Describe what the salesperson will do to achieve the desired change, improvement or learning.

1.   What the salesperson will do (the goal):

2.   How he or she will do it. Any steps, methods or proce-
     dures to be followed to achieve the goal:

3.   The way the situation will be if this action plan is success-
     ful (standards to be met):

4.   When these things will be done (dates, times, deadlines):

FIVE: MANAGER'S ACTION PLAN

1.   What you will do to help the salesperson achieve his or her
     action plan:

2.   When these things will be done (dates and times):

REFERENCES

Introduction	Walton, Mary. *The Deming Management Method*. Dodd, Mead & Company.
	Barr, C. Charles III, Dallas, TX.
	The H. R. Chally Group, 500 Lincoln Park Blvd., Dayton, OH 45429-3479, (513)299-1255, fax (513)299-0630.
Chapter 3	Wilson, Larry. *Changing the Games: The New Way to Sell*. Simon and Schuster.
Chapter 5	McGraw Hill, 1221 Avenue of the Americas, New York, NY, (212)512-2000. (A sales call costs from $99 to $452.)
	Dartnell Corporaton, 4660 N. Ravenswood Ave., Chicago, IL 60640, (312)561-4000.
	Sales and Marketing Executives International Association, Statler Office Tower, Cleveland, OH 44115, (216)771-6650.
	Electronic Representatives Association, 20 E. Huron St., Chicago, IL 60611, (312)649-1333.
Chapter 6	Wall Street Journal. March 22, 1990. Communispond Inc. (New York) survey.
Chapter 7	Olivier, Sir Laurence. British actor.
	Berman, Jack. President and Owner, Berman Publications, 15720 Ventura Blvd., Suite 311, Encino, CA 91436, (818)905-5388, fax (818)905-5380.
Chapter 10	Zunin, Leonard. Contact: The First Four Minutes. (We make a lasting impression on others during the first three to five minutes.)
	Mehrabian, Albert. *Silent Messages*. Wadsworth. (7% by what we say, 30% by the tone in which we say it and 55% by facial expression and body language.)
Chapter 23	James, William. American Psychologist and Philosopher.

396 WORLD CLASS SELLING

ADDITIONAL RESOURCES

National Speakers Association

Sales and Marketing Management Magazine

Personal Selling Power

Selling Magazine

Success Magazine

Inc. Magazine

Marketing Times

Bethel, William. Questions that Make the Sale. Dartnell.

Corbin, Carolyn. Strategies 2000. Eakin Press.

Covey, Stephen R., Ph.D. The Seven Habits of Highly Effective People. Simon and Schuster.

Davidson, Jeffrey P. Marketing to the Fortune 500 and Other Corporations. Dow Jones Irwin.

Drucker, Peter F. Managing for the Future. Truman Tally Books/Dutton.

Gerber, Michael E. The E Myth. Harper Business

Hill, Napoleon. Think and Grow Rich. Fawcett Publication.

Karrass, Gary. Negotiate to Close. Simon and Schuster.

LeBoeuf, Michael, Ph.D. The Greatest Management Principle in the World. Putnam.

Mackay, Harvey. Swim with the Sharks without Being Eaten Alive. William Morrow and Company, Inc.

McCormack, Mark H. What They Don't Teach You at Harvard Business School. Bantam Books.

Naisbitt, John and Aburdene, Patricia. Megatrends 2000. Morrow.

Peale, Norman Vincent, Ph.D. The Power of Positive Thinking. Hawthorne Books.

Peters, Tom. Liberation Management. Knopf.

Richardson, Jerry and Margulis, Joe. The Magic of Rapport. Kampmann and Company, Inc.

Rodgers, Buck. The IBM Way. Harper and Row.

Rosen, Robert H., Ph.D. Healthy Companies. Putnam.

Rosenbluth, Hal F. The Customer Comes Second.

Schwartz, David J. Ph.D. The Magic of Thinking Big. Wilshire Book Company.

Stevens, Howard and Cox, Jeff. The Quadrant Solution. American Management Association.

Tschohl, John. Achieving Excellence Through Customer Service. Prentice Hall.

WORLD CLASS SELLING
MAX SACKS INTERNATIONAL

Max Sacks International is a sales and marketing training and consulting firm. We provide practical high quality, state of the art programs, products and services that are dedicated to developing skills, enhancing performance, and providing on-going reinforcement to individuals and their companies. We are committed to excellence, integrity and one hundred percent client satisfaction.

Max Sacks International offers the following programs and services:

- 3-day public Track Selling System™ workshop — in Los Angeles, Seattle, Minneapolis and San Paulo, Brazil
- 3-day in-house Track Selling System™ seminar — customized for your company
- Track Selling System Graduate Program™ — 3-day workshop in advanced selling skills (in-house only)
- World Class Selling™ — ½-day or 1-day in-house program in building client partnerships
- The Guaranteed Close™ — ½-day or 1-day in-house seminar in closing professionally, logically, and without pressure
- Telemarketing Excellence™ — ½-day or 1-day customized in-house program
- Customer Service Excellence™ — ½-day or 1-day customized in-house program
- Sales Management Coaching™ — customized in-house program
- Speakers who educate as well as motivate
- Consultation in sales, sales management and marketing

If you would like more information about the services of Max Sacks International, or to order additional copies of *World Class Selling*, please return the postage paid return card on the following page or contact:

Max Sacks International
5647 40th Avenue West, Suite 1000
Seattle, Washington 98199 USA
Phone: (206)217-0288 Fax: (206)217-0286
E-Mail: maxsacks@serv.net
Web Site: http://www.maxsacks.com/worldclass